radio

Media Industries

David Sumner,
General Editor

Vol. 4

PETER LANG
New York • Washington, D.C./Baltimore • Bern
Frankfurt am Main • Berlin • Brussels • Vienna • Oxford

William A. Richter

radio

A Complete Guide to the Industry

PETER LANG
New York • Washington, D.C./Baltimore • Bern
Frankfurt am Main • Berlin • Brussels • Vienna • Oxford

Library of Congress Cataloging-in-Publication Data

Richter, William A.
Radio: a complete guide to the industry / William A. Richter.
p. cm. — (Media industries; v. 4)
Includes bibliographical references and index.
1. Radio broadcasting—United States—History.
I. Title. II. Series.
PN1991.3.U6R53   384.540973—dc22   2006017733
ISBN 0-8204-8834-8 (hard cover)
ISBN 0-8204-7633-1 (paper back)
ISSN 1550-1043

Bibliographic information published by **Die Deutsche Bibliothek**.
Die Deutsche Bibliothek lists this publication in the "Deutsche
Nationalbibliografie"; detailed bibliographic data is available
on the Internet at http://dnb.ddb.de/.

Cover design by Lisa Barfield

© 2006 Peter Lang Publishing, Inc., New York
29 Broadway, New York, NY 10006
www.peterlang.com

Printed in the United States of America

Contents

In the Beginning

Introduction

Perhaps no other mass medium has affected American society like radio. Evolving from a series of dots and dashes transmitted over wires to today's satellite-delivered programming, radio now reaches roughly 277,990,086 of Americans twelve years old and older each week and more than 73 percent of us each day.[1]

A few statistics about radio

About 13,748 radio stations in the United States reach a total of 94 percent of Americans twelve and older each week. Of these stations, 4,759 are commercial AM stations, 6,243 are commercial FM stations, and 2,746 are considered noncommercial FM.[2] More than 600 million radios are owned in the United States, with each home owning an average of 5.6 receivers.[3]

- Ninety-five percent of American cars have radio.[4]
- Radio reaches over eight out of ten American adults in their cars each week.
- The average person listens to nineteen hours and thirty minutes of radio per week.

- Between 6 A.M. and 6 P.M. more people use radio than television, newspapers, or magazines. In fact, forty-four percent of their media time is spent with radio.[5]

Radio is considered by some to be our first national medium. Newspapers are generally community-specific. Magazines are written for and distributed to a much wider audience, but are subject to temporal constraints. If one wishes to find the medium that linked the country together instantaneously, it has to be radio. Radio brought us together as a nation. While just a few thousand people braved the weather to attend Abraham Lincoln's swearing-in ceremony, some 15 million people heard Calvin Coolidge's 1925 reelection inauguration on the radio while sitting in the comfort of their living rooms.

Radio gave Americans something that they never had before: the ability to experience one special moment as a country. Prior to radio, it might take days or weeks for news to reach across the country. But as radio grew from stations into networks, everyone shared the same experiences at the same time. For this reason, radio is considered to be the first national medium.

Television programming of today owes much to the early days of radio. Chapter 2 will illustrate how many of the types of programs popular on television today got their start on the fledgling radio.

Radio has helped define what type of music is popular in our society, given groups a common bond, and been used to advance political messages of both the mainstream and fringe groups.

As chapter 2 also points out, the genre of talk radio not only has been a source of information, but has served and continues to serve as a safety valve for those who wish to express their opinions.

Radio is in our homes and our cars. We can carry a radio with us almost all the time and may listen to it twenty-four hours a day, seven days a week. Radio never sleeps.

In its original usage, *broadcasting* is a farming term. When seeds are scattered over a general area without a specific pattern, it is called broadcasting. Perhaps you have seen a broadcast spreader being used to spread grass seed in a front yard. The seed pattern is circulated without regard to where it lands. Therefore, when a station is broadcasting, it is sending out a message to a wide range of potential listeners, without regard for who hears it. In fact, this is vital if a medium is to be considered a mass medium.

Radio was not originally envisioned as a broadcast medium, but as a narrowcast, point-to-point method of communication, as we will see later in this book.

Broadcasting of any kind requires several elements. First, there must be electricity or power. Someone standing on a street corner shouting a manifesto may be reaching the public, but one would hardly consider this broadcasting. Second, as in all forms of communication, a set of symbols must be understood by all parties involved (Morse code, spoken language, pictures, music, and so on). Third, transmissions must be made at regularly scheduled times. Many of the early pioneers lacked this portion of the equation, often going on the air sporadically or when they had spare time to kill. Finally, there must be a transmission-reception device. A radio program being broadcast without receivers can hardly be considered to be a mass medium. As we shall see, the early pioneers of radio envisioned receivers that were tuned to only one transmitter. It was envisioned to be point-to-point communication, more similar to a cell phone than radio as we know it.

The Inventors

> *If I have seen farther than others, it is because I have stood on the shoulders of giants.*
>
> —Sir Isaac Newton

Radio does not have *one* inventor, but many. While no one truly knows how many people were experimenting with the idea of broadcasting and radio waves, most acknowledge the Italian inventor and entrepreneur Guglielmo Marconi as the father of the wireless. But before looking at Marconi's work, one must first exam the work of those who came before him. Experiments using electricity and the idea of wireless transmission date to as early as the late 1700s. There is hardly a grade-school student today who hasn't heard tales of Benjamin Franklin and his kite. But there were many others who shared a fascination with lightening and electricity.

Maxwell (1831–1879)

In the mid-1860s Scottish physicist James Clerk Maxwell started theorizing about the existence of electromagnetic waves. Born in Edinburgh, Scotland, Maxwell attended the Edinburgh Academy and the University of Edinburgh. Fascinated with the fields of optics and electricity, he invented the fish-eye lens and took what is believed to be the first color photograph. But it was his theoretical work with the electromagnetic field that led the way for others to invent today's modern radio.

Christopher Sterling and John Kittross explain that there are three different types of electrical transmissions: conduction, induction, and radiation.[6] Conduction means using a medium through which electricity may pass. The telegraph used wires as a means of conduction. Induction creates a signal between two similar circuits when one is charged. This is done without wires but generally can only be achieved over a short distance. Using mathematical equations, Maxwell postulated the existence of an electromagnetic field and that the speed of sound, light, and heat were close to equal. He was talking about radiation. Maxwell was attempting to prove the ideas of Michael Faraday when he wrote his *Dynamical Theory of the Electromagnetic*

Field. These equations would later become the basis for the work of Heinrich Hertz and, consequently, the basis for all broadcasting.

Hertz (1857–1894)

The work Heinrich Hertz did to further that of Maxwell was some of the most important research done in the field leading to the invention of the wireless. Born in 1857, he began his experiments as part of a demonstration during a class he was teaching. Eventually he was able to prove that Maxwell had been correct, that electromagnetic waves did travel near the speed of light. He also proved that these waves obeyed the same laws of physics as light waves, but that they had a much longer wavelength.

While the scientific community was slow in accepting his work, these waves were eventually named for him. One cycle of a wave is called a Hertz. Today, Hertzian waves are an international standard in radio broadcasting. When you tune in to your favorite station, such as 99.7 FM or 1060 AM, the station number refers to its frequency—in this case 99.7 megahertz (MHz) and 1060 kilohertz (kHz). A kilohertz is 1,000 cycles per second, while a megahertz is 1 million cycles.[7] The AM band reaches from 535 to 1,605 kHz (although not all of the frequencies are being used and frequencies have been set aside up to 1,700 kHz for future use), while FM is transmitted between 88.1 and 107.9 MHz.

Popov (1859–1906)

Of all the figures involved in the invention of radio, Alexander Popov is perhaps the most elusive. Little is known of his life and work. Popov was born in Russia in 1859, and after completing his education he taught at the Russian Torpedo School, where he began research into using electricity aboard ships. After a visit to the Chicago World's Fair, he returned to Russia with an interest in perfecting the wireless.

Some report that he demonstrated wireless transmission in March 1896, but no one took notes at the time and the results were not reported until thirty years later. If true, this would mean that Popov beat Marconi's first public demonstration by several months.

Marconi (1874–1937)

Guglielmo Marconi was born in Italy in 1874 to a wealthy country gentleman, Guisppe, and an Irish mother, Annie Jameson, of Daphne Castle. At an early age Marconi became fascinated by preliminary experiments with electricity. He had private education and showed a fondness for the sciences. Taking an interest in electricity and the work of Maxwell and Hertz, he set up a laboratory in the family home when he was a young man. His experiments proved both successful and destructive in nature. His father would often find Guglielmo's experiments and destroy them. His mother, who was more nurturing of her son's inquisitive nature, often helped him hide these tests.

Performing experiments at his family's country estate and improving upon the experiments of Hertz, Marconi successfully sent a wireless signal across his attic laboratory when he was just ten years old. Over the next few years, he kept increasing the distance of his Morse code signals by devising new ways of increasing the power of his transmitter. By 1896 he had achieved an unbelievable feat of transmitting a signal over two miles without wires.

Shortly thereafter, he and his mother left for England. Various sources offer different reasons for the move. Some say that his father refused to back him financially, while others claim that his father did indeed support him and his experiments. Everyone agrees that the Italian government's refusal to accept his invention was a key decision in his move to England. In any case, after arriving in England he applied for and received the first patent for wireless telegraphy. Using the contacts his mother's family provided, he proceeded to demonstrate his wireless to an official of the British Post Office. That official—William Preece—had done his own experiments in wireless communication and was impressed enough with the invention that he helped Marconi better his system and introduced him to more powerful people in England. Soon they set up a demonstration off the coast of Wales.

Following this public demonstration, the Wireless Telegraph and Signal Company—soon to become the Marconi Wireless Telegraph Company, Ltd.—was formed. Marconi kept refining his process and eventually sent a signal across the English Channel, in 1899, to ships at sea. However, there were still improvements to be made to the system. Interference was one problem. Multiple stations could not operate without interfering with each other's signal. In 1900 Marconi received the famous patent number 7777 or the Four Sevens, for a tuned circuit. In 1901 he sent a transatlantic signal, the letter "S," from the coast of England at Cornwall to the coast of Newfoundland—about 2,100 miles.

Even though Marconi had little training, he proved to be not only a brilliant scientist but also a cunning businessman. His frequent demonstrations led the British royal family, the American navy, and the Canadian government to express interest in the wireless.

In 1899 Marconi established the American Marconi Company and soon thereafter the Canadian Marconi Company. In an attempt to keep his monopoly of the wireless, Marconi never sold the equipment, but rented it to customers with the stipulation that only Marconi-trained operators could be used. The Marconi operators were not allowed to communicate with operators from other companies unless there was an emergency.[8]

In 1912 the American Marconi Company acquired the United Wireless Telegraph Company. This increased the number of stations from five to over sixty, and Marconi wireless–outfitted ships from five to four hundred, giving it a near monopoly of ship-to-shore wireless on the Atlantic Coast of the United States. While a savvy business move at the time, this expansion would later prove a detriment to the company.

Marconi had arrived on one of his trips to the United States, planning on staying just a few days and traveling back to Europe on the ship's trip back. However, entangled business dealings delayed his return. Not long after news came that the ship had been torpedoed and sunk by the German navy on its return voyage. That ship was the Lusitania.[9] It is widely speculated that this was a failed assassination attempt on Marconi life.

In 1914 Marconi entered the Italian army as a lieutenant, was promoted to captain, and in 1916 transferred to the navy with the rank of commander. He was even a member of the Italian delegation to the Paris Peace Conference at the end of the war. But he was still very much involved with the perfection of the wireless.

The wireless was limited, however. The invention could only send the dots and dashes of Morse code. Perhaps even more limiting was the fact that Marconi's system used a spark gap transmitter. This created a loud electrical noise. Even Marconi realized the limitations of his system and began experimenting with ways of sending voices through the air.

The Marconi Company had some grand plans and great insight into possible uses for the wireless. In a 1919 article, the company's managing director was quoted as saying that they hoped to achieve wireless telephone service in New York and London the following year and could imagine a day in the near future when

> pocket wireless telephones will be in wide use. A business man's secretary, walking along the street. . .will hear a bell ring in his pocket, will put a receiver to his ear and hear 'his master's voice' give him instructions, probably from an airplane hundreds of miles away.[10]

The outbreak of World War I had a major effect on the Marconi companies. In the United States, the navy mandated that all wireless stations be taken off of the air. In addition, the government suspended all patents dealing with wireless for the duration. Upon war's end, the Marconi interests were trying to negotiate the purchase of several Alexanderson alternators. General Electric, although needing the money, did not wish to become involved in the communication industry. In what one can look back in retrospect and call a bad decision, the Marconi Company offered even more money, with the stipulation that it had the exclusive right to purchase these components, known to be the best available. Marconi held a virtual monopoly over wireless, and following the war, this move to consolidate it struck a note of concern in many people, including President Woodrow Wilson and the acting secretary of the navy, Franklin D. Roosevelt.

Owen D. Young, head of the GE legal department and ultimately the chairman of the board of GE, was eventually approached by the U.S. Navy and asked to help GE form a company to purchase Marconi's patents. British Marconi by now realized that the U.S. government would never allow its plans to continue. In fact, officers of British Marconi were led to believe that if they didn't sell their company Congress might enact a law forbidding foreign companies from controlling wireless businesses or stations on any U.S. soil. After months of negotiations, GE purchased 364,826 shares of American Marconi's stock.[11] Following that, it began buying the shares of the company's American stockholders.

But the story of Marconi does not end here. He developed many more technical innovations that created better and longer transmissions. For instance, in 1932 he established the first microwave radio-telephone connection between the pope's summer home and the Vatican. Following this, his work resulted in demonstrations of the use of microwaves for navigation of ships and even radar.

Tesla (1856–1943)

Nikola Tesla, born 1856 in Croatia to Serbian parents, is an obscure player in the mainstream history of radio. While many textbooks ignore his role in the development of radio, to many enthusiasts he is revered as its true father. Indeed there is a cult-like following surrounding the man.

Tesla's father was an Orthodox priest, his mother an amateur inventor and housewife. At an early age Nikola showed an extreme talent for memorization and mathematics and could perform complicated calculations in his head. While most inventors and engineers would painstakingly create drawings and models before undertaking tasks, it was not uncommon for Tesla to create from pictures he had created and stored only in his mind. Tesla's father, much like Marconi's, did not wholly endorse his son's fascination with electricity and machinery. He wanted Nikola to follow him into the priesthood. Eventually Tesla was allowed to attend the Austrian Polytechnic School to study engineering. He never completed his degree. By age twenty-four, he had invented the induction motor, an idea so revolutionary that it brought him fame.

He had in essence developed an alternating current (AC) motor. Prior to this, the industrialized world was using Thomas Edison's direct current (DC) motors. This would later cause a major problem for Tesla.

Tesla immigrated to the United States. As a child he had imagined that the power of Niagara Falls could be harnessed. But more important, he wanted to meet Edison. He arrived with little money and a letter of introduction from a mutual acquaintance, Charles Batchelor. The letter said in part, "My Dear Edison: I know two great men and you are one of them. The other is this young man!"[12]

But Edison wanted nothing to do with Tesla's ideas about AC power. Tesla tried to explain that with Edison's system of direct current power stations had to be set up every mile, and that the farther away one was from the station, the less power was available, leaving lights darker and the current weaker. With Tesla's alternating current, one power plant could supply power over great distances, with each user receiving the same strength. Finally tiring of the fight, Tesla decided to work on bettering Edison's plan. When he said that he could improve the system by at least 15 percent, Edison said that if he did he would give him $50,000, which was an enormous sum of money at the time. Tesla did indeed improve the system, but when he asked for the money, he was told that it was a joke and that he "didn't understand American humor." Tesla quit.[13]

Tesla continued his work on AC and continued to file patents. Eventually George Westinghouse, the inventor of railroad air brakes, offered to purchase all of his patents. Tesla sold his patents to Westinghouse, starting a bitter battle between the Edison Power Company and the Westinghouse Company. Edison staged public demonstrations of the dangers of AC current by electrocuting cats, dogs, a cow, a horse, and even a rogue elephant that a circus was going to kill.[14] Even the first person condemned to die in the electric chair was included as part of his campaign.

Yet despite all of the negative publicity, Tesla and Westinghouse scored a major coup when they bid upon and received the contract to light the Chicago World's Fair. On the opening night, May 1, 1893, President Grover Cleveland pushed a button and 100,000 lights came to life. The battle between AC and DC had been decided.

Building on the work of Maxwell and Hertz, Tesla, like Marconi, began to work on the transmission of electricity through the air without wires. It was his belief that using a high frequency would be a more efficient and safer method. Working toward this goal, he eventually invented the Tesla coil— a step that allowed for the production of high frequency and high voltage. These inventions led to the first neon lights and the first fluorescent lighting, and even allowed Tesla to light a bulb without wires—an experiment that is still demonstrated in science museums around the world.

Turning all of his attention to transmitting wireless energy, Tesla applied to the U.S. Patents Office for his "System of Transmission of Electrical Energy" and "Apparatus for Transmission of Electrical Energy." He received a patent for the former in March 1900 and the latter in May of the same year. When Marconi filed to patent his radio in November 1900, his application was turned down, due in part to Tesla's patents. In fact, over the course of the next three years Marconi was turned down repeatedly. Still, the more flamboyant Marconi, with his flair for business and publicity, thrived. Even though he was using many of Tesla's patents, the Marconi companies continued to prosper. Then in 1904, for dubious reasons, the U.S. Patents Office reversed earlier decisions and granted Marconi a patent for radio. As if to add insult to injury, Marconi was awarded the Nobel Prize for his work. Tesla brought suit against the Marconi Company, to no avail.

Tesla went on to later lay the foundation for robotics when he demonstrated a radio-controlled model boat, demonstrating what he called "teleautomation." Tesla envisioned using this invention to create "the first race of robots, mechanical men which will do the laborious work of the human race."[15]

He also developed a new turbine engine, attempted to set up a world-wide wireless system, and theorized about radar. But many of Tesla's claims met with ridicule. He reported picking up radio signals from outer space and started to become more and more eccentric in his private life. One topic that has created a great deal of debate is Tesla's "peace beam." He claimed to have discovered a new source of energy that could be used to shoot a beam of energy through the air to bring down enemy airplanes. The legend says that Tesla had made an arrangement with Admiral Robert Peary and his party, who were attempting to reach the North Pole for the second time. Tesla said that he would make contact with them on a certain date. On that date, in 1908, he and his assistant aimed his "peace ray" across the Atlantic Ocean toward the North Pole. After not hearing any news, he concluded that his experiment had failed. But news started to spread that an explosion, heard up to 620 miles away, had devastated a 500,000-square-acre section of forest in Siberia on that same evening. Scientists claim that this was probably the result of a meteorite or a piece of a comet, but no impact site or debris that usually would be found by such a hit was found. Estimates are that the explosion was equivalent to ten to fifteen megatons of TNT, which was more powerful than a nuclear bomb. Fearing that the explosion was the result of his peace ray going astray, Tesla dismantled his machine, never to use it again. Those who believe in the peace ray often claim that it was the origin for the Star Wars defense program initiated by President Ronald Reagan and the new weapon that Russian president Vladimir Putin has made reference to.

Whether one believes the story of the peace ray or not, Tesla does deserve his place among those who helped make radio a reality.

Fessenden (1871–1932)

Imagine you are a radio operator aboard a ship. It is evening, Christmas Eve, 1906. Surrounded by darkness, you are wearing your headset listening for the dots and dashes of the wireless. But instead of the usual sounds, you suddenly hear a violin solo, Bible verses being read, a singer, and a wish of "Merry Christmas." With this leap of technology, Canadian Reginald Fessenden sent what is believed to be the first radio broadcast. While the legend is that this was unannounced and took radio operators by surprise, we know today that Fessenden had alerted ships and reporters days earlier. Nonetheless, this development not only astounded those listening but also prompted many scientists to refocus their research efforts.

Fessenden was born in 1866. While he is one of the lesser-known players in the early invention of radio, he may be the most important. He was a scientist, scholar, and inventor, hot-tempered and a bit of a wanderer. Initially invited by Bishop College to teach math and language, he moved on to another school in Bermuda.

Fessenden became enamored with experiments with electricity. He soon decided that he must work with Edison. Quitting his teaching job, he headed to the great man's Orange Park, New Jersey, factory with expectations of meeting Edison. But even though Edison had no time to meet with him, fortune was smiling on Fessenden that day. A tester had just quit his job with Edison, and Fessenden was immediately hired.

At the time, having electricity in one's home was rare, but many of the wealthiest families had their own generators. One such man was banker J. P. Morgan. Fessenden was sent on a service call to the Morgan estate. Looking at the generator, he not only made the repairs but also made some improvements. Morgan then asked him to look at the wiring. Fessenden made some improvements to the wiring, such as adding insulation, that today we take for granted. Morgan was so impressed that he gave Fessenden a reward for his efforts. When Morgan's words of praise reached Edison, Fessenden was promoted to Edison's assistant. Edison had a team he called "muckers" so that he could give notes to them and they could hammer out the details. He had turned inventing into an assembly line. Eventually Fessenden was promoted to chief chemist, despite his objections that he wasn't a chemist.[16]

But like many of the great inventors of his day he was more interested in the possibilities of the wireless. A bad turn in the economy left Fessenden unemployed. But with his talents he was soon hired by the United States Company and within a year moved to Massachusetts to start work at the Stanley Company. All this time, Fessenden kept researching wireless and began getting his papers published in scientific journals. He felt that he could improve on the Marconi system by making it more powerful with less interference. It wasn't long until he was offered a professorship at Purdue University, despite the fact that he had never finished his own degree. At the end of the year, he left when the University of Pittsburgh made him a better offer.

In 1900 the United States Weather Bureau hired Fessenden to develop a better way to forecast and communicate the weather reports. He moved to Cobb Island, Maryland, where he once again set up shop. That December he successfully sent voice over the wireless between two stations set up one mile apart. His assistant reported hearing Fessenden state, "One, two, three, four. Is it snowing where you are Mr. Thiessen? If it is would you telegraph back to me?[17] Although the signal wasn't great, he continued setting up transmitters down the East Coast, at Cape Hatteras and Roanoke Island in North Carolina and Cape Henry, Virginia.

But soon Fessenden became embroiled in an argument with the Weather Bureau concerning who owned the patents to his inventions. He left and began work on perfecting his system with hopes of one day starting his own company.

Fessenden had envisioned a new principle: the heterodyne. Edwin Armstrong would later perfect this idea. But in order for him to build a better transmitter he would need a piece of equipment more powerful than any ever seen. For the continuous supply of AC power necessary to accomplish this, he would need an alternator that was capable of generating 100,000 cycles (100 kHz). He contracted with General Electric, but the company was only able to supply him with a 10,000-cycle alternator. Within a year, the new machinery had burned out. General Electric engineer Ernst Alexanderson joined the project, and over the course of several years he and Fessenden gradually built more and more powerful alternators and eventually reached the 100,000-cycle goal.

The new machinery was delivered to Fessenden's Brant Rock, Massachusetts, laboratory beginning in 1906. The Alexanderson alternators were huge. Each one could fill a small building, looking very much like power plant generators or other pieces of industrial machinery. With the key to his new more powerful transmitter in place, he turned his attention to another task. Signals coming in were often quite weak and required operators to wear headphones to try and pick up the faint dots and dashes of Morse code. He invented a new means for amplifying incoming signals that quickly became the standard.

His dream of starting his own company came to fruition when two Pittsburgh bankers funded the creation of the National Electric Signaling Company (NESCO). Once again Fessenden's temper flared when the business partners didn't agree with his ideas for how his inventions should be used. He wanted to sell equipment, but the partners wanted to sell entire wireless systems.

During this tumultuous time, Fessenden made his historic broadcast, though accounts differ as to who heard it. Some historians say only those on board the ships and a few amateurs heard it, while others say the press had been alerted. In either case, this historic broadcast didn't give Fessenden the publicity he deserved.

Fessenden continued to be at odds with the partners. In fact, when he decided to try to beat Lee De Forest in the race to send a transatlantic broadcast, he set up his own company back in Canada without telling the two men. When they found out about the Fessenden Wireless Company of Canada, they became enraged and fired him. He in turn sued NESCO for wrongful termination and after many years won a settlement.

Eventually, through a long series of patent sales and mergers, NESCO's patents became the property of RCA.

De Forest (1873–1961)

Many people accept Dr. Lee De Forest as the inventor of modern radio. In fact, he titled his autobiography *Father of Radio*. Years later, he also claimed to be "the Grandfather of Television." De Forest was a person who never seemed to fit in with his surroundings. Born in the Midwest, his father accepted the position of president at Talladega College, a historically black school in Alabama. He was not allowed to socialize with the children at the school and was shunned by other children in the community.[18] His father sent him to boarding school, where he excelled in his studies but again did not quite fit in with the other students. Upon graduation, he was admitted to Yale, where he eventually earned a Ph.D. in physics and began a series of jobs for various companies.

The young De Forest was enthralled by wireless technology. As a young man he invented a system to compete with Marconi's. In a move for publicity, he arranged to transmit reports of a 1901 yacht race in New York from a boat in the harbor. Marconi, however, had had the same idea and put a transmitter on another boat. Both transmitters acted to cancel each other out. De Forest, in a fit of anger or disgust, tossed his into the water.[19] But the publicity that he received resulted in the backing to start his own wireless company. That financial backing came from Abraham White. While De Forest focused his attention on experimentation, White oversaw the business side of the company. Even though the company had many high-profile customers, it folded within five years. Undaunted, De Forest formed another company, the De Forest Radio Telephone Company. Several lawsuits were brought against De Forest and the company, not the least of which were charges of stock fraud. This was doomed to be another in a string of failed businesses, and the company lasted only four years. De Forest eventually started at least five businesses that failed—and four marriages, the last which was successful, despite the fact that he had he married his fourth wife without bothering to divorce his third.

In a 1906 paper presented to the American Institute of Electrical Engineers, De Forest announced that he had invented the Audion tube. He later gave credit for the name in a footnote: "For its name, Audion, a title as beautiful as it is appropriate, I am indebted to my assistant, Mr. C.D. Babcock, who has been of utmost service to me in the development of this device almost from its inception"[20]

In essence he had taken the Fleming vacuum tube and improved upon it. Ambrose Fleming had invented the tube while working for the Marconi Company. The Fleming tube enabled one to control electrical current so that it flowed in only one direction. Being able to create bursts of electricity was a huge step in making the telegraph and voice reliably audible.

To this invention, De Forest added a grid. While this tube allowed for better wireless transmissions, allowing signals to be amplified, De Forest himself did not quite understand how or why it worked. This later became a serious factor in subsequent patent infringement lawsuits brought by Edwin Armstrong.

Perhaps what makes De Forest more memorable than others working on wireless at the time was his ability to promote himself and his love of opera. While most inventors of that time saw the wireless as a useful tool for communicating with ships, especially those in trouble, De Forest had a more sentimental vision of the possibilities of this new medium. In 1906 he wrote, "My present task is to distribute sweet melody broadcast over the city and sea so that in time even the marine far out across the silent waves may hear the music of his homeland."[21] In 1907 he partially achieved that dream when he broadcast the great tenor Caruso live from the stage of the Metropolitan Opera in New York. Of course, few people had receivers, but De Forest made some available to his friends. In another publicity stunt, he and his new wife played records from atop the Eiffel Tower. What he lacked in scientific knowledge, he more than made up for in showmanship.

Armstrong (1890–1954)

Edwin Howard Armstrong is another of the great inventors of radio whose name has been all but lost to the history books. But many believe that Armstrong had the scientific knowledge that De Forest lacked. Armstrong was just a young boy when Marconi made his first transatlantic demonstration, but it spurred an interest in him that would consume his entire life. Armstrong's parents sought to develop this love for science in their son. His father, vice president of Oxford University Press, gave him books about inventors. When De Forest announced the development of the Audion tube, Armstrong was allowed to purchase the expensive piece of equipment and add it to his laboratory in his bedroom. While attending Columbia University, he was allowed to erect a 125-foot antenna in the family's yard so that he could continue research into perfecting wireless communication. He built the antenna himself and was known to hoist himself to the top using a boson's chair. (If Armstrong had another passion that was greater than his love of the wireless, it was his love of heights.) Armstrong turned his attention to De Forest's Audion tube. While the tube itself was adequate, he felt that he could improve it. Eventually he reached one of his great discoveries. By taking the output of the tube and repeatedly sending it back in, he created a feedback, or "regenerative circuit." This allowed for reception that was so superior that he could hear signals from halfway around the globe. Additionally, he found that this tube could be used to transmit signals as well. After graduating from Columbia, he applied for two patents, and demonstrated his new inventions to David Sarnoff, the chief inspector for the American Marconi Company. The two men became close friends, and eventually bitter enemies.

Soon after he filed for his patents, De Forest filed a patent application stating that he had invented the oscillating Audion a year earlier than Armstrong. The patent question was put on hold when the navy took all radio broadcasting off the air and commandeered all radio patents. Armstrong enlisted in the Army Signal Corps and was assigned to a research post in France. There he worked on upgrading communication capabilities of both ground and air forces. His love of heights was evident in the fact that he insisted on testing all of his airplane equipment himself. But this wasn't his most significant contribution.

The Allies believed that the Germans were sending signals using a very high frequency (VHF) because the Allies could not receive the signals in that range. Armstrong met an engineer for British Marconi, Captain H. J. Round, who informed him about the progress the British had made toward intercepting these signals. Realizing that the British were far ahead of the Americans, Armstrong invented what he called the superheterodyne circuit. This not only allowed receivers to listen to German VHF, but also gave them the opportunity to listen to even higher frequencies should the Germans ever access them. He quickly filed for a patent in France, and upon returning to the United States (with the rank of major) he filed for a U.S. patent. During the next twenty years the superheterodyne circuit continued to be perfected, which allowed radios to be tuned to a certain frequency, making radio has we know it today possible.[22]

Armstrong won the patent infringement suit brought by De Forest. This meant that he was free to license the use of his regenerative circuit. He took the idea to Sarnoff, who had become the general manager and vice president for the new Radio Corporation of America (RCA). The two friends worked out a deal that gave Armstrong money and enough stock to make him the largest private stockholder in the company. Sarnoff also introduced Armstrong to his secretary, who would soon become Armstrong's wife.

While courting her, Armstrong would often try to impress her by climbing to the top of RCA's radio towers, causing Sarnoff to ban him from such stunts. As a wedding gift, Armstrong presented his wife with the world's first portable heterodyne radio, which was about the size of a small trunk.

But this is not where the Armstrong story ends. He refused to sign the final judgment made in the patent case and also refused to license his invention for De Forest's use. In fact, he wanted nothing to do with him. De Forest backed against a wall with nothing to lose, he once again brought suit against Armstrong. This time the courts agreed with De Forest. Armstrong lost the rights to his invention. He brought a new suit, this time against RCA, the new owners of De Forest's patent, but lost again.

Feeling humiliated, he went before the Institute of Radio Engineers to return a medal that they had awarded him for his invention. When the president of the association refused to accept it, the other engineers rose to their feet, giving Armstrong a standing ovation, and expressed their conviction that they knew the true inventor even if the courts did not.

Meanwhile, Armstrong was working on his third and perhaps greatest contribution to the world of radio. He was constantly annoyed by static on the radio. This problem became even worse during the summer months or when lightening was in the air. He wished to develop a system to remove the static from broadcasts.

Up until this time, all broadcasting was done by amplitude modulation, or AM. In this method the intensity of the radio wave is increased or decreased in order to achieve a broadcast signal. After a great deal of experimentation, Armstrong found that he could eliminate the static and provide a superior sound by changing or modulating the frequency of the sound waves instead; the system was called frequency modulation, or FM.

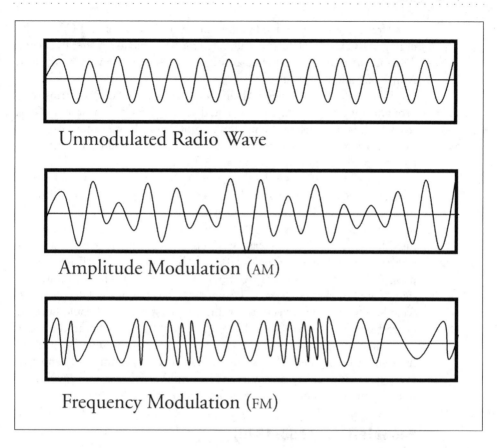

Unmodulated Radio Wave

Amplitude Modulation (AM)

Frequency Modulation (FM)

Once again he took his new invention to his friend Sarnoff. Sarnoff gave Armstrong laboratory space atop the Empire State Building. From this post two signals were sent—one AM and then one FM. A receiver was ready for those they invited to hear the difference. Not only did FM eliminate the static that the AM signal carried, it also offered a broader range of sound. It was obviously a superior system. Yet Sarnoff did not want it, claiming that RCA already had too much money tied up in other ventures.

This ended what was left of the friendship between the two men. Armstrong was told to remove his equipment. Using his own money, he began to perfect his new system. He was granted a license for station W2XMN and began to broadcast in FM. Soon the New England–based Yankee Network was broadcasting in FM. It looked as if FM would be a sure hit.

But Armstrong's dreams were once again shattered. While he was making deals with radio manufacturers, RCA refused. Again they brought patent cases against him. The outbreak of World War II halted the trials. Armstrong generously donated his patent rights to the military, feeling that it was wrong to profit from war. Once again he turned his scientific knowledge and creativity to developing new technology for the military.

After the war, the Federal Communication Commission (FCC), at the urging of RCA, moved the space allocated for FM radio to a higher frequency. This meant that all previous transmitters and receivers were worthless. Armstrong had lost again.

When RCA began using FM circuits for their television sets, Armstrong brought suit yet again. Armstrong had divested himself of most of his RCA stock by this time, using the money to fund his FM experiments; the rest of the stock was sold to help pay the expenses of his lawsuits. This time the trial dragged on until Armstrong was left financially ruined.

Armstrong's health was declining since suffering a stroke.[23] Even his once idyllic marriage was in ruins. On Thanksgiving evening, 1953, during an argument over money, he struck his wife with a fire poker and she left him. Two months later, on January 31, 1954, Armstrong wrote a letter of apology to his wife, put on his hat and coat, and stepped out of his apartment window on the thirteenth floor of the building.[24] He landed on a third-floor overhang and his body wasn't discovered until the next day. He left a note that said: "I am heartbroken because I cannot see you once again. I deeply regret what has happened between us. I cannot understand how I could hurt the dearest thing in the whole world to me. I would give my life to turn back to the time when we were so happy and free. God keep you and may the Lord have mercy on my soul."[25] His widow, Marion, kept fighting RCA and others. Later that year, the suits were settled, and Marion was awarded $1 million. Eventually all of Armstrong's patents for FM radio were upheld.

Stubblefield (1860–1928)

Yet another claim to the first broadcast comes from a telephone repairman with no formal training. Nathan B. Stubblefield of Murray, Kentucky, claimed to have invented a wireless system that he demonstrated in 1892. He gave his device to a friend, Rainey T. Wells, and told him to go outside. He later claimed that the first words that were broadcast, words that understandingly startled him, were, "Hello, Rainey." However, it wasn't until 1902 that he made a public demonstration of his device. This first demonstration was over a distance of only two hundred feet, but it was a transmission nonetheless. He later went on to demonstrate his device in Philadelphia, Washington D.C., and New York. He didn't market his invention himself, fearing it might be stolen. He finally was persuaded to allow the formation of the Wireless Telephone Company of America, of which he was director and a stockholder. In exchange, he gave his patents to the company. Stubblefield left the company and returned to his shack in Kentucky because he felt he was being cheated. This may be true, as evidenced in the fact that several of the company's executives were eventually convicted of mail fraud.

Stubblefield held many patents. He even had patented what later would become a common demonstration in grade-school classes and an early amusement for children: a phone made by connecting two tin cans with a taut string.[26] Despite his successes as an inventor, he returned to Kentucky and lived as a recluse, always fearful, some say, that someone would steal his ideas. Shortly before he died of starvation in 1928, he is quoted as saying, "I've lived fifty years before my time. The past is nothing. I have perfected now the greatest invention the world has ever known."[27] Following his death, a monument was erected on the grounds of Murray State College declaring him the Inventor of Radio. Today we understand that what Stubblefield had actually achieved was induction using the ground as a conductor. While it was wireless communication, it is not what we would generally call radio broadcasting.

Others

Many more people could be included among the first innovators in the field of radio. Joseph Henry (1842) achieved induction, sending electricity a distance of two hundred feet. Samuel F. B. Morse had been working on the same type of experiment, sending current across a canal that same year and across the mile-wide mouth of the Susquehanna River the next. Other early inventors include Mahlon Loomis, who sent a signal eighteen miles in 1866, and Amos Dolbear, who made his discovery accidentally. While working in his laboratory at Tufts University, he heard sounds from a disconnected receiver. After working on this induction system, Dolbear was able to send his signal up to one mile, but the system lacked a good receiver.

The Companies

Although early interest in wireless was limited to ship-to-shore broadcasts, domestic broadcasts were soon developed. By 1915, the American Telephone and Telegraph Company (AT&T) had sent a spoken signal across the United States for the first time. This feat was achieved through the use of sites that would receive and repeat the signal every thirty miles. This took 2,500 tons of copper wire and 130,000 telephone poles.[28] With the outbreak of World War I, the U.S. Navy took control of all wireless patents and equipment in the country. Following the war, the navy made an attempt to retain control but was thwarted by Congress.

As mentioned earlier, with some assistance from the government, which unofficially oversaw the creation of a monopoly, RCA was formed at the end of the war. The charter of the new corporation required a representative of the government to be on the board of directors. Included in the formation of the new entity were the American Telephone and Telegraph Company, which, along with patents, brought access to quality phone lines; Westinghouse, a manufacturer of appliances and radios; and United Fruit, which used wireless to contact banana boats as soon as crops were being harvested.

At the time, GE, however, had little interest in the operation of broadcast stations. It was concerned primarily with the manufacture of alternators. The new company's officers included Owen D. Young as chairman of the board, Edward J. Nally as president, and David Sarnoff as commercial manager. In fact, part of the deal was that all of the American Marconi employees would be transferred to the new RCA. Soon after purchasing all of the patents, RCA received all wireless stations previously owned by American Marconi.

RCA focused its early resources on international transmission, due to its ownership of the patents for the Alexanderson alternator, among others. Meanwhile, Westinghouse began to develop its domestic broadcasting efforts. During this time, there were many amateur broadcasters. Radio—both broadcasting and listening to it—had become a popular hobby. Many of these early amateur broadcasters didn't have regular schedules or even planned programming. Most of these hobbyists were more concerned with the electronics than the content. Their goal was reaching out as far as possible. They would ask people to send postcards letting them know how far their signals were reaching. Of course, radio didn't remain a hobby for long.

Broadcasting Pioneers

When discussing the pioneers of radio broadcasting, one must look not only at the people, but also at the institutions that they were involved with. For unlike the early experimenters, sitting in laboratories trying out various configurations, it required a great deal of money to move the early stations from a hobby to a commercial enterprise.

Conrad (1874–1941)

One of the early amateurs was Frank Conrad, a Westinghouse engineer. Conrad left grammar school to work for Westinghouse and worked his way up from bench hand to chief engineer. Later in life, he was awarded an honorary doctorate for his work, along with many other medals of distinction.

During World War I, Westinghouse had contracted with the U.S. Navy to provide point-to-point communications. Wishing to keep his watch as accurate as possible, Conrad built a receiver that would allow him to pick up broadcasts of the official time by the Naval Academy. Conrad conducted wireless experiments out of his garage in the Pittsburgh suburb of Wilkinsburg, Pennsylvania. The experimental station was given the designation 8XK. Since he was working with the navy, Conrad was one of the few people who was able to remain active in radio during the war. As the war came to an end, the navy cancelled its contract with Westinghouse. Almost immediately after the war, during the summer of 1919, Conrad put his station back on the air. Like other amateur or "ham" operators, he was primarily concerned with distance rather than content. His original broadcasts consisted of his reading newspaper stories over the air. Several turning points in broadcast history occurred during this time.

Not only were the usual amateurs listening in, but a whole new group of men, trained by the navy to build and operate radio receivers, had joined the growing audience. Another factor was that listeners started to become bored with Conrad's "newscasts." One listener wrote in suggesting that he play music. Conrad placed the microphone in front of the speaker and became a disc jockey. Whether he or Fessenden is entitled to the title of first DJ is debatable. Soon he was offering music broadcasts on Wednesday and Sunday evenings, later adding sports scores and live music performed by his sons. His broadcasts became so popular that the Joseph Horne Department Store took out an ad in the *Pittsburgh Sun* selling radio receivers for "$10 and up."

Harry Davis (1915–1944)

Upon seeing the Joseph Horne Department Store advertisement, Harry Davis, vice president of Westinghouse, recognized an opportunity. Realizing that his company still had radio receivers left over from the war, he believed that offering better programming would create a demand for receivers, which in turn Westinghouse would manufacture and sell. Westinghouse received a license from the Department of Commerce to operate under the call letters KDKA.

The station and transmitter were moved to the roof of the Westinghouse factory in east Pittsburgh. This move offered a higher location that resulted in a wider coverage area. In addition, the station increased the transmitter power. The first broadcast occurred on November 2, 1920. The presidential election-night coverage of the presidential race between Warren G. Harding and James M. Cox lasted from 8 P.M. until after midnight. In an ironic twist, Conrad was not at the new studio but at his garage location acting as a backup in case of equipment failure.

This new station, literally a shack on the factory roof, was replaced with a large tent. When it was blown down in a storm, the station was once again moved, this time to an indoor location. Soon Westinghouse added more stations to KDKA and formed a broadcasting group. Among them were stations in Newark, New Jersey; Springfield, Massachusetts; Chicago, Illinois; Cleveland, Ohio; and Hastings, Nebraska. The Nebraska station repeated the KDKA signal coming from Pittsburgh.[29]

By sharing a broadcast, either by repeating the signal of another station or linking the stations for a simultaneous broadcast, a much wider audience was reached. Chain broadcasting was quite appealing to the owners of multiple stations, since it reached a wide audience for a relatively low cost. (This was still before the days of satellite and microwave feeds.) These stations were literally linked together via telephone lines.

KDKA holds many "firsts." In addition to the election-night returns, it was the first to broadcast from a theater, the first to have a regularly scheduled church service broadcast, the first to air a live sporting event, and more.

David Sarnoff (1891–1971)

David Sarnoff, a Russian immigrant, is one of the more flamboyant players in the story of radio. Controversy surrounds many aspects of his life. Ever the self-promoter, many believe that Sarnoff might have played with some of the facts of his life in order to appear as a larger-than-life figure. This section will attempt to distinguish what is known as fact from that which he may have enhanced.

Sarnoff's father came to the United States, leaving his family behind, when David was just four years old. The next year, Sarnoff was sent away to rabbinical school. In 1900, when David was nine, the elder Sarnoff sent to Russia for the family to join him in New York. The young David had to work in order to help support their family in their new home. He took jobs as a delivery boy for a butcher and a paperboy for a Yiddish newspaper and began school to learn English. His hard work paid off. By age eleven, he was employing his own father at a newsstand that he had purchased for $200.

The driven Sarnoff soon took a job as an office boy for the Commercial Cable Company. Noticing that the operators made more money than he did, he taught himself Morse code and how to use the telegraph. By the time he was seventeen, Sarnoff was working for the Marconi Company. He was stationed on Nantucket Island and even volunteered to be the Marconi operator aboard a sealing expedition ship to the Artic. David asked to be transferred to a station in Brooklyn, even though it meant a cut in pay. Before his twentieth birthday, he was the manager. From here he moved to the busiest wireless telegraph station in the country, the Marconi station in Wanamaker's Department Store. He sought additional training, and quickly moved up the ladder to instructor, onboard ship equipment inspector, station equipment inspector, assistant traffic manager, assistant chief engineer, and finally, when he was twenty-six, commercial manager.

Stories in many books claim that Sarnoff was the lone telegraph operator on the evening of the *Titanic*'s sinking. Some say that he stayed at his post for three days relaying messages from the ship and from those who came to its rescue. This is disputable. As a letter from the curator of the Sarnoff collection in Princeton points out, there is no hard evidence that Sarnoff was in the building when the distress signals started coming in.[30] Even more questionable is why Sarnoff, a management member, would be working a receiver, and why he would be working at night.

Another story involves a memo that he wrote in 1915 outlining a "radio music box." His memo described to his boss, Edward J. Nally, Marconi's vision that the wireless could be used for more than point-to-point communication. In his memo he suggested that the wireless could be marketed like a piece of furniture that would play music being broadcast. An article by

Louise Benjamin questions the authenticity of this claim. Neither the original memo nor the reply can be found. There is a report that Sarnoff later provided to his superiors at RCA in 1920. In that report he mentions the earlier memo and offers it as a possible plan. Benjamin, among others, notes that this was at a time when radio as we know it was "right around the corner." [31] A memo from 1915 would show much more foresight than one from 1920. Did Sarnoff write the famous 1915 memo? Unless a record of it is uncovered, we may never know for sure.

Sarnoff was already commercial manager at American Marconi by the time RCA was formed. When he joined the new group with the same title, he was just twenty-eight years old. Sarnoff continued his meteoric rise to become a major force behind radio broadcasting and the development of the networks.

During World War II, he was called to active duty in the Signal Corps from June to July 1942, again from August to October of the same year, and again from March to December 1944, when he was asked to help develop electronic news coverage of D-Day and the liberation of Paris. On December 7, 1944, he was promoted to brigadier general.[32]

Upon his return from the war, he insisted that everyone at NBC refer to him as "the General."[33] One has to wonder if this was in emulation of his idol, Guglielmo Marconi, who had earned the rank of admiral in the Italian navy, or if it was a slap at Major Armstrong, or perhaps a little of both.

The Birth of Radio Broadcasting Networks

The Radio Corporation of America (RCA)

The Radio Corporation of America (RCA) was formed at the end of World War I, but did not make an appearance on the domestic broadcast scene until the following year. On July 2, 1921, RCA broadcast the Jack Dempsey–Georges Carpentier heavyweight boxing match using an experimental station with the call letters WJY. On December 14, 1921, RCA's broadcast station WDY began operations in Roselle Park, New Jersey, using the WJY transmitter. This station only lasted two months. On February 24, 1922, RCA joined Westinghouse in the operation of their station WJZ. Eventually RCA became the sole owner of the station.

Meanwhile, another of the RCA partners, AT&T, had begun to manufacture and sell radios, calling them "wireless telephones." AT&T claimed that the earlier patent agreements gave it the exclusive right to "toll broadcasting," to manufacturing and selling radio transmitters, and to linking stations together by telephone wire for chain broadcasts. In 1922 it started toll broadcasting and sold commercial advertisements on station WEAF, New York. The first advertisement was for a housing development on Long

Island. The ad, running fifteen minutes at a cost of $100, was aired on five consecutive evenings, and then once again a month later. Although KDKA is referred to as the first commercial station because it operated with the intent of making money by selling radio receivers, WEAF was the first station to air a commercial. The following year, AT&T used its phone lines to link up WEAF and WNAC, Boston, for a simultaneous broadcast of a five-minute saxophone solo. This was an early predecessor of the radio networks to follow.[34]

The first permanent connection between stations was established on July 1, 1923, linking WEAF and WMAF of South Dartmouth, Massachusetts. What many consider to be the first broadcast network premiered on December 6. At that time, WEAF was grouped with WJAR (Providence, Rhode Island) and WCAP (Washington, D.C.).

By 1924, AT&T had linked twenty-two stations, both owned and operated (O&O) and affiliates, in what became known as the "Telephone Group." The stations of RCA, GE, and Westinghouse became known as the "Radio Group." While telephone wires designed for voice and music linked the Telephone Group stations, the Radio Group was forced to use the Western Union lines. These lines were not intended for such a use and proved to be vastly inferior to those of AT&T.

In May 1926 AT&T renamed the Telephone Group stations the Broadcasting Company of America (BCA). Faced with the possibility of government action against their emerging monopoly, AT&T sold their stations to RCA for $1 million. The telephone giant also agreed to stay out of the broadcast market for a period of eight years. In fact, it was 1990 before AT&T made its return. In exchange for the sale, AT&T was granted exclusive rights to provide the means of connecting the RCA stations together. These connected stations later became the NBC network.

Long before there were television networks, there were radio networks. Three of these networks went on to become television networks, but there were many more that didn't make the move to the new medium.

NBC

After acquiring the Telephone Group, RCA, along with the General Electric Company and Westinghouse Electric Corporation formed the National Broadcasting Company (NBC). RCA retained control by being the major shareholder, owning 50 percent of the stock; GE owned 30 percent and Westinghouse the remaining 20 percent of the new company.

The justice department began to scrutinize the NBC and the three individual companies under the existing antitrust laws. In 1930 the justice department brought an antitrust suit against the three corporations, resulting in RCA buying out the other two partners. This made RCA the sole owner of NBC. In an interesting turn, in 1985 GE bought NBC, once again becoming its owner.

The man chosen to head NBC was Merlin Aylesworth, the managing director of the National Electric Light Association. Ironically, he did not even own a radio receiver.

This new entity—the first organized with the purpose of operating a broadcast network in the United States—went on the air on November 15, 1926, at 8 P.M. EST. An announcement of the formation of the National Broadcasting Company boasted "Radio for 26,000,000 Homes." That evening, NBC conducted its first network broadcast, joining the AT&T Telephone Group stations with 3,600 miles of telephone lines. The all-star lineup broadcast lasted for a total of four hours and was reported to have cost in excess of $50,000—about $500,000 in today's money.[35] In January 1927 another network was launched by NBC that united the stations that had been owned by RCA. The two semi-independent networks were identified as the Red Network, the original, and the Blue Network. WEAF became the flagship station of the former and WJZ the latter (see table 1.1).

The names for the two networks were derived quite accidentally from a map of the United States used by NBC engineers. Before the days of satellite and microwave transmission, the stations in a network had to be physically linked by telephone wires. Signals would be relayed from one station to the next, or daisy chained. On a train ride from New York to Washington, RCA chief engineer Alfred Goldsmith and AT&T operations manager Elam Miller set to work planning the potential network routes using a map. One network was drawn with WEAF as the flagship station. The connections from WEAF were drawn using a red pencil. In order to easily distinguish the two networks, the stations connected to WJZ were linked together using a blue pencil. Most people can easily remember that NBC had the Red and Blue networks, but many don't remember that NBC also operated an Orange Network and a Gold Network. These two networks were independent of the Red and Blue because they were operated on the West Coast, and linking with New York would have been too costly. NBC also had a White Network, sometimes called the "Watchtower Network," that carried religious programming—although some sources claim that the White Network was NBC's International Network.[36] The Pacific Coast Network eventually merged the Orange and Gold networks. This new network lasted until 1928, when NBC was able to achieve a coast-to-coast network due to the transcontinental telephone line mentioned earlier.

CBS

CBS had a rather unusual beginning. In 1926 Arthur Judson thought he saw a unique opportunity with the formation of NBC. Judson formed a talent agency with the goal of getting clients booked on the NBC network. Unfortunately, NBC did not accept his offer. Taking a page from many successful business people, Judson, along with three partners, decided that if NBC wouldn't do business with them, they would compete against them.

Table 1.1

Original Red Network Stations

WEAF	:	New York, NY	:	(O&O)
WCAP	:	Washington, DC	:	(O&O)
WJAR	:	Providence, RI	:	
WFI-WLIT	:	Philadelphia, PA	:	
WTIC	:	Hartford, CT	:	
WTAG	:	Worcester, MA	:	
WEEI	:	Boston, MA	:	
WCAE	:	Pittsburgh	:	
WGR	:	Buffalo, NY	:	
WOC	:	Davenport, IA	:	
WTAM	:	Cleveland, OH	:	
WWJ	:	Detroit, MI	:	
WSAI	:	Cincinnati, OH	:	
KSD	:	St. Louis, MO	:	
WCCO	:	Minneapolis, MN	:	
WGN-WLIB	:	Chicago, IL	:	
WCSH	:	Portland, ME	:	
WDAF	·	Kansas City, MO	·	

Original Blue Network Stations

WJZ	:	New York, NY	:	(O&O)
WBZ	:	Springfield, MA	:	
WBZA	:	Boston, MA	:	
KDKA	:	Pittsburgh, PA	:	
KYW	:	Chicago, IL	:	

Early the following year, they formed the United Independent Broadcasters (UIB).

UIB soon signed several stations to its network, including WOR in New York. But there was one major factor keeping the fledgling network from taking off: money. Without the capital to pay for necessities such as airtime, and $8,000 per week for telephone wire connections, UIB appeared doomed. AT&T did not feel that the network was worth the risk and refused to supply connections without money up front.

While UIB was trying to get started, rumors began circulating that RCA was planning to merge with the Victor Talking Machine Company. The Columbia Phonograph Company was Victor's main competitor, and officials at Columbia realized that such a merger could ruin them. Columbia, not wanting to let Victor get the upper hand, knew that UIB was trying to get its network up and running. The Columbia Phonograph Company offered to supply capital in exchange for part ownership in the network and a change in the network's name to the Columbia Phonograph Broadcasting System, Inc. (CPBS). UIB was given $163,000 in startup money, and on April 5, 1927, the two companies officially merged. Columbia hoped that the new name would help it in selling records and phonographs.

With the much-needed money, the UIB—now CPBS—could begin building the network using the leased AT&T lines. On September 25, 1927, CPBS went on the air for the first time. The network, however, was far from the success that all had hoped for. In the first month, CPBS lost $100,000, and the Columbia Phonograph Company soon decided to abandon the sinking ship.

Facing the network's failure once again, Judson went in search of a new financial backer. He found several investors, including millionaire Jerome H. Louchheim as the largest investor. Without the phonograph company as a partner, Judson decided to drop the word *phonograph* from the network's name, but kept Columbia. Thus, with a new influx of money, the new Columbia Broadcasting System (CBS) was born. But the network continued to lose money, while NBC continued to flourish. The frustrated backers soon put their shares in the network up for sale. The network had only a few advertisers, but one of them, the Congress Cigar Company, had had great results with its ads. Realizing the potential of the network and the power of radio advertising, the vice president and secretary of the Congress Cigar Company (who also happened to be the son of the company's owner) purchased the controlling share of CBS for $300,000.

William Paley. Just days shy of his twenty-seventh birthday, William Paley had to repeatedly ask his family for assistance, but eventually he invested around $1.5 million in CBS.[37] With the money and Paley's enthusiasm, the network finally began to make money.

Paley was an innovator in many ways. Realizing that NBC had the lion's share of the market, the astute businessman began to offer incentives to stations. NBC had required stations to pay for the privilege of airing network programming. After all, the network was supplying a product. Paley offered affiliated stations free programming. In exchange, the network received a portion of the individual stations' broadcast schedule in order to sell its advertising. Today this is known as barter syndication. By doing this, Paley was able to increase the number of CBS affiliates, to make it the largest radio network in the United States by 1935.

Soon Paley and David Sarnoff would become bitter combatants. NBC had several years' head start on CBS. In that time, the older network had been able to lure most of the big vaudeville stars to radio. Paley embarked on a series of "talent raids" in order to try to lure some of the big-name stars from NBC to CBS. He was quite successful, and this caused bitter resentment from Sarnoff. He was so successful, in fact, that CBS became known as the "Tiffany Network," either because of the high level of programming it set or, according to some sources, because of the fact that CBS demonstrated color television to the public for the first time at the Tiffany building in New York.[38]

ABC

NBC had been toying with the idea of making NBC Blue a separate network for most of the 1930s. Then in 1939 the Blue Network named Mr. K. Kiggins the network's director and opened a sales department separate from NBC, beginning the process of creating an entirely new network. This caught the eye of the FCC, which started an investigation into chain broadcasting, "to determine what special regulations applicable to radio stations engaged in chain broadcasting are required in the public interest, convenience or necessity."[39] In the meantime, the Blue Network established all of the departments needed to become an independent network (programming, advertising, sales, station relations, promotion, and publicity). The only thing that kept it part of NBC was ownership. And this was the part that troubled the FCC.

Report on Chain Broadcasting. On May 2, 1941, the FCC issued its *Report on Chain Broadcasting,* an event that changed the network landscape forever. While the FCC could not directly regulate the networks, it could control the individual stations. The report said, in part, "No license shall be issued to a station affiliated with a network organization maintaining more than one network." This meant that NBC had to do something to rid itself of one of its networks.

Shortly after the United States became involved in World War II, and after appealing the decision of the FCC all the way to the Supreme Court and losing, the new network was incorporated. Many at RCA wanted to call the network the United Broadcasting System. Others realized the importance of using the familiar Blue Network brand.

All of the stations and personnel of the NBC Red Network and the NBC Blue Network were divided up over the next year. NBC vice president Mark Woods was made president of the Blue Network and was told to sell the company. Sarnoff decided to set the price of the network at $8 million.

The Blue Network had grown from seven stations to three O&O stations and 168 affiliate stations by the time it was put on the block. Some very powerful and well-known groups were among the twenty-eight that expressed interest in purchasing the network. Interested parties included publisher Marshall Field; Paramount Pictures; the banking house of Dillon, Read and Company; and a partnership made up of James McGraw, president of McGraw-Hill publishing company, and Edward J. Noble, the candy magnate. Noble, who had made his money as the owner of the Lifesavers Candy

Company, had purchased a radio station, WMCA, in December 1940 and apparently wanted more.

Edward J. Noble. The story of how Noble made his money with the familiar candy is quite interesting. He was working in advertising sales when he called on Cleveland candy manufacturer Clarence Crane. In the days before air conditioning, chocolate would melt in the summertime. So Crane produced a hard peppermint candy. Noble became interested in the little candies with the hole in the middle that resembled a life preserver. The hole was actually the result of a pill-making machine that Crane employed. Noble thought that with a little promotion and the addition of different flavors the sale of Crane's candy could greatly increase. But instead of buying into Noble's idea, Crane offered to sell the recipe, trademark, machine, the candy in stock, and all of the rights to him. Noble and a friend pooled $1,900 and in 1913 purchased the Lifesaver brand. But Noble found that the candy had a problem. Even though they were packaged in cardboard rolls, they had a very short shelf life. He started wrapping the candies in tinfoil and launched an empire. Eventually Noble would also own the Rexall drugstore chain as well.[40]

During negotiations for NBC Blue, McGraw and Noble parted ways. Noble wanted the network and offered $7 million—a full $1 million less than the asking price.

At the same time that Noble was making his offer, Dillon, Read and Company made a $7.75 million offer—the highest anyone had offered for NBC Blue. Woods, who had been negotiating the deal with the company, accepted their offer and telephoned Sarnoff with the exciting news. But by the time he got through to Sarnoff, he learned that Noble had agreed to the full $8 million and was the new owner of NBC Blue. This was the largest amount anyone in the radio industry had ever paid for a property.

Noble said that the money wasn't his number-one concern. In fact, he didn't purchase the network for profit but for sheer entertainment. An article in a 1943 *Tide* magazine said, "Shining with an enthusiasm that belies his [Noble's] years, the candy manufacturer allowed last week that he could afford to lose quite a bit of money on the Blue and 'still pay the butcher on Saturday night.'"[41]

For the same reasons that NBC did not change the network's name when it broke off to become a new network, Noble decided to keep the Blue Network brand.

In 1945, the network decided that by staying with the Blue designation, the audience might still consider it to be an NBC station. So it started to look for a new name. As World War II came to a close and it was becoming obvious that the Allies were going to win, the network settled on a name that would play upon the listening public's patriotism. In a press release, Woods announced that as of June 15, 1945, the Blue Network would be renamed the American Broadcasting Company (ABC). In another release, Woods said the name was chosen because,

> American so completely typifies all that we hope, and believe, this Company will be and represent to the people of the world. The tradition of independence and free enterprise, liberality in social philosophy, belief in free education for all and in public service—all this and much more is inherent in the name. It is our responsibility to see that our operation of the American Broadcasting Company is such that it will conform to standards and ideals that have come to mean throughout the world—The American way of life.[42]

The Mutual Broadcasting System

In 1934 the most powerful of the independent radio stations, WGN, Chicago, WOR, Newark, WLW, Cincinnati, and WXYZ, Detroit, joined forces to form a network of their own. The Mutual Broadcasting System was more of a co-op than a network. The name *Mutual* was chosen because each of the stations was an owner of the network even though WGN and WOR retained the majority of the shares. While Mutual never became a powerhouse able to compete with NBC or CBS, many of the smaller independents across the country subscribed for the news and programming it offered. *The Lone Ranger* and *Lum and Abner* were two of the better-known programs aired on the network.

Things began to fall apart for the Mutual Broadcasting System in 1935. WXYZ, the station that owned *The Lone Ranger*, left to join NBC Blue. CKLW, a Canadian station, came on board as a replacement. The next of the original four to leave was WLW, which dropped out the following year.

Things began looking up later that year when the Colonial Network of thirteen stations in New England and the ten stations of the Don Lee Network from the West Coast united with Mutual. The number of affiliates began to grow rapidly. The Mutual Broadcasting System reached 300 stations in 1946 and added 100 more in 1947. Just four years later, in 1952, the Mutual Broadcasting System had 560 affiliates. Just as it had added the regional networks of Don Lee and Colonial, Mutual would continue to add more and more smaller networks from all parts of the country. This small but steady growth made Mutual "the world's largest radio network."

The network never became a success in television as the other three radio networks did, but the Don Lee Broadcasting System did go on to experiment in the new medium.

In 1950 the company that owed the Macy's department stores decided to rid itself of its broadcasting division. Don Lee Broadcasting purchased the stations and changed its name to General Teleradio. In 1952 the holdings of the company were sold with 50% (including the a Hollywood production facility) ironically being purchased by the General Tire and Rubber Co.

In 1958 the broadcasting company became RKO General when it bought RKO Films from Howard Hughes. The studios were sold to Desilu

Productions (Desi Arnez and Lucille Ball). Eventually the radio network had several more parent companies: the 3M Company, Amway, and finally Westwood One. Westwood One operated Mutual from 1985 until 1999, when it announced that it was retiring the Mutual Broadcasting System name.[43]

Questions for Further Thought

1   Of all of the inventors/innovators mentioned in this chapter, can any be identified as the "Father of Radio"?

2   There are no women mentioned in this list. Why do you think this is true?

3   What was the most significant step in the development of radio as we know it today?

4   Radio is used more than television, newspapers, or magazines between the hours of 6 a.m. and 6 p.m. Why?

5   Was Tesla a "mad scientist" or did he really invent a "peace ray"?

Shop Talk

Affiliates: Broadcast stations owned by individuals or companies other than the networks that air network programming.

Audion tube: Technical advancement of the Fleming tube. By adding a grid, Lee De Forest was able to amplify signals. The tube was the center of much controversy in that De Forest could not explain why his invention worked.

Barter Syndication: A system where networks supply free programming. In exchange the network sells ad time to run within the program.

Broadcasting: A farming term used to refer to the wide pattern spreading of seeds. This term was borrowed to define the somewhat wide approach of sending radio signals.

KDKA, Pittsburgh: First commercial radio station in the United States.

Narrowcasting: Term used to describe programming to a highly defined audience.

Owned and operated (O&O): Stations owned and operated by one of the networks.

Radio Corporation of America (RCA): Company formed by the pooling of patents held by Westinghouse (acquired from American Marconi), General Electric, AT&T, and the United Fruit Company. Became parent company of the National Broadcasting Company (NBC).

Report on Chain Broadcasting: FCC report of 1941 that stated that the commission would not issue a license to any station affiliated with an organization that owned more than one network. This essentially forced NBC to divest itself of its multiple ventures.

The Beginning of Radio Programming

Perhaps no medium has had such a diverse history of different types of programming as radio. As chapter 1 illustrates, the earliest broadcasts were made by amateurs and hobbyists playing with the new medium. They put their voices and perhaps music into the air to see how far it would reach and who, if anyone, was listening. But this was soon to change.

When World War I broke out, there were over eight thousand wireless radio stations on the air in the United States. But the war put an abrupt halt to the burgeoning broadcast industry. When the navy took over the radio industry, everything ground to a screeching halt. For the duration of the war years, 1917 to 1919, the development of radio for all intents and purposes halted.

Radio was more popular than ever following the war. The increasing number of stations meant that broadcasters had to give the audience an ever growing menu from which to choose. While the goal of the original stations might have been to sell radio receivers, the goal of future stations was to sell airtime to potential advertisers. More listeners resulted in higher advertising rates, and so stations were constantly trying to come up with new and better ideas for programming.

Schools, churches, department stores, newspapers, and even hotels owned many of the earliest stations. Some of the earliest radio programming included religious services, educational programs, music (both live symphonies and recorded), and even nightly bedtime stories. Soon these evolved into more exciting fare. Many of the programs and genres of radio's golden era would later make the transition from radio to television. Most of today's television programs owe their creation in part to early radio programming.

Some radio programs even made the transition from radio to the big screen. *The Lone Ranger* was a motion picture serial as well as being a radio serial. Other programs that were both on radio and the screen include *Blondie*, *The Aldrich Family*, and *Tarzan*. Some movies, like *The Thin Man*, subsequently became radio series. One program, *Screen Director's Playhouse*, took popular movies and abridged them for radio. Drama, comedy, adventure, game shows, news, even variety programming was found around the radio dial.

Children's Programs

Early on, broadcasters saw potential in broadcasts aimed at children. After all, who better to get parents to purchase the new home innovation than the whining child resident in their own homes? Many parents broke down and purchased a radio so that *Little Orphan Annie*, *Superman*, and *Sky King* could come in and entertain. Children were eager to be amused by the new medium and also eager to purchase the products advertised. If *Jack Armstrong: All American Boy* was eating Wheaties, then it almost seemed downright unpatriotic not to do the same; if *Little Orphan Annie* said to drink Ovaltine, then, by golly, Ovaltine it was!

It's hard to say which children's radio program was the first to be broadcast. But one thing is certain: it happened almost immediately upon the advent of radio. Many of the early broadcasts from amateurs and commercial stations included some sort of bedtime story reading.

Sponsors wanted a younger audience, so station and network programming became more sophisticated. Youngsters rushed home from school to tune in to shows such as *Red Ryder* or *Sky King*, featuring his niece Penny (the show's announcer was longtime *60 Minutes* cohost Mike Wallace), or *Little Orphan Annie* (one of the few shows that had a strong female lead).

Many of the children listened in on homemade crystal radio sets. Using a few items from around the house—a piece of wood, a cardboard tube, some insulated wire, a pair of earphones, nails, thumbtacks, a used razor blade, a safety pin, and a pencil—one could make a crude "foxhole" radio. Adding a crystal called a galena for about $1 would greatly improve the homemade device. Something about the properties of galena picked up the powerful radio signals, and acted in the way today's semiconductors do. The eager child would move the "cat's whisker" (actually just a wire) around the stone until the signal came in strong. Moving the pencil tip over the razor allowed the radio to be tuned. These sets did not have amplifiers, so the only way to listen was through a headphone or earpiece.[1]

Most of the early children's shows were fifteen minutes long and, as was common at the time, had only one sponsor. While this could be artistically limiting, since the sponsor had final approval of all scripts, it allowed the sponsor to incorporate advertising into the programs. Many programs offered premiums to its young listeners for exchange of box tops or labels from the sponsor's product. *Little Orphan Annie* and later *Captain Midnight* each had decoders. Somewhere during or after the program a secret code was given that the child would decode with the ring. Usually it was a clue to the next exciting episode. By having this hint, a child with the decoder was king of the schoolyard.

Many of these programs offered membership in fan clubs. Today the radio show premiums—the *Little Orphan Annie Ovaltine Shake up Cup*, the *Tom Mix Straight Shooters Medal*, or the *Captain Midnight* decoder, for example—are highly sought-after collectibles.[2]

The content of the early programs tended to stress values such as good citizenship, healthy behavior, and good triumphing over evil. However, with the coming of World War II many of the shows became, if not overtly, then subtly propagandistic. The villains became Asian, German, or Italian. The content of many of these shows was as violent as—if not more violent than—many of today's children's television programs, culminating in gunfights, explosions, and aerial dogfights. Interestingly, *Captain Midnight* had an episode before the Japanese attack on Pearl Harbor in which he found plans for attacking the harbor at the headquarters of his nemesis, the Barracuda, in Japanese-occupied China.[3]

Not all programming had violent content. Many were designed for the younger child. Programs like *Let's Pretend* and the *Singing Story Lady* focused on fairy tales. Perhaps the strangest of all children's programs was *The Hartz Mountain Master Radio Canaries*, sponsored by Hartz Mountain canary food. This program, which went by different names over the course of its run, featured birds singing current hit tunes.[4]

Even into the 1970s and '80s, there were various attempts to program radio content specifically for children. In the mid-1980s one Chicago station broadcast an inventive talk show for children. The actors who did the voiceover work on various cartoons would be the show's guests, not as themselves, but in character. Children could call in and talk with He-Man, Spiderman, the Smurfs, or others. The show's hosts had another program. Broadcasting live from Chicago's Lincoln Park Zoo, the program was a replacement for the earlier show. While the children in the audience were entertained, those listening to the show on the radio had trouble getting excited about a continuous explanation of what animals looked like.

Table 2.1 Children's Radio Programs

Adventures in Reading	Adventures of Superman
Animal News Club	Ann of the Airlines
Blackstone, the Magic Detective	Bright Idea Club
Buck Rogers in the 25th Century	Captain Midnight
The Cinnamon Bear	The Cisco Kid
Coast to Coast on a Bus	Curley Bradley, Singing Marshal
Dan Dunn, Secret Operative 48	Dick Steele, Boy Reporter
Dick Tracy	Doc Savage
Dorothy Hart, Sunbrite Nurse	Dr. Dolittle
Dr. Six Gun	Flash Gordon
The Flying Family	Green Hornet
Green Lama	Hopalong Cassidy
House of Mystery	Howdy Doody
Jack Armstrong	Jerry of the Circus
Jungle Jim	Junior G-Men
Junior Nurse Corps	King Arthur, Jr.
Kukla, Fran, and Ollie	The Lady Next Door
The Land of the Lost	Lassie
Let's Pretend	Little Orphan Annie
The Lone Ranger	Mandrake the Magician
Mel Blanc's Woody Woodpecker	Mickey Mouse Theater
No School Today	Og, Son of Fire
Omar the Mystic	Once upon a Time
Phantom Pilot Patrol	Popeye the Sailor
Red Ryder	Rin-Tin-Tin
Robinson Crusoe, Jr.	Roy Rogers
Sgt. Preston of the Yukon	Sky King
Smilin' Ed's Buster Brown Gang	Space Adventures of Super Noodle
Space Patrol	Starr of Space
Story Time	Tarzan
Terry and the Pirates	Tom Corbett, Space Cadet
Tom Mix	Treasure Island
Will Bill Hickok	Wizard of Oz

Drama

Drama played an important role in the rise in the cultivation of an audience for radio. Technically, many of the above children's programs were dramas. Drama on radio can be considered any plot-driven episodic or serialized programs with central characters. They differ from programs like game shows or news.

Soap Operas

The radio drama consists of many subgenres. The housewife was the target of one type of drama, the soap opera, which began during the late 1920s and early '30s. This genre was developing just as Americans were taking advantage of new modern conveniences such as ready-made soap, electric washing machines, and the like. Companies needed a way to reach their desired customers. The name *soap opera* was a reference to the detergent companies that sponsored many of the serials. In 1940, 90 percent of commercial radio programs were soap operas.[5]

This was also a time when an influx of immigrants was coming to America. Many of the women listening to the radio while doing their daily housework were learning about American society and, often, how to speak English.

The soap opera usually followed a standard format:

> The defining quality of the soap opera form is its seriality. A serial narrative is a story told through a series of individual, narratively linked installments. Unlike episodic . . . programs, in which there is no narrative linkage between episodes and each episode tells a self-contained story, the viewer's (or in our case listener's) understanding of and pleasure in any given serial installment is predicated, to some degree, upon his or her knowledge of what has happened in previous episodes.[6]

Irma Phillips. In 1930 WGN, Chicago, began airing a fifteen-minute program called *Painted Dreams*. The series was notable primarily because the three characters were female and the scripts were written by an ex–speech teacher, Irma Phillips, who also acted in the series. Phillips would go on to become the person many believe to have been the most prolific writer of the radio era. She created *Today's Children, Women in White, Right to Happiness, Road of Life, Lonely Women,* and *The Guiding Light*. Phillips dictated up to six scripts a day and wrote 3 million words per year according to some reports.[7] Not only was she a prolific writer, but Phillips was also responsible for many of the techniques other soap operas used. She created the cliffhanger ending, whereby a story line would reach a climax just before an episode would end, ensuring that listeners would tune in next time. This is a technique still used in the daytime television soap operas, usually to hold a viewer from Friday to Monday. She introduced the crossover, in which characters from one program appeared on another show (another technique still used in television programming). Yet another technique she invented was the use of music between scenes, or "bridges," that let the listener know that a transition was taking place.[8]

Many of the producers, writers, and stars of soap operas were women. Ironically, however, these powerful working women were creating a make-believe world to appeal to the stay-at-home housewife. This is also true for another format to be examined later—infotainment.

The Hummerts. No review of radio soap operas would be complete without the mention of the husband-and-wife team of Anne and Frank Hummert. Frank was quite successful as a copywriter and advertising executive. Anne was his assistant and later became his wife.

Frank Hummert accepted an offer from a rival ad agency to head a new radio production unit. The Hummerts pitched ideas for shows to clients, then hired writers and actors and oversee their production. Eventually they broke out on their own, starting a soap opera dynasty. At one point they had close to a hundred employees, twenty of them writers, and eighteen shows on the air at once.

The couple were complicated people. Far from being ideal bosses, they were reclusive by nature, doing their work from home and sending it to

Table 2.2 Radio Soap Operas

The Affairs of Doctor Gentry	*Against the Storm*
Amanda of Honeymoon Hill	*Aunt Jenny's Real Life Stories*
Backstage Wife	*Big Sister*
Brighter Day	*Couple Next Door*
Dr. Kildare	*Doctor Paul*
Doctor Susan/Love of Dr. Susan	*The Doctor's Wife*
Front Page Farrell	*The Goldbergs*
The Guiding Light	*Hilltop House*
John's Other Wife	*Joyce Jordan, M.D.*
Judy and Jane	*Just Plain Bill*
Life Can Be Beautiful	*The Light of the World*
Lora Lawton	*Lorenzo Jones*
Ma Perkins	*Myrt and Marge*
One Man's Family	*The O'Neills*
Our Gal Sunday	*Nona from Nowhere*
Painted Dreams	*Pepper Young's Family*
Perry Mason	*Portia Faces Life*
Pretty Kitty Kelly	*The Right to Happiness*
The Romance of Helen Trent	*The Second Mrs. Burton*
Second Stage	*Stella Dallas*
The Story of Mary Marlin	*The Strange Romance of Evelyn Winters*
This Is Nora Drake	*Today's Children*
Valiant Lady	*We Love and Learn*
Wendy Warren and the News	*When a Girl Marries*
The Woman in My House	*Woman in White*
A Woman of America	*Young Doctor Malone*
Young Widder Brown	

their New York studio. Their company, Air Features, paid employees poorly. They would not allow actors to deviate from the scripts at all. Actors had to have perfect diction. The Hummerts had faults, but they were fiercely loyal to their employees. Risking their careers, they refused to fire employees who had been blacklisted during the Communist witch hunts.

The radio soap opera tradition is still carried on today by BBC radio. The program *Westway* is described as a "drama set in the vibrant community around a busy health centre in West London."[9]

Many African nations have soap operas airing as infotainment. One such soap opera, funded by the U.S. Department of State, involves a teacher, Mr. Suma, who is HIV-positive. The program, airing in Liberia, Sierra Leone, the Democratic Republic of Congo, Angola, and Burundi, deals with Mr. Suma's personal life. It attempts to educate the listener about HIV/AIDS, how to avoid contracting it, and what a person with HIV might face and how he or she can continue to live a productive life.[10]

Adventure

Adventure programming was another aspect of drama. Most of these programs followed the exploits of the main character as he or she fought off the evil in the world, for at least fifteen minutes at a time.

Some of the programs were westerns, some were set in outer space, and others were concerned with the cases of private detectives. The most famous of these detectives were in novels, movies, and radio. *Sam Spade*, created by Dashiel Hammett, and *Phillip Marlowe*, a Raymond Chandler character, set the prototype for all private detective characters for years to follow.

The adventure programming and children's programming of the day overlap to some extent. Some of the programs followed the stories of characters from the "funny pages" of the newspaper. Most of the programs on radio at the time were family friendly; after all, radio listening was an activity that the whole family participated in. While today's families may have television sets in every room, at the time, most families who could afford a radio had only one, which was situated in the living room or den. Sitting around the radio and listening to a program was a family event.

There were adventure programs like *The Shadow*, with its well-known opening: "Who knows what lurks in the hearts of men? The Shadow knows . . ." followed by ominous laughter. This program was about crime fighter Lamont Cranston, who learned the secrets of hypnosis on a trip to "the Orient." Using his power, he was able to render himself invisible to those around him. The wonderful thing about radio is that it used theater of the mind. The actor portraying Cranston didn't have to disappear, but to those listening at home, he did!

The Lone Ranger

MUSIC: William Tell Overture Theme Song

SFX: HORSE GALLOPING

Lone Ranger: "HI HO, SILVER, AWAY!!"

SFX: SHOTS (6)

ANNOUNCER: A fiery horse with the speed of light—a cloud of dust and a hearty, "HI HO SILVER" . . . The LONE RANGER!!

MUSIC: William Tell Overture (whole thing)

ANNOUNCER: With his faithful Indian companion Tonto, the daring and resourceful masked rider of the plains led the fight for law and order in the early western United States. Nowhere in the pages of history can one find a greater champion of justice. Return with us now to those thrilling days of yesteryear.

SFX: Fade in Hoof Beats

ANNOUNCER: From out of the past come the thundering hoof beats of the great horse Silver. The Lone Ranger rides again!

SFX: Hoof Beats

LR: (from a distance) Come on, Silver! Let's go, big fella! Hi Ho, Silver—AWAAAY!

SFX: Hoof Beats fade—music up and under as announcer sets scene for this week's adventure.[11]

The Lone Ranger's call to his horse, delivered by Fred Foy, is perhaps the best known line in radio history. Arguably no show captured the minds and hearts of its audience like *The Lone Ranger*. Almost three thousand episodes eventually aired on radio, in addition to the movie, television, and comic book stories. The story was that of a Texas Ranger whose posse was attacked, leaving everyone, including his brother, dead and him the only survivor. Tonto, an Indian the ranger had assisted at one time, found him and nursed him back to health. Later the Ranger donned a mask made from the remnants of his brother's vest so that he could remain dead in the minds of his enemies while fighting injustice and seeking out those who had killed his brother. Each show would usually end with someone asking, "Who was that masked man?" Another person would reply, "I don't know, but he left behind this silver bullet." The bullets were made of silver to remind the Lone Ranger that life was valuable and to never shoot to kill.

The official Lone Ranger creed, written by Fran Striker, stated:

- I believe that to have a friend, a man must be one.
- That all men are created equal and that everyone has within him-

self the power to make a better world.

- That God put the firewood there but that every man must gather and light it himself.
- In being prepared physically, mentally, and morally to fight when necessary for what it right.
- That a man should make the most of what equipment he has.
- That "This government of the people, by the people, and for the people" shall live always.
- That men should live by the rule of what is best for the greatest number.
- That sooner of later . . . somewhere . . . somehow . . . we must settle with the world and make payment for what we have taken.
- That all things change but truth, and that truth alone, lives on forever in my Creator, my country, my fellow man.[12]

Striker was another prolific writer. Working on several programs, he averaged about sixty thousand words per week.[13]

Radio was and still is a popular medium, and one reason is because it is inexpensive. While it would be costly to shoot a movie serial of *The Lone Ranger* or any other adventure story, radio can do it cheaper. A great show needed only a script, actors, and a good sound effects person. One of the main reasons many shows didn't make the transition to television was that the cost was much too high. Some of those that did make the move were little more than dialog with one set.

Coconut shells clapping together stood in for horse hoofs; a piece of sheet metal vibrating was thunder. The audience heard a show that sounded like it was coming straight from the Old West, but in fact it was broadcast from a studio in Detroit. In the absence of visual images, the audience was highly suggestible and able to imagine clearly what the sounds represented.

Later, the same Detroit radio station would update the Lone Ranger character and introduce *The Green Hornet*, the great-nephew of the Lone Ranger. Instead of the *William Tell Overture*, they used *Flight of the Bumblebee* as a theme song. Instead of a horse he had a car, Black Beauty, and the Japanese valet-chauffer Kato replaced Tonto. (When World War II broke out, Kato suddenly became a Filipino.)

Another program that was similar in format to *The Lone Ranger* was *The Cisco Kid*. The Kid was a Mexican cowboy whose actions more than resembled those of the Lone Ranger. His sidekick was Pancho. One difference was that Tonto was stoic, while Poncho was a more affable partner. Mel Blanc, the voice of Buggs Bunny, Elmer Fudd, and the whole stable of early Warner Bros. cartoons, played Pancho in one episode. Blanc also appeared on many other shows and had one of his own that lasted only a year. Later, he would become the voice of Barney Rubble on *The Flintstones*. He was just one example of the many artists who honed their skills doing various character voices and found that their talents were quite useful for cartoons.

Adventure shows, like most of the radio programs of the day, were generally performed live. This could result in some sticky situations. If the actors read too fast that week, the show wouldn't be long enough. Actors who worked with Paul Rhymer, writer of the series *Vic and Sade*, said that Rhymer would sit in a closet and type additional dialog and hand it to the actors if needed.

One radio legend that almost everyone in the industry has heard in one form or another tells the story of a sound effects nightmare. The villain confronting his victim says, "This is the end; take this lead you rat." But for some reason the sound effects man couldn't get the pistol to fire. Quickly ad-libbing, the actor added, "Nah, shooting's too good for you; I'm going to stab you with this knife." Just then the gun went off.[14]

Adventure programming, like most other formats, quietly went off the air with the introduction of television. Some made the transition to television, while others just faded into memories. Yet from time to time there have been attempts to resurrect the genre. In 1981, George Lucas allowed PBS to adapt his *Star Wars* movies for its program *NPR Playhouse*. The thirteen episodes averaged an audience of 750,000, almost twice that of any other program. PBS still airs the popular *Prairie Home Companion*, a music variety show that has two reoccurring skits that pay homage to the adventure programming of old, *Guy Noir, Private Eye* and a skit about two lonesome cowboys, Lefty and Dusty, who ride the range while trying to adapt to today's modern society. Yet another program, while not a drama, does have many elements of the form. *This American Life*, produced at Chicago's WBEZ, allows people to produce mini-documentaries that are woven together under the umbrella of each week's topic.

While not radio broadcasts, there are also numerous organizations, such as *LA Theatre Works*, that adapt plays and movies and record them on CD, a medium that has been dubbed "audio theater." Of course there are also the ever popular books on tape or CD for the traveler.

Comedy

Comedy took several different tracks on radio. The first radio comedy artists were straight from vaudeville. As was the style in vaudeville comedy acts, many of these were teams. Usually one person played the part of the straight man or foil, while the other character, often the dumber of the two, would get the big laughs. Some famous examples of these acts are George Burns and his wife, Gracie Allen (who once announced she was running for president on the Surprise Party ticket); Lou Abbott and Bud Costello, famous for their "Who's on First?" baseball routine; and Jack Benny, his wife Mary Livingston, and African-American actor Eddie Anderson as Rochester. Benny was a genius with the new medium of radio. He used the art of self-deprecating humor to create the image of being miserly and of playing the violin poorly, and even started an on-air radio feud with Fred Allen, another radio host. Rochester, his valet, at a time when this was not the norm for African-American actors, would often get the best lines and sarcastic digs in at his boss.

Early pioneers in radio comedy often just did a rehashing of their old vaudeville routines. But there was an inherent problem. The vaudevillian toured around the country and could usually make a good routine last for years with few variations. Each act performed on radio was the equivalent of months

---

Table 2.3 Adventure Programs

The Adventures of Bill Lance	The Adventures of Father Brown
The Adventures of Frank Race	The Affairs of Anne Scotland
Alias Jimmy Valentine	All Star Western Theater
The Amazing Mr. Smith	The Avenger
Boston Blackie	Box 13
Broadway Is My Beat	Calling All Cars
Case Dismissed	Casey, Crime Photographer
CBS Radio Mystery	Charlie Chan
The Cisco Kid	Cloak and Dagger
The Crime Classics	Crime Club
Crime Does Not Pay	Danger Doctor Danfield
Danger with Granger	Dragnet
Ellery Queen	The Fat Man
Five Minute Mystery	Frontier Town
Gangbusters	Green Hornet
Gunsmoke	The Haunting Hour
Have Gun, Will Travel	Hearthstone of the Death Squad
Helen Holden, Government Girl	The Highway Patrol
Inner Sanctum	It's a Crime, Mr. Collins
I Was a Communist for the FBI	Johnny Madero, Pier 23
Jungle Jim	The Lone Ranger
Mark Sabre of Homicide	Mike Mallow, Private Eye
Mr. Chameleon	Mr. Moto
Mystery House	Philip Marlowe
Philo Vance	Ranger Bill
Red Ryder	Rogues Gallery
Sam Spade	Sgt. Preston
Secret Agent K-7	Sherlock Holmes
Tales of the Texas Rangers	The Thin Man
This Is Your FBI	True Detective Mysteries
Unsolved Mysteries	The Whistler?
Weird Circle	

of touring. New routines were in demand. This is still true for comedians of today who appear on a nationally syndicated programs like the *Tonight Show* or *The Late Show*.

Employing teams of writers helped keep on-air talent sounding witty and intelligent. Radio may have killed vaudeville because it was free entertainment delivered right to living rooms across America during the Depression, but many of those displaced found a home on radio.

Comedy/Variety Shows

Many of the comedy programs were what we term a comedy/variety show. These generally followed a standard format: "they usually opened with a musical number, followed by a monolog (or dialog), then more music, one or more comedy skits, usually featuring guest stars from other shows or movies, still more music, and a short closing bit with the guest star before saying good night."[15] This style is not to be confused with the strictly variety show. This format did not include sketches but was talent-driven. The show could have a singer or performer as the host, but there were other musical guests. The first of these shows on to be broadcast on a national basis was *The Fleischmann Yeast* program starring Rudy Vallee. Newspaper columnist Ed Sullivan, known for his awkward on-camera presence during his twenty years on his television show, first debuted on radio.[16]

Situation Comedy

The situation comedy, or sit-com, is another style of comedy. As the name implies, these are shows that put their protagonists in outrageously funny but often unlikely situations. Some of the more popular shows were *The Life of Riley, Amos and Andy, Ozzie and Harriet*, and the longest running, *Fibber McGee and Molly*. Many of the shows took place in a family home. Part of the formula required either a stable, mild-mannered father dispensing wisdom or a central character with a never-ending stream of get-rich-quick schemes. Usually a gullible but well-meaning best friend would assist this character in his quest. The wife was often the voice of reason, the one person who realized that everyone else involved was crazy. Running gags such as Fibber McGee's overstuffed closet that, through the handiwork of a sound effects device known as a crash box, would overflow whenever he would open it, let the audience feel they knew something that the character didn't. One knew the closet door was going to open, that everything would come crashing out . . . the only question was when would it happen?

Stars from the silver screen also appeared on sit-coms. *Beagle, Shyster, and Beagle* was the original title of a radio program staring two of the Marx Brothers. Groucho played a less-than-honest lawyer, named Waldorf T. Beagle. (The NBC Blue Network changed the program's name to *Flywheel, Shyster, and Flywheel* after an attorney named Beagle threatened litigation.)

The program used many elements and scripts that came directly from the Marx Brothers' previous movies, and some of the program even made it into the movies that followed. An example of this crossover can be seen in a piece of dialog from episode 1, which is repeated almost verbatim in a scene in *Duck Soup*, a film that was made during the year the radio program was on the air. In the scene, Chico, playing the part of Ravelli, Groucho's inept assistant, reports on shadowing a woman for a client: "Monday I shadow your wife. Tuesday I go to the ballgame—she don't show up. Wednesday she go to the ball game—I don't show up. Thursday was a double header. We both no show up. Friday it rain all day—there'sa no ball game, so I go fishing."[17]

The cast was relatively small, with only two of the brothers, Groucho and Chico, appearing. Harpo Marx, who was inadvertently given no dialog in their first movie and remained the silent clown throughout the rest of his on-screen and stage career, obviously wasn't suited for radio.

The brothers were living in Hollywood during this period, while they were making films. Most network programming, however, was being broadcast from New York, which meant that the brothers had to travel cross-country every week. To accommodate them, the show was moved to Hollywood, but writing a radio program, performing, and working on films was too strenuous. Chico was also a notorious womanizer and gambler, and a weekly show surely put a crimp in his activities. According to Harpo Marx in his autobiography, *Harpo Speaks*, Chico's antics were such that one film director put them in a cage to ensure he wouldn't escape before the scene was shot.[18]

The two brothers made other appearances on radio, but the most memorable was Groucho's radio quiz show, *You Bet Your Life*, which later became a TV program. Famous for the line "Say the magic word [pronounced "woid"] and win $100." The show started as a quiz show but soon became a vehicle that showcased Groucho's quick wit, often laced with double entendres, more than that of his contestants, who were often celebrities.

Think of your favorite situation comedy and you'll probably notice many similarities with the radio sit-coms of the 1930s, '40s, and '50s. Many of the comedy programs were funny and still elicit laughter today, while others do not stand the test of time. The "humor" often relied on unflattering stereotypes of minorities or the newest ethnic groups to arrive in the United States. Even in programs where there were African-American characters, white men often played the roles. The most famous were Amos and Andy. The main characters were African-American men who moved to the south side of Chicago from their homes in the South, seeking a better life. White actors Freeman Gosden and Charles Correll played these characters, using stereotypical Southern black dialects. Ex-vaudevillians, they originally created the characters for a radio program in exchange for free meals. They soon became a national hit. Christopher Sterling and John Kittross report that some movie theaters stopped films for fifteen minutes so the audience could listen to the show.[19] Black actors didn't take over the roles until the move to television necessitated it.

Another example was the show *Beulah*, a spin-off from *Fibber McGee and Molly* that aired on radio from 1945 to 1953. Beulah was a black maid to a middle-class white family. But a black actress didn't portray the character; a white actress didn't portray her either. Marlin Hurt, a white *man*, played Beulah. Hurt had played the part on the *Fibber McGee and Molly* program as well. Hattie McDaniel, an African-American actress, took over the role in 1946. She continued in the role until she died in 1953. Interestingly, in 1950 the program began running on ABC television, but starring another actress, Ethel Waters, making it the first television sit-com to star an African American, beating *Amos and Andy* by eight months. The television version ended in 1953 after going through several different stars.[20]

There are even more instances of absurdity on the radio. Edgar Bergen, father of actress Candace Bergen (known for her role on television's *Murphy Brown*), was a ventriloquist. He and his dummy, Charlie McCarthy, had a comedy variety show. While part of the allure of a ventriloquist's act may be his or her comedy, the biggest draw is usually the skill at which he or she can make the audience believe the dummy is alive by using his skills as a puppeteer and, most important, controlling his or her lip movement. Nonetheless, the Bergen-McCarthy show was a hit on radio.

Comedy and variety shows differed from adventure and soap operas in that they were often performed before a studio audience. This is similar to today's television programming. Comedians, comedic actors, and musicians often rely on the feedback of audience members. The very first shows did not have audiences, but soon performers, especially comedians, demanded a live audience.

Table 2.4 Comedy Programs

Abbott and Costello	The Aldrich Family
Amos and Andy	Blondie
Bob and Ray	Bob Hope
Burns and Allen	The Couple Next Door
Duffy's Tavern	Fibber McGee and Molly
Flywheel, Shyster, and Flywheel	Fred Allen
The Goldbergs	Great Gilder Sleeve
Jack Benny	Life of Riley
Melton Berle	Our Miss Brooks
Ozzie and Harriet	

Politics and Broadcasting

Fireside Chats

President Franklin D. Roosevelt was the first president to use the new medium of radio to his advantage. He was also the first president to appear on television when he officially opened the 1939 World's Fair in New York. As the governor of New York, he had found that the radio was an effective way to reach a large number of people. As a politician and public speaker it was also a benefit that he had a voice and speaking style that the audience welcomed.

Many silent movie stars had strange-sounding voices or thick accents. They had to quit the industry because they didn't sound right for "talkies." Some radio stars had to give up their roles after the move to television because they sounded the part but didn't look the part. Roosevelt sounded like a president. In fact, since polio kept him confined to a wheelchair, he felt that radio was the best way to present himself.

During some of the country's hardest times—the banking crisis, the Depression, and World War II—Roosevelt used the radio as a way to talk with the American people, not in a press conference environment, but in what became known as fireside chats. His thirty-minute broadcasts gave the people a sense that even in hard times, the president could get them through it.

Researcher Herbert Gans identifies eight enduring values that people enjoy while reading the newspaper. One of those is "altruistic democracy." The people want a leader who has their best interests at heart.[21] In many ways, Roosevelt was giving this to his audience. He was the father figure who would make sure everything was all right.

This was the first time that the president's office used the radio, but certainly not the last. The practice of radio addresses fell out of favor until 1982, when Ronald Reagan, who had worked in radio in his youth, brought back a Saturday-morning radio address. The addresses continue today.

News

Newscasts were popular on the radio from the beginning. However, news radio as we know it today was nothing like the news on early radio broadcasts. As noted earlier, KDKA came on the air with the presidential election returns and followed that with Frank Conrad reading the newspaper—until listeners got bored. For quite some time, this was the extent of radio news. Newscasts would consist of either reading stories from newspapers, something that is against copyright law if permission isn't granted, or doing what was referred to as "rip and read." Back in the days when the telegraph was new, several newspapers joined together to share the cost of sending news from city to city. The group called itself the Associated Press (AP). More newswire organizations developed into worldwide networks linked together by Teletype machines. Radio announcers ripped the latest news copy off of the machine or "wire" and read it on the air.

A different type of newscast started with Lowell Thomas in 1930. His fifteen-minute broadcasts were the beginning of extended nightly news. In 1930, both NBC and CBS were simulcasting the program *Lowell Thomas and the News*. The agreement was that CBS would broadcast only to the western half of the country and NBC to the eastern half. Soon the show became solely an NBC production. Other networks soon followed suit. With the exception of some special broadcasts, like the famous Scopes "monkey trial," the Bruno Hauptmann trial surrounding the Lindbergh baby kidnapping, or the famous recording of Herb Morrison, of WLS, Chicago, reporting on the landing and explosion of the dirigible Hindenburg ("the frame is crashing to the ground . . . not quite to the mooring . . . oh the humanity"), little changed until the years leading up to World War II.[22]

When it became apparent that radio was making inroads into territory of the newspapers, many newspapers decided to undercut the radio stations by not listing radio schedules. In order to bring an end to the rift, the networks signed an agreement that put strict limits on their news broadcasts. This only lasted for about a year. After the agreement ended, radio stations had the option of taking a story and rewriting it, adding a local angle to it, or reading it straight off the wire. In the race to be the first to bring a big story to listeners, the announcer sometimes read it for the first time live on the air. In an interesting twist, following the ban, a record number of radio stations were owned by newspapers, which apparently took an "if you can't beat them, join them" attitude. A. A. Schechter became the head of the NBC news operations in 1938. His accomplishments include the use of long-distance telephone reports and introducing human interest stories.[23]

At CBS, Paul White introduced the use of on-the-spot reporters, live via short-wave radio from Europe. In 1937 he named Edward R. Murrow, then twenty-eight years old, as the CBS European news director.[24]

As Mathew Brady had brought photographs of war to magazines and to the home front, Edward R. Murrow and his reporters brought World War II into the American living room live, via radio.

German bombs dropped all around Murrow while he reported on his *This . . . Is London* program. Many Americans listened at home and were exposed to something they had never been exposed to: war. Today many turn on the television and watch war as if it is a movie or video game. There have even been recent battles in which the press has arrived prior to the military. But in Murrow's time it was new and it was frightening.

War coverage boosted the number of listeners tuned in to the radio, the amount of radio content being aired, and the number of people involved in the production of the news. News radio was here to stay, at least for the time being.

The U.S. government used the medium for a variety of reasons—civil defense programs, propaganda, and advertising war bonds chief among them. Motivations for the sale of war bonds were many. The government did need money to keep the war effort going, but with nearly full employment and goods like tires, sugar, and gasoline being rationed, people had excess savings. Buying bonds encouraged investing money while the government was heading off inflation. As an added bonus, by investing in the bonds the individual and families were buying into the idea of war. They were supporting the government in its undertaking.

Two government agencies were in charge of selling war bonds. The War Finance Committee was in charge of the sale, and the War Advertising Council, as the name implied, did the advertising. The adverting for war bonds created the largest advertising campaign in the history of the country. CBS aired a sixteen-hour marathon program as part of the effort. This broadcast made Kate Smith's singing of *God Bless America* famous across the country and became her theme song for the rest of her career. The marathon raised almost $40 million through the purchase of bonds.

Hybrid programs mixed news and drama. Shows like *You Are There* and *Time Marches On* were programs that attempted to reenact historical events or the important news of the week. In *Time Marches On*, sponsored by *Time* magazine, actors portrayed newsmakers. With the audiences' awareness that these were recreations and an assurance that every effort was being made to ensure the accuracy of the portrayals, the question of ethics never arose.

In 1951 Murrow began a safer—but nonetheless still interesting—radio project. He asked the American people, from celebrities and politicians to the average person on the street, to write short essays and submit them to a program called *This I Believe*. National Public Radio (NPR) resurrected the program in April 2005.

Infotainment

It may seem that cable channels like DIY (Do It Yourself) or TLC (The Learning Channel) invented the infotainment format, which is programming that teaches the audience in an entertaining manner. This type of programming, however, began on radio long ago. Broadcasts to housewives during the 1930s and '40s dealt with topics such as health, fashion, child rearing, cooking, and consumer education. Talk shows and those following Hollywood gossip were also quite popular.

What makes many of these programs even more important than the idea that they were pioneering a format is that, like the soap opera, many of these programs were produced and hosted by women.

Some of the early shows were *Morning Market Basket*, *The Mary Lee*

Taylor Show, which, even though it only lasted from 1948 to 1949, was the longest running cooking show on radio, and *Pickens Party*, a music and variety program. *The Child Grows Up* and *Children in Wartime* dealt with rearing children.

Many give Walter Winchell credit for the invention of the gossip column. Leaving school in sixth grade, he toured the country with vaudeville and later got a job writing for the *New York Daily Mirror*. CBS hired him in 1930 to do a fifteen-minute business news program, *Saks on Broadway*. NBC Blue hired him away in 1932 to do *The Jergen's Journal*, in which he combined hard news, gossip, and entertainment. He is remembered for his abrupt style, stories that were usually no more than a few seconds long, and his famous greeting of "Good morning, Mr. and Mrs. America and all the ships at sea."[25]

Audience Participation

While most of the early programming on radio was one-way communication, a new format arose that allowed for the audience to join in on the fun. The audience participation program allowed the listener to have some investment in the program. This is very similar to the magician or public speaker who asks for a volunteer from the audience. To the rest of the audience, that person becomes their representative, making sure that everything is aboveboard. The contestant on a radio program became a representative of the men and women listening in at home.

Quiz Shows

Audience participation programs take many different forms. The quiz show is perhaps the best known, and one that is still prevalent on television. Local stations had many different versions of the quiz show. *Professor Quiz*, however, was most likely the first quiz show. The program premiered on WJSV, Washington D.C., in 1936. Contestants had the chance of winning ten dollars if they answered the most questions. The networks would often buy local quiz show ideas, and CBS purchased *Professor Quiz* in 1937. Just as in television today, successful programs spawn many imitators, and the quiz show was off and running.

There were shows that showcased the general knowledge of contestants, or specific knowledge (like music or sports), and ones in which the tables were turned and a panel of experts was subjected to questioning. *The $64 Question* was a show similar to *Who Wants to Be a Millionaire*. A host asked contestants a question, with a correct answer worth two dollars. The contestant could then try a second question, going double or nothing, for four dollars. This could go on all the way to $64. Hardly the millions of dollars that today's shows offer.

Pot o' Gold aired during the Great Depression and featured Horace Heidt and his Musical Knights. At the end of the show Heidt would randomly pick a phone number from around the country and award the person who answered $1,000. This merging of telephone and radio was a major innovation, and it was done on a program that wasn't even a quiz show.

In a precursor to today's programs like *Fear Factor*, other shows had contestants performing outlandish (although tame by today's standards) stunts. A radio announcer who would become one of the leading producers of radio and television game shows for decades, Ralph Edwards, developed the original of this type of show. The program, *Truth or Consequences*, presented contestants with a question. When they got the answer wrong, which they inevitably did, they had to perform a stunt. This program became so popular that a town in New Mexico renamed itself Truth or Consequences for the show's tenth anniversary. The program ran on radio from 1940 until 1950, then on television until 1978, with a short-lived revival in the 1980s.

Still another type of participation show, which one can find in many forms on today's television programming, from makeover shows to talk shows such as *Oprah*, had people who were in financial trouble coming on the programs. Contestants won money, gifts, and even offers of jobs. Many people condemned this type of programming as exploitative of the needy. Yet it was a format that garnered listeners and, more important to the networks, sponsors.

The popularity of participation shows continued to climb until the Federal Communications Commission said that the giving prizes to random listeners was in violation of antilottery laws. Most stations feared the loss of their licenses and no longer wanted to air these programs. The American Broadcasting Company brought suit against the FCC, but the case wasn't settled for six years. The Supreme Court finally ruled in favor of ABC. In order for a contest to be a lottery, three things needed to be present:

1 a prize;
2 chance of winning based on randomness and not skill; and
3 some sort of consideration (money or the like) given for the chance to win.

The court said that there was no consideration exchanged.

Many shows continued to air during the years the case was in the court system, but for all intents and purposes the quiz show had died on radio. One must remember that this was also a time when many shows were making a transition to television and quiz shows were among the easiest to transfer. There was a very low production cost and no star salaries, as contestants supplied the talent.

Talent Shows

American Idol is not a new phenomenon. Years before Simon, Paula, and Randy, there were Major Bowes and Arthur Godffrey and others hosting national and local talent shows.

Local talent shows had been a staple on the traveling vaudeville circuit. Bringing local residents to the stage put family and friends in the seats—and the shows were cheap to produce. Since so many of the people pioneering programming on radio had come from vaudeville, it was just a matter of time before the talent show was brought to the airwaves.

Local independent stations looking for a way to compete with the networks tried many formats. In 1934 WHN aired the talent show *Major Bowes' Original Amateur Hour,* which proved to be a hit. Even though WHN had created the show to combat the networks, it became an NBC Red program the following year. Contestants would come on the show to sing, play music, do imitations, or tap dance. Just as today's *American Idol* hosts can be cruel in their evaluations, Bowes was known for banging a gong to end a performance that either wasn't up to par or if a contestant froze in front of the microphone. The show became a runaway hit for NBC Red, launching the

Table 2.5 Audience Participation Shows

Arthur Godfrey's Talent Scouts	*Art Linkletter's House Party*
Ask-It-Basket	*Beat the Band*
The Breakfast Club	*Break the Bank*
Bride and Groom	*Can You Top This?*
Dr. IQ	*Double or Nothing*
Everybody Wins	*Give and Take*
Grand Slam	*Information Please*
It Pays to Be Ignorant	*Kay Keyser's Kollege of Musical Knowledge*
Ladies Be Seated	*Live like a Millionaire*
Major Bowles' Original Amateur Hour	*Melody Puzzles*
Mr. Hush	*People Are Funny*
Pop Question	*Professor Quiz*
Queen for a Day	*Quiz Kids*
Second Honeymoon	*Stop the Music*
Strike It Rich	*Take It or Leave It*
The $64,000 Question	*True or False*
Truth or Consequences	*Uncle Jim's Question Bee*
Vox Pop	*What Am I Offered?*
What's My Line?	*Who Said That?*
You Bet Your Life	

careers of Frank Sinatra and others. The *Major Bowes Amateur Troupes* was a road show featuring some of the favorite radio contestants. While other shows followed in its wake, none had the following or the staying power of the original.

Talk Shows

One can trace the talk show in one form or another to the 1920s. John J. Anthony, not having the capability of putting a caller on the air, nor the advantage of a delay button, asked listeners to his music program to call in. He then repeated their comments on the air.

Another form of talk show was the panel discussion. The shows reached out to the educated and less educated alike. *The University of Chicago's Roundtable* and *Meet the Press* were two of the more academic. Part of the stations' motivation in airing these shows was to meet the FCC's requirements for serving the community, but a lot of the driving force was that such shows gave a network or station an air of dignity.

Another pioneer of radio talk was Barry Gray. Gray was working on WMCA, New York, when he started putting callers on the air without the station management's knowledge. One evening he randomly placed a phone call on the air as he had done in the past. The caller just happened to be Woody Herman, bandleader of the Thundering Herd. This led to more celebrity phone calls being put on the air, leading to more listeners, which of course made management happy. This new format of celebrity interviews led to today's radio and television talk show format. Gray was also a vocal opponent of racism and the red scare. Such liberal opinions led conservative Walter Winchell to publicly criticize him for his views.[26]

In 1959 KLIQ, out of Portland, Oregon, rolled out its all-talk radio format, becoming the first station in the country to go twenty-four-hour talk. This was unusual in many ways. First, the station did not play music. Second, it had thirty announcers on the payroll. Third, the station made deals with different magazines to get articles in advance of publication to use as topics on the shows (see "Agenda Setting" in chapter 12), and they even had special features flown in from the British Broadcasting Corporation (BBC) every day.

Sports

It was years before radio had the technical capability to carry live sporting events. Nonetheless it did anyway. Before the invention of satellite feeds, microwave feeds, or even cheap telephone connections, there were stations airing live coverage of baseball and football games. Sportscasters would be in the local studio receiving play-by-play copy by telegraph. The announcer would get the play and then call it as if he were there. A sound effects person making the sound of a ball hitting the catcher's mitt or the crack of a bat would sometimes be added to make the broadcast even more realistic. Sometimes sound effects records of crowds were also used. Some stations went so far as to send sound engineers out to ballparks to record as many sounds as possible.

President Reagan often remembered his days working in Iowa covering Chicago Cubs games. One day the telegraph went down in the middle of the game. Not wanting the morning newspapers to have a different report than he did, he had the batter foul the ball into the stands. According to Reagan, it was almost seven minutes before the machine came back on and for all that time, he continued to call the same batter fouling balls at the plate.[27]

Questions for Further Thought

1   It is said that radio programming before television was more active because it made the audience use their minds more. Do you agree or disagree?

2   Are any current television or radio programs similar to those of the early days?

3   How has the audience for soap operas changed over the years?

4   Would any of today's television programs be able to make it on radio?

Shop Talk

Crash box: Sound effects device. Boxed filled with miscellaneous items (glass, metal, and so on) that make the sound of things falling or an accident.

Crystal radio set: Homemade radio receiver using a galena crystal and no power supply.

Fireside chats: Radio addresses given to the public by Franklin D. Roosevelt during the Depression. So called because he liked to think of the American family, sitting by a fireplace listening to him speak.

Soap operas: Serial dramas first introduced on radio during the late 1920s. The name is derived from the fact that soap operas were written for housewives, and advertisers tended to be producers of detergents and other household items.

Spin-off: Program in which a popular character from one program becomes the main character on a new program. Producers will also sometimes try out a character on an existing show before committing to produce the new program.

Theater of the mind: The concept that people listening to a radio broadcast will fill in the visual elements, often adding creativity to the original endeavor.

3

Radio Comes
of Age

The Evolution of Content

The content of radio programming was slowly evolving in the years prior to and after World War II. Station executives and sponsors were making the most of these changes. Outside factors were influencing on-air content as well. Many artists viewed getting their records played on the air as a win-win situation. The stations were getting free programming, but in exchange they were receiving free publicity. Caesar Petrillo, the president of the American Federation of Musicians (AFM), feared a time, however, when live music would be phased out, leaving many musicians without gigs.

Caesar Petrillo

Petrillo demanded that royalties be paid to the musicians for every record sold to the public, but the record companies refused. He called a general strike forbidding artists from making records for the large labels. In 1937 he began a "standby" policy, in which Chicago radio stations were required to have paid musicians on hand in case the record playback equipment should fail. The technology was still new enough that its reliability was questionable. The stations had little recourse. If they refused, Petrillo could ban musicians from playing on their live broadcasts. Soon the AFM ruling went into effect nationwide. The strike lasted for over two years, until the record companies agreed on a $1\frac{1}{2}$- to 2-cent royalty for each record sold. This money went to pay musicians for free public performances in parks and similar venues.[1]

Congress passed and enacted the Lea Act, sometimes referred to as the "Anti-Petrillo Act," in 1946. The act was in response to Pertillo's strong-arm tactics that forced stations to hire unnecessary musicians. The Supreme Court upheld the act on appeal in 1947 as constitutional. The act was added to the Communications Act of 1934, "Coercive Practices Affecting Broadcasting §506(a)." The addition stated that it was illegal to put pressure on broadcast licensees to hire more people than they needed, but did not say that the stations could not be unionized.

> It shall be unlawful, by the use or express or implied threat of the use of force, violence, intimidation, or duress, or by the use or express or implied threat of the use of other means, to coerce, compel, or constrain or attempt to coerce, compel, or constrain a licensee
> (1) to employ or agree to employ, in connection with the conduct of the broadcasting business of such licensee, any person or persons in excess of the number of employees needed by such licensee to perform actual services.[2]

The courts reversed the Lea Act in 1980. DJs could not play music at some major-market stations prior to that time: they simply announced the tunes, while an AFM union member actually played the music. Often the International Brotherhood of Electrical Workers (IBEW) also unionized these stations. Only union electricians could do tasks as commonplace as plug in a piece of equipment.

The DJ

Television had a major impact on the radio industry. Just as radio had taken audience members and talent from vaudeville, television could have easily been the death of radio. For a while, some stars appeared both on television and radio. Whether they were using the radio as a safety net in case television failed, or whether they wanted to be loyal to their radio listeners, is debatable. What is clear is that the networks were putting the majority of their resources into the new medium and leaving radio stations with less content. Even those stars who had been doing shows on both media began moving to television. Even the shows that the networks were supplying no longer had the drawing power of radio's golden age. Stations were faced with a huge challenge: how to keep afloat in the waves that television was making.

One solution, and one that ultimately saved radio, was to reinvent itself. Dramas, adventures, comedies, and shows using live orchestras would no longer be affordable. Stations could not count on being a member of the national networks; instead they began turning back to a localized format. One of the least expensive formats was a disc jockey (DJ) playing recorded music, occasionally giving the time, weather, and perhaps local news. During the late 1940s and into the '50s this format became the standard. It also made radio a more intimate medium. The family no longer gathered in the living room to listen to radio—radio was no longer a family event. That was reserved for television. Now radio was more of an individual experience, with one person talking to a large audience, one person at a time.

Radio Takes to the Road

Another huge boon for radio was the addition of radios to cars. Inventors began experimenting with portable radios early on. The St. Louis World's Fair in 1904 was the scene of one of the first public demonstrations of a portable radio. Paul Galvin, Elmer Wavering, and William Lear (who later made a name as an airplane designer) invented a superior system that was commercially viable. Taking the word *motor* and the brand name *Victrola*, they called their radio "Motorola."

During World War II, Americans were limited in the use of their cars. The war effort required rubber for tires, as well as gasoline. The government rationed gasoline and lowered speed limits. Driving was only for necessity. Following the war, however, driving could be for pleasure. American society became a mobile society, rife with drive-in movies and drive-in restaurants, as more and more people relied on their cars. Radios were a part of that experience.

By 1952, over half of all cars sold had a radio installed. An in-car record player, the Highway Hi-Fi (high-fidelity), was offered by Chrysler 1956. The record player was mounted under the dash and played special seven-inch records. A suspension system that would overcome the everyday bumps common in driving made the player possible, according to company claims. However, there were problems with the system.

The records were smaller than normal (7$^1/_2$ inches), unbreakable, and recorded at a new speed. Before this, record speeds were 78 rpm (revolutions per minute), 33$^1/_3$ rpm, and the newly introduced 45 rpm. The Chrysler system recorded at 16$^2/_3$ rpm. Playing the records at home was impossible. Additionally, there was a very limited catalog of music available. A new 45-rpm in-car player hit the showrooms in 1960. It also failed.

Changes in Musical Tastes

The war had exposed many soldiers to different types of music. The soldier from New York may have been in a unit with one from Alabama, a white sailor from California might have become friends with a black sailor from Mississippi. In this way a musical cultural exchange occurred. Exposure to genres like jazz or western swing meant that some vets were more likely to listen to them when they came home than they might have been otherwise. "Hillbilly" music, rhythm and blues, and other regional music began making its way onto the airwaves.

At the same time, another movement was underfoot. In general, every generation rebels against the music of its parents. As hard as it is to believe, parents at the time viewed big band music as not being respectable. The same was true for the generation of teenagers of the 1950s. Where big band music had been popular during the war, and artists such as Pat Boone and Frank Sinatra were still popular with some teens, a new type of music was crossing racial barriers.

As R&B was beginning to make headway into the mainstream, white artists began to cover the songs—though in a much less "hip" way. These records often got airtime while the original records did not. Pat Boone was one of the artists who were bridging the gap between the big band era and that of rock and roll. He was the all-American kid, with a cardigan sweater and smooth, crooning style of singing. Yet he released many R&B songs, such as Little Richard's "Tutti Frutti" and "Long Tall Sally" and Fats Domino's "Ain't That a Shame." In a bizarre irony, his version of the Domino song was at number one on the charts while Domino's own version was at number ten.

Desegregation was still in the distant future while white teenagers were first being exposed to black artists. Some white bands began covering songs of these artists, and many parents were not happy about the development. This new music was a rebellion against parents and society, just as, later, punk rock and grunge were movements against the establishment and parents.

Some names emerged at this time as being instrumental in the development of radio and what teens were listening to: Alan Freed, Sam Phillips, Barry Gordy, Wolfman Jack, Murray the K., Todd Storz, and Gordon McLendon.

On the Air

Alan Freed

Alan Freed was a disc jockey who had worked at a number of stations when he landed a gig hosting a late-night request show at Cleveland powerhouse station WJW. A local record-store owner reported that both black and white teens were buying rhythm and blues albums. Records referred to as "race records" were not getting airplay in Cleveland at the time. Freed soon began *The Moondog Show*, which became a huge success. He refused to play the covers of songs done by white artists, instead airing the originals. In 1952 he put together the Moondog Ball in a twelve-thousand-seat venue. It drew over 25,000 people. In 1953 he moved to New York station WINS. Freed was sued over the use of the name *Moondog*, and soon "Alan Freed's Rock and Roll Party" was born. Where the term *rock and roll* comes from is up for debate; some claim that a secretary came into Freed's studio saying that the whole station was rocking and rolling, while some say Freed knew that he could not get away with playing rhythm and blues on the air so he dubbed it rock and roll.

Yet others say that the phrase has a long and more interesting origin. *Rocking* and *rolling* are terms that sailors had used for centuries to describe how a ship responded during high seas. At some point *rocking* made it into the African-American gospel music. Becoming connected with God was "rocking," an expression of joy and jubilation.

In the late 1940s blues artists began to slip in the word *rocking* as a double entendre to refer to sex. The first of these songs was probably "Good Rocking Tonight." The song, first recorded by Roy Brown in 1947, did not become popular until an artist by the name of Wynonie Harris did a cover with a gospel beat instead of the original blues beat.

Freed went on to appear in several movies and have his own television show. He lost everything, though, in the "payola" scandals. (Chapter 10 examines payola.) Freed refused to sign a statement saying that he had not taken part in the practice and was fired. Following this, he also faced charges of income tax evasion.

Murray the K

To replace Freed, WINS moved the late-night DJ, Bruce "Cousin Brucie" Murrow into his slot and hired a young DJ from another station, Murray "the K" Kaufman. Kaufman soon built a large fan base and moved into the early time slot, 7:00 P.M. to 11:00 P.M., when Murrow left for another station. Murray the K became more than just a DJ; he became a part of rock and roll. He produced and promoted concerts that had interracial acts and audiences during the early 1960s. He produced compilation albums, marketed items with his name, and even became a member of the Beatles' entourage. He appeared in their movie *Help!* and was even called the fifth Beatle.

During one stretch, Murray the K's rating was twenty points above that of his nearest competition, something that is unheard of today. His influence lives on in many of today's DJs, and the Ramones song "Rock n Roll Radio" immortalizes him, along with Alan Freed.

Wolfman Jack

Wolfman Jack, whose real name was Bob Smith, was born in Brooklyn, New York. He began his broadcasting career as "Daddy Jules" on station WYOU, Newport News, Virginia.

As "Big Smith," he started working on air for KCIJ, Shreveport, Louisiana, in 1962.[3] Soon he would develop the persona of "Wolfman Jack" on a Mexican radio station, XERF, licensed to the city of Ciudad Acuña,

Coahuila, across the border from Del Rio, Texas. His deep scratchy voice, howling, and patter made his show instantly recognizable. Smith was a huge fan of Alan "Moondog" Freed and took his on-air name as an homage to him and the blues legend Howlin' Wolf.

His choice of vocal style was due to two factors. First it was to keep his true identity a secret from the audience and make him more mysterious. Second, he already had a daytime program at KCIJ. Smith wanted to disguise his voice from his present boss in order to keep both jobs.

An owner of a competing station that had gone off the air, Larry Brandon, contacted an attorney, Arturo Gonzalez, who had an agency that represented the Mexican station to U.S. advertisers. Brandon purchased all the nighttime hours that he could and started sending one-hour taped programs to him in Del Rio. He in turn would bring the tapes to the station in Mexico. According to a report from one of the DJs, Don Logan, "the taping came to an end when Brandon began offering XERF listeners an autographed picture of Jesus."[4]

Smith then went to Gonzalez, who had him cross into Mexico each evening to host his show live. He left the station after only two years, in part because of the dangerous neighborhood surrounding the station, and began appearing on a station in Minnesota; he soon left it to return to border radio and larger audiences. The second time he was on XERB, Tijuana. Due to his voice and eclectic choices of music, most of the audience across the United States believed that Smith was an African American. It wasn't until the movie *American Graffiti* that most people first got a glimpse of the Wolfman, a white man with a beard that was reminiscent of a beatnik and greaser hairdo from the 1950s. He later went on to appear on *Burt Sugarman's Midnight Special*, a weekly program that presented musical acts and videos pre-MTV.[5]

Behind the Scenes

Gordon McLendon and Todd Storz

Gordon McLendon, a man recognized as the innovator behind much of radio's programming beginning in the late 1940s, along with Todd Storz, is generally credited with coming up with the idea of what is known as Top 40 radio. The story says that Storz and McLendon were sitting in a bar one night when they suddenly realized that people would tend to play the same songs over and over on the jukebox. This gave them the notion that people were not interested in hearing a lot of different music on radio, but rather wanted to hear the familiar songs, or songs that were popular hits. By limiting their playlists to just the top forty songs, they would get more listeners. The rest, as they say, is history. Later McLendon applied the show's format to an entire radio station.[6]

However, to at least one researcher, this story is a myth. Richard Fatherly claims that the origins of Top 40 came from a study conducted in 1950 at the University of Oklahoma and a station in New Orleans that aired a show playing the week's Top 20.[7]

Sam Phillips

Meanwhile, Sam Phillips, an announcer and engineer for WREC radio in Memphis, opened a business at the now famous 706 Union Avenue. His Memphis Recording Service started recording blues artists who were playing Beale Street and the surrounding area. Some of the artists making their first records were B. B. King and Howlin' Wolf. Another historic event occurred in 1951 when he recorded the song "Rocket 88" by Jackie Brenston. Many people consider this to be the first rock and roll song. Soon after, Phillips founded his own label, Sun Records. Looking for a new sound, he eventually hit upon a mix of country and rhythm and blues. He termed this new music "rockabilly." Sun Records had a stable of artists that included Johnny Cash, Carl Perkins, Jerry Lee Lewis, and a young truck driver named Elvis Presley. Phillips claimed he "could make a fortune" if he could "find a white man who sang black,"[8] and he found this in Elvis. One also needs to give credit to another young artist, Otis Blackwell. Elvis could not read music. Blackwell, an African-American songwriter and singer, wrote songs and recorded them. Presley then received the tapes and mimicked his style, receiving cowriter credit on the records, even though, according to Blackwell, the two men never met.

Among the songs Blackwell wrote for Presley were "Don't Be Cruel," "All Shook Up," and "Return to Sender." He also wrote "Great Balls of Fire" and "Breathless," recorded by Jerry Lee Lewis, and many more. This new form of music, part R&B, part country, with a little gospel thrown in, had an ever-growing audience that crossed racial barriers. This rhythmic sound helped to engrain the place of the DJ show even more into the teen culture of the time.

Barry Gordy

Barry Gordy is yet another person who helped form the music that took radio by storm. Gordy was a somewhat successful songwriter by the mid-1950s. His first hit record was "Reet Petite," recorded by Jackie Wilson and later paid tribute to by Van Morrison in the song "Jackie Wilson Said (I'm in Heaven when You Smile)." His next hit was "Lonely Teardrops," which Wilson also recorded. He continued to have modestly successful records, but when the record store he was managing went bankrupt he decided to start his own label, just as his sister had done. He started Tammie Records, but later changed the name to Tamla and added the Gordy, Soul, and

Motown labels.[9]

With borrowed money he rented a house in 1959 and built a recording studio. The small studio, located at 2648 West Grand Boulevard in Detroit, is a mecca among music buffs. The studio was named "Hitsville U.S.A," and his Motown label became a huge success. In an industry that is often hit or miss, Hitsville lived up to its name: 75 percent of the singles Motown released went on to appear in the Top 40 charts at one point.[10] The Supremes, the Miracles, the Four Tops, and later Stevie Wonder and Michael Jackson are among the artists who signed with Motown. Today the Universal Motown Record Group boasts artists such as Brian McKnight, India Arie, and Three Doors Down.[11]

Holland, Dozier, and Holland

Part of this was due to three talented teens that Gordy hired to write songs. The team of Eddie Holland, Lamont Dozier, and Brian Holland were paid two dollars per week plus 1/2 cent per record and had to punch a time clock just like they would at any other factory job. The songs they wrote, including twenty-five top ten hits, and the artists who recorded them, reads like an all-time greats list.

Included among their hits:

Where Did Our Love Go	Diana Ross and the Supremes
Reach out I'll Be There	The Four Tops
How Sweet It Is (to Be Loved by You)	Marvin Gaye
Heat Wave	Martha Reeves and the Vandellas
Ain't Too Proud to Beg	The Temptations
Baby I Need Your Loving	The Four Tops
This Old Heart of Mine	The Isleys
Take Me In Your Arms (Rock Me . . .)	Kim Weston

In 1967 the trio left Motown to start their own label. This resulted in a lawsuit with Motown, but eventually they started Hot Wax and Invictus records. The Holland-Dozier-Holland (HDH) Company has produced artists ranging from the Chairmen of the Board, to Freda Payne, to Parliament.

Today's Radio Formats

The type of programming a station airs, music or news, rock or urban, or the subgroups within genres, is called a format, which essentially represents a break from broadcasting, as it is actually narrowcasting. With the number of stations growing after World War II and the rise of television, radio programmers needed to find ways to reach a specific audience instead of the wide approach of the past. The format a station chose was based on several criteria, among them being what other stations in that market were playing. If everyone else is playing a version of rock, perhaps playing a different type of music would be a better option. One cannot expect everybody to like the same music. Another criterion is who the target audience is. While news and talk formats tend to have fewer listeners, the ones that do listen tend to be older, with more education and higher incomes. Therefore, stations can charge potential advertisers a higher rate to reach these desirable customers.

When industry people talk about formats, they usually make distinctions based on the style of music being played, (for example, country or rock), the subgenre within that style (classic country or soft rock), and the age of the music (1970s, '80s, or current). It is important to note that one cannot decide what format a station is programming just by reading the name of a song or artist. Country artists often cover rock and urban songs and vice versa. Style plays a key role.

Today there are many formats available to the listener. *Radio and Records*, an industry magazine, and Arbitron, the radio ratings service, each list fourteen broad categories of station formats, although they are not the same. Arbitron breaks its fourteen into fifty-five subcategories. In the *2002–2003 Broadcasting and Cable Yearbook* there are forty-nine categories listed.[12]

The *2006 Radio Marketing Guide and Fact Book* gave the following numbers for stations reporting a format:

Rank/Format/# of Stations

1	Country 2019	2	News/Talk 1324
3	Oldies 773	4	Latin/Hispanic 703
5	Adult Contemporary 684	6	CHR (Top 40) 502
7	Sports 497	8	Classic Rock 461
9	Adult Standards 405	10	Hot AC 380
11	Soft Adult Contemporary 324	12	Religion (Teaching, Variety) 318
13	Black Gospel 286	14	Rock 270
15	Classic Hits 262	16	Southern Gospel 207
17	Contemporary Christian 174	18	Urban AC 153
19	Modern Rock 152	20	R&B 150
21	Ethnic 112	22	Alternative Rock 104
23	Jazz 84	24T	Pre-Teen 59
24T	R&B/Oldies 59	26	Adult Hits 59
27	Variety 38	28	Gospel 36
29T	Modern AC 28	29T	Classical 28
31	Easy Listening 20	32	Other/Format Not Available 3[13]

Audience Testing

So how do stations decide what format is right for them and what music to play? Programmers first examine the market looking for underserved niche markets. Often they find an existing audience they feel their station can better serve. Surveying potential advertisers can tell if they are willing to advertise on a station with a specific target audience. Focus groups are sometimes brought together to ask members of the key demographic their opinions of the current radio market. But often it is just a gut decision by a station executive.

After the format decision, the station must then decide what to play. Some stations do call-out research that asks people in their audience demographic questions about certain songs. They may ask, "Have you heard of 'XYZ'?" or more often play hooks from different songs. Hooks are just a part of the song that is easily recognizable, often the part that gets stuck in your head all day. They may then ask, "On a scale of one to five, how do you feel about the song?"

Determining if a song has been receiving too much airplay is another important factor. So a question may be included that asks the person to rate how tired they are of hearing the song. While this is a rather inexpensive technique, it does have drawbacks. One drawback is that a song may not have been on the air long enough for the listener to recognize it or even have an opinion about it. As in all research of this type, listeners may give answers that they think the interviewer wishes to hear. The call-in is another version of this research. Here listeners call in to the research office to take the test at their convenience or log on to the station's website. The drawbacks of this technique are similar to those of request and talk shows: the people who call are usually not a true representation of the audience as a whole.

Auditorium testing invites a large group together to listen to hooks and rate them. This is a good technique when older songs are involved. If researchers assume the audience already knows the music, they can play more songs. A drawback to auditorium tests is that they often use hundreds of songs, instead of a handful played during a call-out. This requires a much larger time commitment by participants. To entice participants incentives usually are given.

Another technique is to take song requests that have come into the station and tally them to come up with a top ten most requested song list. *Billboard* magazine, the *College Music Journal* (CMJ), and other industry sources rate songs as to their popularity by format. These lists become a bible of what to play at some stations, especially contemporary hits stations.

The final way a station may decide what music to play is by subscribing to a service. For a fee, usually a percentage of the station's revenue, a station can have a larger company with more resources do all the programming and supply it to the station. Records or tapes were the delivery method in the past. Today's programming may come digitally via satellite or over the Internet.

Many stations have even done away with local DJs. Beginning in the 1980s, stations were able to receive live broadcasts that included music and DJ patter and song introductions. The Satellite Music Network, located in Mokena, Illinois, and operated by Bonneville broadcasting, was one such operation. Operating out of a strip mall, the network had DJs playing music in several studios, each with a different format. The DJ was careful never to say the time, instead using phrases like "It's fifteen minutes after the hour" or "Coming up on the hour we'll have music by . . ." This allowed stations in any time zone to subscribe.

The secret to the SMN formula was that each station received several "liners" each month. The DJs would record things such as station call letters, promos for local events, even a variety of vague weather reports. At a certain time during the hour, the DJ would push a button on the control board triggering tape machines across the country. So an audience member in Minnesota may have heard the DJ say, "I hope you're out enjoying this beautiful sunny day," while someone in Arkansas may have heard "Don't forget about the chili cook-off at the VFW on Friday night." This, along with a chance to include local newsbreaks, gave the stations the illusion of being live and local, but still very polished.

The following is a list and brief discussion of some of the more popular radio formats. One thing to notice when reviewing the artists under each format is today's trend toward crossover artists. Therefore, where it was once easy to classify artists as falling into a certain category of music and one particular format, today it is harder to attempt to pigeonhole music and formats.

Adult Contemporary (A/C)

This format can trace its roots back to the 1950s, when stations wanted to keep playing current music but did not want to play the louder, rhythmic rock music. These stations turned to a mellower type of format, known by many different names, including middle of the road (MOR) and easy listening. "Elevator music" is another of the names critics gave the genre, referencing the nonoffensive music played in elevators.

Songs on the air at easy listening and MOR stations often were on the air at soft rock stations during the 1970s. *Crossover* is the name of this phenomenon. Grouped under the category of "adult standards" along with "nostalgia" and "variety," some easy listening and middle of the road stations still remain.

In the 1970, the format took on the new name of adult contemporary (A/C). In its present form, A/C mixes current songs with recurrents, songs returning to the station's airplay list after several months to two years. These songs are still fresh enough in the listeners' minds to elicit a "Hey, I haven't heard that song in a while" response, thus bringing a listener from passive to active participant. Research shows that the typical audience member for A/C is female (two thirds of the listeners), thirty-five to forty-four years old, does not like oldies, is not a fan of instrumental music except for New Age music, likes up-tempo music, and is more loyal to the song than a particular artist so wants to hear the titles identified. Front announcing, where a DJ tells the audience what songs are about to be played, or back announcing, where the on-air personality announces what has just been played, can easily achieve this. Arbitron breaks this heading into A/C, hot A/C, moderate A/C, and soft A/C, depending on the style of music.[14]

Hot A/C tends to play mostly new music or current hits, while soft or "lite" A/C leans more toward the older easy listening format, including music from a period of ten to fifteen years. Moderate falls somewhere in the middle of the two.

The percentage of stations programming each A/C format are:

A/C (7.2 percent)   Hot A/C (3.7 percent)
Moderate A/C (0.6 percent)   Soft A/C (1.4 percent)[15]

Alternative Rock

There isn't one but actually many versions of alternative rock, as the name implies. During the turmoil and disenchantment of many young people, a format arose on the new frontier, FM. Some stations allowed DJs total freedom to play whatever they wished. Sometimes called "freedom radio" or "underground radio," the new format meant DJs no longer were restricted to playing from a strict Top 40 or any other playlist. These stations played what many would consider at the time to be counterculture music. Antiestablishment music featuring bands such as the Grateful Dead or Frank Zappa and the Mothers of Invention aired on these stations.

Program directors soon wanted to regain some control over the on-air content, so stations began to steer away from freedom radio and move into a new format, album-oriented rock (AOR). These stations offered something that Top 40 and other stations did not. The AOR stations would play cuts that were much longer. Iron Butterfly's "In-A-Gadda-Davida" at seventeen minutes or Led Zeppelin's long "Stairway to Heaven" are two classic examples. Some programs would even play an entire album. As the name suggested, these stations would play cuts that were too long for the traditional station.

Songs fitting onto a 45-rpm single had a better chance of getting airtime and becoming popular. Even though 45s can hold up to seven minutes, bands knew that in order to receive airplay the songs had to fit in a three-minute to three-and-a-half-minute window. This left a minute and a half open every five minutes for news, commercials, and announcing.

On rare occasions, a song like "American Pie" was continued on the B-side of a 45. This made it difficult for the DJ who had to put the song on tape, or have two discs ready. When side one faded out, he or she would start turntable two.

The AOR format continues today under the category of "rock," but a new format emerged with some revisions in the music to appeal to a different audience. In the 1980s alternative stations often played music by new wave, punk, or hair bands. Artists such as INXS, Black Flag, the Dead

Kennedys, and Poison began getting airtime. In the early 1990s the Seattle grunge music led by Nirvana, burst onto the scene, becoming a staple of the alternative format.

Today's categories are "adult alternative album" (AAA) and "alternative." Alternative stations play some of the music of the 1970s through today's current hits and target younger audiences.

AAA, in an effort to reach the older adult market, plays a wide range of music. Besides the music of the standard alternative station, it may also include blues, jazz, folk, country-rock, and more. Some publications call this "progressive" radio. The percentages of stations with each type of alternative format are:

Alternative (3.1 percent)   AAA (0.9 percent)[16]

Contemporary Hits Radio (CHR)

Of all the formats, CHR is perhaps the closest to Top 40. Radio-station owners usually seek a new format when there is a slip in listeners or in advertising sales. In the 1980s radio stations began to use a variation of Top 40 introduced by radio consultant Mike Joseph. This new format moved away from some of the standard features of Top 40. The rotation saw oldies and declining records removed. The top thirty songs replaced the top forty. The music was more up-tempo and the format became almost exclusively heard on FM. Within a matter of a few years, it became the number one format, targeting an audience of thirty-four and older.

While it may sound odd to limit a station to thirty songs, one must remember that the average listener to a CHR station only tunes in for a portion of the day. Even if one tunes to a station all day, one is usually passively listening while doing something else. A song can be on a playlist for weeks before the average listener starts to remember it, like it, and request it. It's a totally different story for the DJs who play the repetitive format, however.

Of course, as more stations adopted this format, the competition for listeners became stiffer. Many stations began tweaking their formats, inventing newer versions of CHR. While the original format was aimed at all listeners, some decided to target only adult listeners, or those twenty-five to thirty-four years old, and became "CHR adult," playing a slightly different set of songs and using different on-air personalities that encouraged audience participation. Today's CHR station plays mostly popular music that is on the charts.

CHR/pop is another version of CHR. CHR/pop skews toward an older female audience by simply drawing its music from a deeper pool going back ten to fifteen years. Music on a pop station tends to be more up-tempo than the traditional CHR station.

Contemporary hits radio (CHR)/rhythmic is also very much like the CHR format, but this version plays more dance music and music with a stronger beat.

The percentages of stations programming each CHR format are:

CHR/pop (5.8 percent)   CHR/rhythmic (4.5 percent)[17]

Country

One can trace many of the early bluegrass and "hillbilly" ballads back to England, Ireland, and Scotland. Passing music down from generation to generation, in the oral tradition, most of these came to America in the 1600s and 1700s. But there had to be a transformation for these ballads to become what we consider to be country music. According to the Country Music Hall of Fame, "Country music is rooted in the folk traditions of the British Isles. In the new world, those roots became entangled with the ethnic music of other immigrants and the African slaves."[18] In fact, early settlers attempted to replicate the bagpipe music of Scotland by using the fiddle, a staple of country music. The banjo was actually a variation of an African instrument, sometimes known as the "banjar," that featured strings stretched over a drum. Today that influence is not heard in new country as much as it is in bluegrass.

Country music is one of the oldest radio formats. The "hillbilly" music first aired in 1922. This format has also undergone many changes in artists and styles of music. It is hard to say what station began playing country music first. The phrase *country and western* eventually replaced *hillbilly* to describe the music in the 1940s. This format mostly played the music of southern Appalachia, as sung by the Carter family, Jimmy Rogers, and Fiddlin' John Carson, as well as the songs popularized by the singing cowboys such as Gene Autry, Roy Rogers, and Tex Ritter on radio and in the movies.

As early as 1923, WBAP, Fort Worth, was airing a barn dance variety show. In 1924 *The National Barn Dance*, a precursor to *The Grand Ole Opry*, was aired from Chicago's WLS. In 1933 the ABC network aired it across the country. WSM, Nashville, hired the shows announcer, George D. Hay, in 1925, to create a similar show for its station. According to *Radio Digest* voters, Hay was the number one announcer in America. The NBC network picked up the show in 1927. The show followed the National Symphony Orchestra on the lineup. Popular legend says that one night Hay came on the air and said, "For the past hour you have heard music, largely taken from grand opera; now we will present the Grand Ole Opry."[19] The name stuck, and the program has become the longest-running live program in history.

With the Great Depression and the Dust Bowl a new form of music arose, called Texas swing. Bob Wills and the Texas Playboys helped pioneer this combination of cowboy music blended with jazz. Lyle Lovett, Junior Brown, and others have picked up the torch on today's music scene.

After the war, a style of music known for its distinctive piano emerged;

honky-tonk laid the groundwork for the cheating songs and country blues of the 1950s and '60s. During this period the sound and locations of country stations began to change.

Country began to lose the western music, although holdouts like Marty Robbins and Willie Nelson remained well past this time. A new "Nashville sound" was born. Stations in major cities also began to program country music in major cities in the north and south. WJJD in Chicago was reportedly the first large city station to play a country format.

The music began to have a more universal appeal. The association early country music had with gospel and folk tunes gave way to a closer association with the blues. It was about everyday troubles and hardships that people went through regardless if they were northern or southern. "D-I-V-O-R-C-E," by George Jones and Tammy Wynett, is a fine example. Country music was not without its critics. In fact, an old joke that started around the early 1970s played on the back masking supposedly done by the Beatles and other bands. It asked, "What do you get when you play a country record backwards? You get your wife back, your job back, your dog back . . ."

The 1970s and '80s saw stations playing a country-rock mix. Many of the artists from the period were able to cross over to the pop charts. Artists like Linda Ronstadt and her backup band, which would later become the Eagles, and others made country more acceptable to a wider range of listeners, increasing the popularity of country stations.

The 1980s also saw two divergent movements in country music. One group, classified as "neo-traditionalists," started to return to the bluegrass roots of country, while another "new country" movement arose.

By the 1990s, country music was one of the most popular formats in radio. A report by the Simmons Market Research Bureau noted that country music radio outpaced the second-place format, A/C, by over 7 million listeners in 1996.[20]

This success did not come without some controversy, however. In the mid-1990s stations began to cater to an audience that was more appealing to advertisers, women eighteen to thirty-four who live in the suburbs. Advertisers view this group as having more buying power than others. They have a larger income and, if married, do most of the shopping. To appeal to this group a whole new set of artists got airplay. Young, good-looking men and women replaced the older generation of artists like Johnny Cash, George Jones, and Loretta Lynn. Country artists not only had to sound good, they now also had to look good for their videos.

Variety lists three types of country music, while *Radio and Records* has an additional category called Americana, sometimes known as American roots music. A relationship exists between the Americana format and the folk music of the 1960s and the hillbilly music of the 1940s and '50s. It features music that has its roots in folk, bluegrass, and western music. This format saw a huge resurgence with the soundtrack to the movie *O Brother Where*

Art Thou? Americana artists such as Allison Krauss and Union Station, Nancy Griffith, and Willie Nelson have all appeared on the charts.

The variations from the mainstream country are classic country and new country. Classic country is the oldies format, playing country hits from the 1960s through the '90s. New country is akin to the alternative or hot formats of other genres. It tends to be the most recent music, and today tends to lend itself to crossover. This format tends to attract a younger audience.[21] The percentages of stations with the three main types of country formats are as follows:

Classic country (0.8 percent)   Country (12.0 percent)
New country (0.4 percent)[22]

News, Talk, and Sports

These three formats all share one trait: they do not center on music. In an industry that is mostly music dominated, they are a bit of an anomaly. Yet this category of stations has higher ratings than any of the other formats measured by Arbitron.

News on radio began at the very beginning. Station KDKA began the format with the presidential election returns and then Conrad's nightly reading of newspaper stories as discussed earlier in this chapter. News could be the longest continuously programmed element on radio.

There are stations that are all news, stations that are all talk, stations that are all sports, and then there are stations that blend the formats. Arbitron's report for fall 2005 shows the blended format as having the highest rating, with almost 16 percent of the market.

Studies have shown that in times of unrest people turn to news more often. This may account for part of this format's current popularity in the United States. But even before recent events, the format was growing in popularity, as evidenced by television shows like *News Radio* and *Frasier,* each of which gave America a humorous look at the industry.

A major step toward today's format of all news was when Gordon McLendon designed a news format for WNUS, Chicago, in 1964. The following year, WINS, New York, took the format but added many features to liven it up, features that we still hear today. WINS used actualities, a collection of clips, also called sound bites, from speeches, press conferences, and interviews. Most public relations people and speechwriters, especially in politics, know the value of speaking in short sound bites. Short clips have a better chance of making the evening newscast. WINS also added soft news features, and live on-the-scene reporting. With a large staff and the resources of the Group W, Westinghouse, stations across the country, the format became an instant hit. It wasn't long before CBS and NBC began their own versions of all-news stations. In many ways, these were the forefathers of CNN, MSNBC, FOXNews, and other all-news cable operations. Many cities even have their own twenty-four-hour cable news operations.

Another tool that news stations use is "nat" (natural) sound. A reporter will record an interview on location so that the listener can hear the sounds of the location. Often the reporter will record several minutes of sound without talking and edit the nat sound in later.

The format of most news stations consists of a rotation of time, weather, and traffic, as well as news on the local, national, and international fronts. Often stations will attempt to take a national or international story and find a local angle to make it more appealing to the listener. Stations may tape the newscast and repeat it, airing a new version every hour or two, or may have multiple anchors relieving one another.

The talk show format really did not mature and flourish, however, until several things occurred. The cost of producing talk radio is much higher than the cost of producing a DJ music program. While a music program only pays for a DJ, most talk shows need a host, an engineer to run the equipment, a producer to coordinate and book guests, and often a researcher, although research is often handled by an intern. This meant that smaller stations could not afford to produce their own talk shows. Syndicated shows, however, became more affordable with the development of satellites. Early shows did not have the luxury of airing callers live. Afraid that they may say something inappropriate, thus putting the listenership numbers and their license in jeopardy, many talk shows did not take calls or took the calls off the air. The delay machine gave the host the all-important "dump button."

Ironically, the growth in popularity of FM and the near demise of AM radio gave news and talk a great boost. Frequency modulation (FM) is by its very nature better suited for the reproduction of music. There is less static and a broader frequency range, and stations can broadcast in stereo. In the mid-1980s many stations experimented with AM stereo, but due in part to the FCC's decision not to select one standard, the experiment failed. Left with ever dwindling ratings, AM station owners and programmers needed something that AM radio could do well, and they landed on the spoken word.

For a talk show to be successful it needs an appealing host. Talk show hosts usually need to share certain common traits. They should be intelligent and well informed on many topics, and they must be articulate, personable, and easily adaptable, as the radio talk show is not prerecorded—this is the format that is the most interactive with the listening audience.

Stations began to expand into the news, talk, and news-talk formats. News-talk is a term credited to KGO, Los Angeles. In 1960, the station became the first to use it.

Talk shows can take many different forms. There are interview shows, in which a host and guest talk to each other but do not take calls; call-in shows, where the audience is invited to call and ask questions of the guest; shows where the audience is invited to call in and talk to the host; and even shows in which the host is the only voice on the air. Most shows, however, are call-in shows. A typical call-in show may begin with a "tease," when the host lets the audience know what the topic and/or who the guest will be. The station breaks for news or commercials, then returns to the host, who does a brief biography of the guest, telling the audience why this person is important enough to be on the program. If this is a nationally syndicated show, the breaks will allow local stations to insert their own news or commercials during certain times. The host will then interview the guest, asking some prepared questions. Before the next commercial break the host will usually tease that he or she will be taking phone calls when the show returns. The host and guest then field phone calls from audience members.

Of course, there is always the rare occasion when a guest falls through at the last moment. In this case, the host usually opens the show with the announcement that it will be an open phone program, where listeners can simply call in to express whatever is on their minds—a trick of the trade.

Today many current or past radio talk show hosts have become household names: Rush Limbaugh, Howard Stern (although his program is not a talk show in the strictest sense), Bruce Williams, Larry King, and Don Imus. National Public Radio (NPR) and Public Radio International (PRI) also produce and air several outstanding talk shows, *Talk of the Nation, The Diane Rehm Show, Car Talk, All Things Considered, Morning Edition,* and *Weekend Edition,* to name just a few.

The talk show audience varies greatly during the day. In general, the audience member is well educated, better informed about world events, higher paid, and more likely to vote than the nonlistener. Other research has shown that nighttime listeners tend to be lonely and use the talk show for companionship. They consider the host to be a friend and it gives them the illusion of human contact.

Talk radio also offers people a place to have their voice heard, a place to express their opinions. During the 1960s and 1970s, the United States saw an increase in underground newspapers. In any society, when the people feel they are being denied a chance to be heard, there is a real risk of uprising or revolution. Acting as a safety valve, underground newspapers helped release social pressures from building up. Certain radio stations and programs have also served that role and continue to do so today.

The overnight talk show tends to draw a unique crowd. For this reason, many hosts have turned down offers to move to an earlier time slot. The overnight audience consists largely of police officers, bakers, factory workers, truck drivers, and insomniacs. These are people who, for the most part, go to work as the rest of the world is going to bed. It is almost a hidden population, and the host of the overnight show becomes a member of this group. In exchange, the overnight audience is one of the most loyal in radio.

Sports radio can either consist of stations that do sports and news, sports talk, or a hybrid that airs sports talk shows, gives sports news, and airs live sporting events. WFAN, New York, was the first station to take a twenty-four-hour all-sports format. It went on the air on July 1, 1987. However, as the home of the Don Imus show, technically it isn't all sports.

The percentage of stations programming each format include:

All news (1.5 percent) All sports (2.0 percent)
News talk (10.6 percent) Talk (1.8 percent)[23]

Religious

A relatively confusing format is the religious music format. While music has played an important part in most Christian worship services for centuries, religious music is difficult to define as a radio format. Arbitron lists five categories of religious music, going as far as naming separate categories for gospel and Southern gospel, even though gospel accounts for only about 5.5 percent of the listening audience.[24]

Gospel music can trace its roots in radio as far back as any other format. As noted in the history of the country format, it can trace its roots to a blending of old English, Scottish, and Irish folks songs, combined with the music of African slaves. In the early days, gospel music programming was usually heard only on Sundays. Stations would air local singing groups, church services, or records. Many great R&B, blues, and even country acts began their careers singing gospel. Aretha Franklin, Curtis Mayfield, Al Green, the Statler Brothers, and Jerry Lee Lewis (cousin of televangelist Jimmy Swaggart) all started in gospel.

Today this format is no longer limited to just one day. Several stations across the country program gospel for part of every day. The song title "Give Me that Old Time Religion" sums up gospel music programming to many.

Other songs falling under the gospel heading are "Amazing Grace" and "Will the Circle Be Unbroken." But as with any of the formats, a song does not define that format. These songs can and have been recorded by contemporary artists and have fallen under the contemporary Christian, inspirational, and Southern gospel formats depending on the arrangement and delivery style. Many believe the contemporary movement began in the late 1960s and early '70s as a way to bring younger members back into the church.

As Louis Armstrong once said about jazz, "Man, if you gotta ask you'll never know."[25] The same holds true for many industry people when trying to categorize the genre. The Gospel Music Association says that Christian music is any music with lyrics that are "Substantially based upon historically orthodox Christian truth contained in or derived from the Holy Bible; and/or—An expression of worship of God or praise for His works; and/or—Testimony of relationship with God through Christ; and/or—Obviously prompted and informed by a Christian world view."[26] To muddy the waters a further, the *Encyclopedia of Contemporary Christian Music* claims that contemporary Christian music is "music that appeals to self-identified fans of contemporary Christian music because of a perceived connection to what they regard as Christianity."[27]

Like secular radio stations, Christian stations have taken many different programming strategies. Among these are A/C, alternative, Christian hit radio, and more. Arbitron, however, uses the designations of Christian, contemporary inspirational (con INSP), gospel, religious, and Southern gospel.

Christian music is similar to AOR. It has many of the same style components, but the lyrics and messages are different. Contemporary inspirational tends to lean more toward the MOR style, with heavier use of orchestral music and strings. Gospel is the same as classic religious music, but with two divisions. Southern gospel is different from traditional gospel in that it is more like country music. Southern gospel incorporates elements of bluegrass, country, and four-part harmony into its style.

The percentages of stations programming religious formats are as follows:

Christian (2.2 percent)	Con INSP (0.4 percent)
Gospel (0.8 percent)	Southern gospel (0.3 percent)
Religious (1.7 percent) [28]	

Rock

It is important to note that Arbitron has three categories of rock, separate from those already accounted for. Active rock, also known as heavy metal, metal, hard rock, or head-banging music, is one category of the rock format. It is music driven by strong guitars, bass, and drums, intended to be played loud.

The AOR format, as mentioned earlier, was born out of rebellion against the strict format of radio stations of the day. But over time the format has changed somewhat. During the 1980s, a musical divide created a need for more formats. While punk and new wave were heading in one direction, AOR stations started to become more structured, much like the stations they were created to counter. The freeform stations started to go to a more structured playlist, and bands like Styx and Kansas began to dominate the stations.

Today AOR is another oldies format that plays music from the late 1960s through the '80s and tends to attract an older audience than some others. This format has seen a sharp decline since its inception and now accounts for 2 percent or less of the audience.

Classic rock is very similar to AOR. In its first incarnation, AOR stations began losing audience members. An aging audience foreshadowed a problem. The original audience was older, but the younger audience disliked the older, original artists. In 1983, WFAA tried adjusting the format so that it appealed to an older audience. While many rock stations began moving into music by Prince, the Eurythmics, and Culture Club, this station stayed with older artists. Today the classic rock format is AOR with the exception that stations do not play current hits.

The percentage of stations programming rock formats are as follows:

Classic (4.8 percent)   Active (2.0 percent)
AOR (2.2 percent)[29]

Spanish

Spanish radio in the United States has its origins in Texas. In the beginning, Mexican DJs would buy blocks of airtime on stations like KIWW-AM. Paul Cortez, however, made history as the first Mexican American to own a radio station when he put KCOR on the air in 1946. The Office of Censorship was opposed to the license because they feared foreign-language stations. But the FCC granted the license, and Cortez imported DJs from Mexico. At one point the station even had a show aired nationally. *La Hora de Teatro Nacional* was a radio drama in the Mexican *novella* style.

In 1967 Manuel Davila purchased KEDA-AM with a novel idea for programming. Announcing in both English and Spanish, he programmed an eclectic mixture of music combining country, bluegrass, Mexican, and other styles. He called the format *Tejano* (pronounced "tay-HAHN-o").

The Spanish format is an umbrella that incorporates ten smaller genres. Many of these formats, like Spanish news and Spanish talk, are essentially the same as their English-language counterparts, with an emphasis on news of importance to the Latino audience.

There is also a Spanish contemporary genre that shares many similarities with other A/C formats. Programmers of this style air current Latino pop music and English-language dance music. Other formats include Mexican regular, which blends contemporary Mexican music with some English-language music. Spanish tropical is a unique format that specializes in Latin and Cuban music with other styles such as salsa included. Spanish oldies stations play Latin hits of the 1950s through the '70s.

These, along with the other categories that compose the Spanish format, are the fastest-growing type of radio, accounting for 9.6 percent of total stations. The percentages of Spanish programming formats are as follows:

Spanish contemporary (1.6 percent)   Mexican regular (2.6 percent)
Spanish tropical (1.0 percent)   Spanish oldies (0.2 percent)[30]

Urban and Urban Contemporary

Today's urban category can trace its history back to the 1920s. Jack Leroy Cooper began work at WCAP, Washington, D.C., as an announcer in 1925, when he became the first African American to have his own commercial radio program. *The All Negro Hour* was a program he started in Chicago in 1929. "The Dean of African-American Disk Jockeys," as *Ebony* magazine referred to him in 1947, he is credited with starting over 150 radio programs on four different Chicago stations, hiring African-American announcers and salespeople, and at least one source cites him as being the first disc jockey, black or white.[31] Cooper was doing his show when his studio musicians walked out in the AFM strike called by Petrillo. Cooper began to play records and talk in between them.

The networks aired early black music in the form of blues and later jazz and jump music. Duke Ellington, Paul Robeson, Earl Fatha Hines, and others were often heard during the 1940s. Attempting to appeal to both African-American and white audiences, the networks sporadically aired historical dramas. Yet, there was a lack of musical programming. Real change in the programming didn't occur until the postwar era, when advertisers began to court African Americans, a previously ignored segment of the population.

Additionally, this was also a time when television was luring stars away from the network radio shows. Local programming became necessary for many station owners. Also, the cost of television sets put them out of the reach of most African Americans. If the white audience was leaving radio, it made sense to program to the remaining listeners.

In 1948 the legendary Memphis radio station WDIA, today known for giving many blues artists airplay for the first time, aired a program designed for the black audience. Soon it changed its entire format to appeal to African Americans, and other stations around the country were followed suit. That same year, J. B. Blayton became the first African-American radio station owner when he purchased WERD, Atlanta.

During the 1950s and '60s, these stations became more than entertainment. They offered public service programming and served as a community through which the Civil Rights movement could gain momentum. Reports of injustice, violence, and the speeches of Dr. Martin Luther King, Jr., became staples, along with the music.

Also during this time, the music itself began to change. Rhythm and blues was still popular, as were jazz and blues, but the new Motown sound was appealing to a younger audience, both black and white. Soul music, with a sound drawn from R&B and gospel, began during the 1960s, with artists like Ray Charles, James Brown, and Aretha Franklin. The 1970s saw a division in styles, as funk competed with the mellower sounds of bands like the Commodores and the Temptations. During the 1980s, rap made its debut with Grand Master Flash and the Furious Five and the Sugar Hill Gang. This music then began to evolve into hip-hop, club, and gansta rap.

Today Arbitron includes three formats under the category "urban." Urban is a mix of rap, R&B, hip-hop, and dance. Urban old is a format that plays music from the R&B and soul genres. The oldies stations, sometimes called "dustys," feature songs from the 1960s and '70s. The format also includes slower music in an effort to appeal to the older audience. Urban adult contemporary is a mélange of soft contemporary R&B hits along with soft R&B and soul of the previous years. This is sometimes referred to as simply urban contemporary. Teens and adults are the targets of the contemporary hits format.

The percentages of stations programming urban formats are as follows:

Urban (4.4 percent)   Urban old   (0.2 percent)
Urban A/C (3.0 percent)[32]

Other Formats

Additional formats accounting for a smaller share of the audience are classical (1.3 percent); adult standards, including easy listening, MOR, nostalgia, and variety (1.4 percent); new AC/smooth jazz (3.0 percent); oldies (7.0 percent); and other formats (0.1 percent). This last category encompasses children's radio, educational radio, ethnic radio, and R&B. Arbitron at one time used the "ethnic" title to refer to what are today's urban formats. Programming in foreign languages other than Spanish comprise today's ethnic category. Across the country, it is not uncommon to find programming in Asian languages, eastern European languages, or others wherever a large ethnic group is living. The last formats do not traditionally chart well with Arbitron.

Children's radio is especially hard to measure because Arbitron only counts stations that program for audience members twelve and older. Therefore stations have to rely on their own research. Today's only big player in the children's radio game is the Walt Disney Corporation, which also owns ABC Radio. Through the roughly 150 stations that carry Radio Disney and also on Sirius and XM Radio, Radio Disney offers a mix of contemporary hits, talk, and programming for children and parents. Not specifically designed as a venture in which to make money through traditional advertising, Radio Disney is more of a marketing venture. Characters dropping in to the shows, commercial spots talking about Disney products, and remote feed broadcastss from Disney theme parks never let the listeners forget that "Disney World (or Disneyland) is the happiest place on Earth."[33]

Radio programmers continue to face many challenges. A format that is successful today may become boring to the audience tomorrow. While radio listenership has remained steady over the last few years, newer technologies such as Internet radio, satellite radio, and, yes, even MP3 players such as the iPod may erode the traditional radio audience.

Another concern is how to reach a falling teenage audience. *MediaWeek* lists the Internet as the medium teens spend the most time with, followed by television, with radio coming in third. (MP3s and satellite radio are new media that became widely available only after the *MediaWeek* report.) Radio broadcasters will need to address this particular audience if they hope to retain it.[34]

General Trend

The Arbitron report for 2005, *Radio Today*, notes that, as one would expect, one's musical tastes tend to change as one grows older. Preferences by age group also change over the years:

- Teens 12–17 strongly prefer to listen to music that is "current"— formats such as CHR . . . and, to a lesser extent, Urban . . . and Alternative
- As they get older, young adults 18–24 develop an interest in Alternative
- music while maintaining continued enthusiasm for CHR and Urban. Adults 25–34 retain their habit of strong listening to Alternative . . . but are open to a wide variety
- of new sounds and stations: Rock . . . and CHR are strong favorites, but Urban and AC . . . are popular formats, as well.
- After age 35, format preferences start to change. Rock . . . and AC are the most popular listening choices, but Oldies, . . . New AC/Smooth Jazz, . . . News/Talk/Information . . . and Country . . . all perform well among this age group.
- Oldies appeals greatly to baby boomers ages 45–54, as does New AC/Smooth Jazz.
- Classical . . . is an extremely popular choice among older Adults 55–64. New AC/Smooth Jazz and News/Talk/Information also appeal to this set.
- Adults 65+ have a very clear favorite—Adult Standards . . . which derives over half of its audience from this age group. Classical and News/Talk/Information are
- also popular choices among the older crowd.[35]

As the data shows, there is no one format that reaches all of the audience. More outlets vying for the same audience members means stations are faced with a very big problem.

Questions for Further Thought

1 Even though there are plenty of stations, there are a limited number of formats. What can a station do to make it stand out from others playing the same music?

2 In your opinion, does geographic location play a role in radio formats or does music transcend boundaries?

3 Do people's tastes in music change as they age?

4 Are you loyal to one type of station or do you listen to different types of formats?

Shop Talk

Arbitron: Radio ratings service. Originally called the American Radio Bureau (ARB), the name Arbitron came from the electronic system developed in an attempt to process data more quickly and with fewer errors.

Call-out research: Research method where randomly selected homes are telephoned and a member of the household is polled.

Format: A particular style or genre of music or other programming a radio station chooses to air. Formats include country, urban, rock, Christian, news, Spanish, and others.

Motown: Record label started in Detroit, Michigan, by Barry Gordy. The label is responsible for discovering talent such as the Jackson Five, the Four Tops, Stevie Wonder, and other artists. The music produced from the Hitsville U.S.A. studio became known as the "Motown sound."

Sound bites: A short usable quotation or piece of dialog that may be used in a news story.

Sun Records: Record label started by Sam Phillips in Memphis, Tennessee. The Sun label was responsible for the rockabilly sound that included Elvis Presley, Johnny Cash, Carl Perkins, and Jerry Lee Lewis.

4

Who Is Listening and Why?

Many different formats are playing on radio stations around the country, as chapter 2 details. Some stations, in an attempt to get the largest audience and therefore appeal to advertisers, will constantly try to keep ahead of industry trends and play contemporary hits. Other stations, wishing to appeal to an older, more affluent audience, will program news, talk, jazz, or another format. This raises the question of why people choose to listen to radio or a particular radio station?

Uses and Gratifications Theory

Before answering this question, we must first look at a communication theory called "uses and gratifications." When New York newspaper carriers went on strike, a researcher, Bernard Berelson, conducted a series of surveys asking people what missing the news meant to them. Surprisingly, he found that people had many different reasons for reading a newspaper. Some missed the news, some missed the sports, and some missed the comics. From this he concluded that not everyone used the newspaper for the same reasons. This laid the groundwork for years of further study by numerous communication researchers. Studies then went on to look at other media and how people used it, and what gratification they received from it.[1]

When asked why they listen to radio, most people will instinctively answer either "for entertainment" or "for information." However, these early studies suggest that people have different uses for radio and expect different gratifications.

Chapter 2's discussion of talk radio mentioned that for some listeners, the radio keeps them company. They see the radio host as a friend. Connected with other listeners, they do not feel alone.

Think about the many uses for radio that you have. Entertainment and information are two reasons you may listen to radio. Even if you do not routinely listen to a news program, you may have tuned in to a radio station to hear weather or traffic reports. Every schoolchild who lives where there is snow has shared the experience of listening to see if school is closed.

Maybe you have turned on the radio when you are alone just to have some noise. Some people have difficulty studying or working if it is too quiet. They often turn on the radio to break the silence. Some people will turn on the radio during a car trip to stay awake or to keep from being bored, while others may fall asleep to the radio at night. For each of these people, the use and gratification they receive from radio is different.

Radio has passive listeners and active listeners. Listeners who tune in to news, weather, or talk programs tend to be active listeners. They are paying closer attention to the radio than those who turn the radio on for noise. This presents a different set of programs for a station.

In order for advertising to be effective, and even for a station's ratings to register higher, as we will see later, an active listener is most desirable. Contests, giveaways, and other promotions are one way to ensure that listeners are paying attention to the station. "Morning zoo" programming that has a combination of music, weather, traffic, time, news, and funny DJ patter is a proven method. Studies have shown that listeners of all radio stations are more active listeners in the hours between 6 A.M. and 9 A.M. Most people are preparing to go to work or school, or are in their cars already, and want to hear the weather and traffic reports. This airtime slot is called "morning drive" time for that reason.

Since this is the most desirable time slot, stars of the station usually work morning drive. Morning drive commands higher advertising prices due to its high ratings. Drive-time talent usually earn higher salaries than others at the station. According to the 2005 Arbitron *Radio Today*, close to 25 million people are listening to radio at 6 A.M., compared with less than 10 million at 7 P.M.[2]

Audience Measurement

Stations can measure their audiences in several ways. They can base a show's popularity by the number of calls and letters they receive. If the morning show receives one hundred requests per hour and the afternoon show receives two hundred, they might say that the afternoon show is more popular. However, the morning audience usually is preparing for the day ahead or commuting, which means they can't or don't call in. This could skew the results.

Stations can use call-out research much like the programmers mentioned in chapter 3. Instead of attempting to determine music preferences, however, they are trying to determine the number of people tuning in to their station. The method is similar, in that a station employee or intern will telephone random homes asking to speak with someone in their audience demographic. Not identifying themselves as working for the station and often using a vague identifier like "radio research analyst," they will ask the person to rank his or her favorite stations. By using some simple statistical methods, they determine a general idea about their listenership. However, each of these methods has many potential areas for misinterpretation built into it.

Why is audience measurement so important? Remember, the product that most radio stations are selling is you—the listener. The number of listeners determines prices for airtime for commercials, or spots. An estimated 95 percent of Americans listen to the radio at least once a week.

As of March 2006, there were 13,748 radio stations in the United States, including 4,759 commercial AM and 6,243 commercial FM stations The remaining 2,746 were noncommercial FM stations.[3] Radio is a valuable tool for advertisers. As in any other business, advertisers need assurance that they are spending their money in the best way possible. Advertisers wish to get the most bang for their buck, and logically want to know which station is drawing the most listeners who are likely to buy the product they are selling.

The one method that most stations use, and the one that is accepted by American advertisers as being the only reliable method of measurement, is the ratings service provide by the Arbitron company. However, Arbitron has not always been the leader in radio research.

History of the Rating Services

Hooperatings

Advertisers wanted to know the size of the audience their commercials were reaching beginning as early as 1927. Unlike magazines or newspapers, which could point to issues sold, radio could only say that the signal could possibly reach anyone and everyone. This put them at a disadvantage.

The Clark-Hooper Company began in 1934 to measure magazine and newspaper advertising effectiveness, but C. E. Hooper, president and cofounder, also wanted to measure radio.

Another organization, the Cooperative Analysis of Broadcasting (CAB), had already been doing radio measurement since 1930, but many magazine publishers questioned the validity of its findings. Working for CAB, Archibald Crossley had begun doing research via telephone. Telephone phone numbers were randomly chosen and the person answering was asked questions pertaining to their radio listening over the last twenty-four hours. This method, known as "recall," relied on the respondent's memory of what he or she actually listened to and for how long. In an attempt to be fair to all four networks (NBC Red and Blue, CBS, and Mutual), he limited his calls to only those cities that had all four on the air. Additionally, the CAB research was concerned only with networks and network programming.

While Hooper's method also used the telephone, instead of using recall, he used a method known as "coincidental" phone calls. This method called people and asked them questions about what they were listening to at the time of the phone call. Of course, this meant that people had to stop listening to the show in order to talk with Hooper and his associates. People felt that his results were more trustworthy, however. Even CBS signed on as a client. In 1934 the Clark-Hooper organization disbanded, but Hooper continued with his radio research. Using good publicity skills, he made sure that his name and the name *Hooperatings* were synonymous with radio ratings.

While CAB and Crossley measured only the networks; Hooper took his rating service to local stations. When Hooper started making his findings available to the networks and advertisers, Crossley's days in radio audience analysis were numbered.

Just as Hooper had exploited a vulnerability in Crossley's methodology, however, television, and more specifically the A. C. Nielsen Company, would spell the demise of Hooperatings.[4]

A. C. Nielsen

When it was founded in 1923, the A. C. Nielsen Company studied the performance of industrial equipment. A few years after its founding, Nielsen added a Drug Index and a Food Index to project sales of products based on marketing strategies. Researchers took a small sample of data gathered from stores and used statistical analysis to generalize the findings to a larger area.

Clients urged Nielsen to start measuring radio effectiveness, so he started the Nielsen Radio Index (NRI). This method was quite different. In his measurement, Nielsen hooked a special machine to the radios of cooperating households. The machine recorded when the radio was on and to what station it was tuned. The process was time-consuming, however. Machines were set up and then disconnected at the conclusion of the study. Only the Chicago office interpreted the data produced by the machines. This meant that the NRI was costly and could not give results as quickly as Hooper or Crossley could.

An advantage of the Nielsen service, however, was that it included homes that did not own telephones as well as those that did. The Hooperatings only contacted the 20 percent of the homes that had telephones, which skewed the numbers in favor of the wealthy. The tapes also took a form more easily mailed back to the company. This change gave the NRI a more cost-effective and quicker system.[5]

While Nielsen was measuring a nationwide sample, Hooper was only measuring urban areas. Hooper tried to institute a national service for an additional fee. Nielsen, however, offered its national service at no additional fee.

By the time television was introduced, Nielsen had a meter that could measure up to four radio receivers simultaneously and also had the infrastructure in place to determine national television ratings. Hooper realized that further attempts at competition were futile, and in 1950 sold his national ratings services to Nielsen. Hooper died in a boating accident in 1955, and the up-and-coming Arbitron purchased his remaining local rating service.

Nielsen continued to innovate in audience measurements. It developed a system that alerted listeners or viewers when to make notes in a diary that they kept. This gave the company a measurement of usage, but also allowed it to give out demographic information (gender, age, and so on) of the person using the media. Subscribers to the service welcomed this addition.

Nielsen discontinued radio measurement in the early 1960s due to many factors. Chief among them were the Harris Hearings on broadcast ratings in 1963. These congressional hearings questioned the validity of radio and television measurement methods. A *Time* magazine article reporting on the hearings noted that around two hundred firms in Manhattan alone offered local ratings services. During the hearing it was found that the company in question, Robert S. Conlan and Associates, did not have a "staff of experienced 'verifiers,' program editors, tabulators and calculators." The company was actually one person, Hallie Jones, who also managed the office, bookkeeping, and other records. In fact, as *Time* reported, "The way the system works: 75% of the surveys are 'sold before they're made' by informing a station that it has placed first."[6]

Videodex was another competitor of Nielsen. Accusations arose that the company did not conduct the research that it had claimed to conduct. The post office where the company rented a mailbox for returned diaries reported that no such deliveries had occurred. When asked to produce a diary for inspection, company officials could not. Videodex claimed to store old diaries in a warehouse, but management at the warehouse said they had considered the account inactive for many years.[7]

Nielsen, and those companies still in the ratings business after the dust settled, was required to abide by a stringent set of guidelines overseen by the Federal Trade Commission (FTC). The Nielsen Company saw that the number of radio stations was growing while the audience was shrinking, thus making their radio service, in their opinion, less desirable than their television ratings system. In addition, with people spending more time in their cars and elsewhere away from home, radio was becoming more of a portable medium. The Nielsen measurements, based on electrical power, were not practical or possible for this new audience.

While Nielsen continues today as the leader in television rating services, it has gone though many owners and changes. Today VNU, an international corporation with headquarters in the Netherlands, specializing in measurement of many different markets and products, owns Nielsen.[8]

Arbitron

In 1949, as television was beginning to make huge waves, Jim Seiler started the American Research Bureau (ARB). Using a listener diary method to measure the audiences in large and medium-sized markets, Seiler was able to gather a large amount of information from respondents. The company randomly selected households, and participants kept a diary for each member of the household, outlining when and what station they were listening to. Of course, this task was easier then than it is today. At that time, the typical home had only one television or radio in a central location. The number of diaries in a given market varied. Statistical sampling, however, allowed the company to generalize numbers to the whole audience. Families selected to complete ARB diaries had to live within fifty miles of a television station and also have a telephone, just like the Hooper families. An advantage that ARB had was that the families kept the diaries for only one week, resulting in a quick turnaround of ratings.[9]

Originally only measuring ratings of listeners on the East Coast, Seiler came across a company called Tele-Que that was using the diary system to generate ratings on the West Coast. Roger Cooper of Tele-Que met with Seiler. Consequently, the two companies merged in 1951 and established headquarters in Washington, D.C. This gave the new ARB Tele-Que the ability to generate national ratings.

John Landreth started another company, the Television National Audience Measurement Service. Soon he too united with ARB Tele-Que and became a third partner. By 1954, the company had dropped the awkward name and returned to the simpler American Research Bureau.

Due in part to the A. C. Nielsen Company's "Audimeter," ARB developed its own electronic measuring device, called Arbitron. The device surpassed Nielsen's because it instantaneously measured when a receiver was on and the channel it was tuned to. Most stations did want to pay the high price for using this new system. Combined with a patent infringement suit that Nielsen brought against ARB, the new method was a failure, but *Arbitron* became the company's new, futuristic-sounding name.

As Nielsen was getting out of the radio ratings business, Arbitron was entering it. Soon it started to expand heavily into radio audience analysis to fill a gap, while at the same time continuing its television service. Soon

Arbitron was the leader in the field of radio research.

The company moved to Beltsville, Maryland, as part of an expansion that included the installation of one of the first computers. While in theory UNIVAC should have given Arbitron an immediate advantage over Nielsen, the first results were disappointing. The computer returned unusable results that made no sense and took longer than hand counting. Eventually, when the bugs had been worked out, Arbitron was able to give much more detailed demographic information with its reports.

For a short time during the mid-1980s and the '90s, a rival company, Birch-Scarborough, offered an alternative radio ratings service. Birch-Scarborough claimed that their Birch Reports, which used a telephone recall system, were more accurate than others because they were using a statistical method in which traditionally underrepresented audiences were given more weight.

Stations used both the Birch and Arbitron ratings depending on which book showed them with the highest percentage of the audience. Eventually Birch-Scarborough withdrew from the ratings business, but it remains a leader in market research for many other industries. Today Scarborough Research is a joint venture between VNU and Arbitron.

In 1993 Arbitron announced that it was withdrawing from the television ratings business and focusing its attention solely on radio. Still look-

Figure 4.1 Arbitron's PPM system

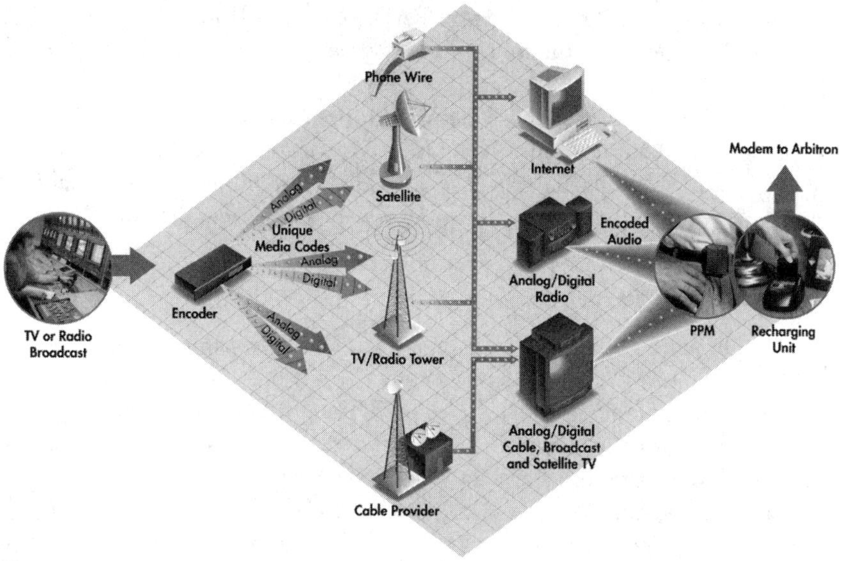

Used by permission, Arbitron, Inc.

ing for ways to refine its measurements, especially of those who are out of their homes, Arbitron has announced that it has developed a new device in another unique partnership with VNU, parent company of A. C. Nielsen. The Portable People Meter (PPM) is about the size of a beeper. Radio and television stations send out unique signals on a frequency above that of human hearing. The device can then measure every station that the person is listening to. It comes with a recharging dock that downloads the data back to Arbitron. It's been used in Canada, the Netherlands, Belgium, and Singapore. The company has licensed the technology for use in select countries around the world and recently initiated it in the Houston market.

Arbitron now also measures Internet radio listening. In a joint partnership with comScore Media Matrix, a new system with the cumbersome name comScore Arbitron Online Radio Ratings was used to measure its three charter subscribers: America Online's AOL Radio Network, Yahoo's LAUNCHcast, and Microsoft's MSN radio and WindowsMedia.com during fall 2004.[10]

RADAR

A measurement system introduced in 1967 by Statistical Research Incorporated (SRI) but not widely used until 1972 is called Radio All Dimension Audience Research (RADAR). This system, designed to measure network and national advertising listenership, allows for a great deal of variability in reports dependent upon clients' needs. It allows for multiple variables in the analysis, including data about other media, the audience, and so on. In 2001 Arbitron bought RADAR from SRI for $25 million. Today RADAR measures the following networks:

ABC Radio Network	Jones Media
America Radio Network	American Urban Radio Networks
Crystal Media Networks	Dial Communications-Global Media;
Premiere Radio Networks	Westwood One Network.[11]

Navigauge

Based in Atlanta, Navigauge is a relative newcomer to radio ratings. Its new in-car measuring device combines a way to monitor the listening habits of participants along with a global positioning satellite (GPS) time stamp that lets the company know when and where the car stops. The company hopes that its data it will interest advertisers as well as radio stations, retailers, and others. According to a press release issued by the company, "The country's first electronic medium, radio, was the only electronic medium not measured electronically until the arrival of Navigauge."[12]

Understanding the Ratings

The following section is from the publication *Arbitron Radio Market Report Reference Guide* (sometimes referred to as *The Purple Book*) © 2002 Arbitron Inc. and is used by permission.

AVERAGE QUARTER HOUR (AQH) PERSONS: The average number of persons listening to a particular station for at least five minutes during a 15-minute period.

AVERAGE QUARTER HOUR (AQH) RATING: The AQH Persons estimate is expressed as a percentage of the population being measured.

$$\frac{\text{AQH Persons}}{\text{Population}} \times 100 = \text{AQH Rating (\%)}$$

AWAY-FROM-HOME LISTENING: An estimate reported for a listening location outside of the home. It could identify listening taking place either in-car, at-work or some other place.

COST PER GROSS POINT (or "Cost Per Point"): The cost of achieving a number of impressions equivalent to one percentage of the population in a given demographic group.

$$\frac{\text{Cost of Schedule}}{\text{GRPs}} = \text{Cost Per Gross Rating Point}$$

COST PER THOUSAND: The cost of delivering 1,000 Gross Impressions (Gis).

$$\frac{\text{Cost of Schedule}}{\text{Gross Impressions}} \times 1000$$

OR

$$\frac{\text{SpotCost}}{\text{AQH Persons}} \times 1000$$

CUME PERSONS: The estimated number of *different* persons who listened to a radio station for a minimum of five minutes in a quarter hour within a reported daypart. (Cume estimates may also be referred to as *cumulative* or *unduplicated* estimates.)

CUME RATING: The cume persons audience expressed as a percentage of all persons estimated to be in the specified demographic group.

$$\frac{\text{CumePersons}}{\text{Population}} \times 100 = \text{CumeRating}$$

DAYPART: A part of the day recognized by the industry to identify time periods of radio listening, e.g. Saturday 6AM–10AM or Monday–Friday 7PM–MID.

DEMOGRAPHICS: This term identifies population groups according to age, sex, ethnicity, etc.

DESIGNATED MARKET AREA (DMA): Nielsen Media Research Inc.'s geographic market design, which defines each television market exclusive of others based on measurable viewing patterns. Every county (or county equivalent) in the U.S. is assigned exclusively to one DMA. Arbitron reports radio listening estimates in the top 50 DMAs (ranked on TV households) in the Radio Market Reports of all Standard radio markets whose Metros are located within the DMA and whose names are contained in the DMA name.

DISCRETE DEMOGRAPHICS: This term refers to uncombined or nonoverlapping sex/age groups, such as Men and/or Women 18–24, 25–34, 25–44, as opposed to "target" of aggregate demographics, such as Men and/or Women 18+, 18–34, 18–49, or 25–49.

EXCLUSIVE CUME: The number of different persons listening to only one station during a reported daypart.

FREQUENCY: The average number of times a person is exposed to a radio spot schedule.

$$\frac{\text{Gross Impressions}}{\text{Net Reach}} = \text{Frequency}$$

FREQUENCY: An FCC-authorized AM or FM band designation assigned to a city service area and a radio station license.

GROSS IMPRESSIONS: The sum of the AQH Persons audience for all spots in a given schedule.

METROS: Arbitron Metros generally correspond to the Metropolitan Statistical Areas (MSAs, PMSs, CMSAs) defined by the U.S. Government's Office of Management and Budget. They are subject to exceptions dictated by historical industry usage and other marketing considerations as determined by Arbitron.

METRO TOTALS and/or DMA TOTALS (Total listening in the Metro or DMA): These total listening estimates include listening to reported stations, nonqualifying commercial stations, noncommercial stations, cable-only stations and unidentified stations.

NET REACH: The number of different persons reached in a given schedule.

PERSONS USING RADIO (PUR): The total amount of listening to radio for a particular demo/daypart/geography. The term PUR can defer to Persons or Ratings, AQH, or Cume. (See "Metro Totals and /or DMA Totals" above.)

RATING (AQH or Cume): The AQH or Cume Persons audience expressed as a percentage of the total population.

SHARE: The percentage of those listening to radio in the Metro (or DMA) who are listening to a particular radio station.

$$\frac{\text{Persons}}{\text{Population}} \times 100 = \text{Rating (\%)}$$

$$\frac{\text{Station AQH Persons}}{\text{Metro AQH Population}} \times 100 = \text{Share (\%)}$$

TARGET DEMOGRAPHICS: Audience groups consisting of multiple discrete demographic cells (e.g., Men 18–34, Women 25–54).

TOTAL SURVEY AREA (TSA): A geographic area that includes the Metro Survey Area and may include additional counties (or county equivalents).

TURNOVER: The total number of different groups of persons that make up a station's audience.[13]

$$\frac{\text{CumePersons}}{\text{AQH Persons}} = \text{Turnover schedule}$$

Putting the Numbers to Work

Broadcast stations, advertisers, networks, and others all subscribe to Arbitron. In major markets Arbitron issues the *Arbitron Radio Market Report* every three months. When the report, often referred to as "the Book" comes out, it produces a lot of anxiety at most stations. It shows important figures such as which programs attract listeners and which ones do not, which demographics are tuning in and which ones are not. While it looks like a confusing set of numbers, there are a few vital ones defined here.

One must define the word *market* before examining the numbers. There are many ways one can define a market, but using geography is the most common method. The federal Office of Management and Budget (OMB) has placed every city, town, and county into a greater metropolitan statistical area (MSA), primary metropolitan statistical area (PMSA), and consolidated metropolitan statistical area (CMSA).

Arbitron has set its own geographic definitions based on the above designations but with its purposes in mind. The stations that subscribe to Arbitron get to vote on whether a county should be included in the ratings for that metropolitan area or not. The two categories that have arisen are the metro survey area (Metro) and total survey area (TSA).[14] The Metro area mirrors the MSA, and the TSA is the Metro plus all contiguous counties that meet a set of criteria as to percentage of respondents who list the Metro stations in their reports.

Stations that rank highly can expect more advertisers, and by the simple economic model of supply and demand, they can charge more for their spots. If a station drops in the ratings, it may see a decline in advertisers, forcing salespeople to work harder. The station may even need to reduce the cost of airtime, resulting in less income. The ratings drive station business plans until the next set are issued.

Stations often replace on-air talent with a declining listenership for more than one book. DJs can lose their jobs for poor ratings in accordance with many contracts. There are even stories of people losing their jobs for one bad rating period.

However, a station does not have to be first in its market to make money. The deciding factor is often the cost of reaching the listener. CPM (M is the Roman numeral for one thousand) tells the advertiser how much money it will cost to reach one thousand listeners on average. A lower cost of reaching listeners at station WHAA than at rival station WHAX may be the deciding factor. However, as discussed in chapter 2, stations often target key demographics. While a dealer of upscale automobiles like Jaguar or BMW may not see spending advertising money on an alternative station as a wise move, a clothing chain such as the Gap may see it as being the perfect station on which to spend money.

One might often hear someone say, "I'm number one with females eighteen to thirty-four," or "I'm number two 9 A.M. to noon." Even if a station isn't doing great, there is a chance that certain parts are doing better than others. Salespeople as well as advertisers will pour over the ratings books looking at dayparts and demographics—advertisers looking for the people they want to sell to, and salespeople trying to determine how to package their station to potential advertisers. They look at things such as the turnover, and the cume, the rating, and the share. Again, the share is the percentage of the audience tuned in to a show of all people that are listening to radio at that time. The rating is the percentage of the whole population, whether they are listening to the radio or not, that is listening. The share should always be equal to or greater than the rating.

Another important term in radio programming is "average quarter hour." A station receives credit for a listener who listens for five minutes during each quarter hour, ending with :15, :30, :45, and :00. Therefore if someone only listens to a station for ten minutes, then listening from :10 to :20 is better for the station's ratings than listening from :00 to :10. Why? In the first example the listener has tuned in for five minutes during the first quarter hour and five minutes in the second. The station gets credit twice. In the second example it receives credit for only one quarter hour. Stations realize this and deal with it in many unique ways. Giving the audience want it wants, news, weather, and traffic will all be aired during these times. Some stations will not schedule commercials during these ten minutes. Some will play music sweeps announcing what songs are coming up. They often will lead the set with something such as, "Now, five in a row from your home of [fill in the format here]." The commercials will be played in the slots of :05 to :10, :20 to :25, :35 to :40, and :50 to :55. Still another technique is a contest that requires the audience to listen for a chance to dial in when they hear a song. Keeping a listener tuned in for just ten minutes—the goal of the station—may involve many methods.

It's crucial for the audience, especially those who are filling out listening diaries, to know the radio station's identity. Since most of the listeners push a button or scan the dial, they may not immediately know the name or frequency of the station. At one time Arbitron would only accept the official call letter and/or frequency of the station in its diaries. Now they also allow names that the stations go by, "River Rock," "Cowboy Country," or any other name, so stations mention their names frequently.

No one at a radio station knows whom Arbitron has chosen for its research. Upon contacting potential diary keepers, the company asks if they, or anyone in their family, are affiliated in any way with a radio station.

Ratings Distortion

The publication *Rating Distortion and Rating Bias: A Handbook on Arbitron's Radio's Special Station Activity Policy* acknowledges the Harris Hearings and lists activities that it feels could put the objectivity of the ratings at risk. Ratings distortion, as defined by Arbitron, is any station activity that it feels "may affect the way diary keepers record their listening, so that recorded listening differs from actual listening." The publication goes on to list several categories of improper behavior.[15]

"Diary-keeper solicitation" can take many forms. This includes any attempt at buying diaries, asking listeners to turn in their diaries as a contest entry form, or even telling listeners, "If anyone asks, tell them you listen to this station for three hours every day."

"Improper promotional activities" can be things the station does that may cause diary keepers to "overreport, underreport, or misreport their actual listening." Examples of this are contests that either give preference or award larger prizes based on more listening, any discussions that talk about the "importance of extensive listening in diaries." Not only does this cover on-air discussions but also other media, such as a column or article.

"Survey announcements" are direct appeals to diary keepers. Saying, "If you've got a diary, remember to put us in," or announcing that a rating period is going to be conducted and urging listeners to fill out diaries accurately are both considered to be a possible bias threat to the research.

"Indirect appeals" are similar to survey announcements but don't address the diary keepers exclusively. They include the entire listening audience. Some stations try to avoid survey announcements by announcing, "Tell anyone who asks, you listen to WHAA," or "Write it down: WHAA is your favorite station." These are indirect appeals and are also seen as a threat.

Other activities that can result in sanctions include answering a caller's question about ratings that "prolongs or expands the discussion" of the ratings, methodology, Arbitron, and so on. Even offhand remarks such as "Write down that you listen to me every day" or "Well, looks like the new ratings period is off to a good start" can be punishable.

Arbitron notes that it takes circumstances of extemporaneous comments such as those above into consideration when making a decision as to what action, if any, to take.

If there is any impropriety, Arbitron can leave the station out of the next rating book, which affects its ability to represent itself to advertisers. In less serious cases, it will place a notice on the cover and/or beside the station's listing, and/or place the station out of alphabetical order at the bottom of the page or "below the line."[16]

A Case Study

Most people think that entertainment, information, or even commercials are the media's primary products. However, the product that the media sells is access to its audience. The way radio stations make money is by selling airtime to advertisers. The cost of this airtime can vary greatly dependent upon the city, the time of day, and the audience demographics and size.

Advertising on a radio station in Los Angeles, California, obviously costs more than advertising in a smaller city such as Knoxville, Tennessee. There are several reasons. The cost of living (things like rent, utilities, food) is much higher in major cities. Therefore it is only logical that that the fees radio stations charge to clients will also be higher. But what about stations that are in the same market or the same city? How and why do they differ in price? The answer is simple economics: supply and demand.

Imagine that you are a media buyer for a major advertiser looking to purchase airtime for your new client, "Baby Breath Mints . . . the breath mint that will make your baby's breath fresh all day long." The first thing you will identify is who the potential buyer is for your product. In this instance we'll say that it is men and women with babies. This doesn't mean that grandparents or friends won't buy our product. However, you have a limited budget and can only purchase time on one station.

You look at each of the stations in town and, based on their format and ratings, identify which will be more likely to have your potential customers listening:

- station A programs classical music;
- station B programs hard rock;
- station C programs urban;
- station D programs news/talk; and
- station E programs country.

This isn't always an easy call. Generally stations that program classical music or news/talk have a smaller percentage of audience members in the young adult segment, but that isn't always a rule. Many younger people with children may listen to classical music or news. However, generally, stations B, C, and E seem to be good bets.

The next step is to examine the ratings. Examining the demographic and daypart data finds that most of the women ages eighteen to thirty-five are listening to station E, so that very well may be the station on which to advertise.

However, say that all three stations have an almost identical share of women in your key demographic. You'll need to use another variable. In this case, look at cost.

Stations use a rate card, which is much like the sticker in a car's window at a dealership. It tells the cost of advertising on the station, offering breaks in the price for greater volume. For instance, one spot may cost $100, but twenty spots may only cost $1,500 instead of $2,000. In our example we will use only one price per station to make things easier.

As an advertiser, you will use that important variable called cost per thousand (CPM). CPM tells the station and advertiser how much money it will cost to reach one thousand listeners. Assume the following is true for our three stations during the time we wish to advertise:

Station B	100,000 women 18 to 34	$100/spot
Station C	120,000 women 18 to 34	$60/spot
Station E	110,000 women 18 to 34	$50/spot

We just need to do some simple math. Station B is charging $1 to reach one thousand audience members. Station C is charging $2 per thousand, and Station E is charging $2.20 per thousand. In this case, Station B may indeed be the winner.

This decision is based on quantitative research. Most advertisers also use some form of qualitative research as well. Psychographics is one type of qualitative research. Psychographics attempts to get into the mind of the consumer. A better understanding of the listener will help tailor the commercial copy that is most appealing. This type of research, however, has its critics.

Pioneered by SRI in 1978 with the VALS system and Clarita's PRIZM, this research goes beyond the demographics of gender, age, and the like and tries to find out what values motivate consumers. VALS breaks the market into eight groups based on resources, motivation, and innovation. They use the labels "innovators," "thinkers," "achievers," "experiencers," "believers," "strivers," "makers," and "survivors."[17]

Identifying "clusters" is part of another type of qualitative research. Clusters consist of a combination of demographic and geographic data, such as location and income, combined with other variables to make a stereotype for the people who live in that area. In theory, people who are similar in income, ethnicity, social class, education, values, and so on will tend to live in areas where they find others like themselves. While this information is useful for certain types of advertising (direct mail) or marketing, it has limited use in buying radio advertising. Broadcasting by nature reaches all parts of the community, regardless of how they have clustered. A surgeon or lawyer may listen to the same music as the person working in a factory.

Ignore the qualitative research for this example, and say that station B is going to be your best buy for the money. Stations usually have many different pricing scales. Just like in any other business, you may find that buying in volume can result in a lower cost. Some stations are willing to bargain to keep or sign on a new advertiser. Station C may be willing to come down in price to match that of station B. Stations also offer different rates for different time periods. If you advertise during drive time, the cost will be much higher than if you advertise in the 9 A.M.–to–12 P.M. or 12 P.M.–to–3 P.M. slot. Perhaps you are willing to exchange a large number of listeners at once for more exposure.

Studies have shown that radio listeners usually need to hear a commercial spot more than once before it has an effect. If you can afford only ten spots during drive time but can afford fifty spots during the other time periods, you may wish to go with a higher exposure frequency.

Another factor that can decrease the price of an ad is the number of open spots or "availabilities" and how close to airtime it is. One may compare radio to a donut shop. Most shops have rules about how long a donut may remain on the shelf. Donuts reaching a certain length on the shelf are thrown away if they are not sold. Radio airtime is also like that. A thirty-second spot at 4:55 P.m. that is still empty when that time comes is gone forever. This inventory is a loss. One can't discount it for sale tomorrow offering it as day-old goods. Therefore, if a station has a few openings in its schedule for that day, there is a chance of getting a reduced price on them.

Run of schedule (ROS) is also sometimes called "best time available" (BTA). For a cut rate, a client can get a guaranteed number of spots throughout the day, but at times that may not be desirable. The package may include a promise of one drive-time, two daytime, and five overnight spots. Generally the station places the ads whenever there is an opening in the schedule. This grab-bag approach may not be a bad deal for our particular product. Many new parents are up for middle-of-the-night feedings and might be listening to the radio at odd hours.

Most stations also offer value-added opportunities. In addition to radio advertising, a client may also receive a live remote broadcast during a big sale, or may trade out a product as a prize during a station contest. Other value-added opportunities may come by way of bumper stickers or even a logo placement on T-shirts.

How Many People Are Listening?

Obviously the number of people listening to radio has dropped since its golden age, when children would run home from school and turn on the radio. Entire families would sit around the set and listen to their favorite shows. Now one's evenings are full of television, video games, the Internet, and other pastimes.

Technology and Programming

New technology often threatens the life of the technology that came before it. In the case of radio, the first threat came from television. The high level of technological advancement on behalf of radio directly aided the development of television. Radio had reached almost every household by the end of World War II. As more and more television stations went on the air, and more households could afford television sets, radio saw its first major drop in listenership. However, several things happened that kept radio from going the way of the wireless.

Local news and events were more important to stations. DJs were creating a relationship with their audiences. New music appealing to a younger audience became popular and stations began playing it. Possibly of more importance, America, especially American teenagers, became a society centered on cars, especially cars with radio. The mid-1950s and '60s saw a resurgence in the medium.

Many factors may have contributed to this resurgence. The late 1950s and early 1960s saw the invention and development of the portable radio. With the invention of the transistor, small, affordable pocket-sized radios became a reality. Usually these radios had a small earphone included. It only used one earphone because broadcasts were still AM and mono. While the sound quality was nowhere near that of today's MP3 players, they were just as popular as MP3 players in their time.

Many families began to move to the suburbs during this period. This meant a longer commute and longer time spent in the car. The car radio was the perfect companion, and thus drive time was born. While people did not listen to the stations at night as they once had, enough were still listening during the day.

Cheap, recorded music and tape players for the home and car were introduced in the mid-1960s. Forming a group, Ampex Tape Company, RCA Records and Lear Jet invented the eight-track tape, which was much more practical than Chrysler's phonograph. Once again, William Lear, the man who helped bring a practical radio system to the automobile, was back at the drawing board.

Famous around the world for his jet design, Lear worked on a system for playing music in the jets and in the cars of his executives. Prior to this, most taped music was on reel-to-reel player. The first company to offer the eight-track player as an option was Ford, in its 1966 line. Now drivers had the option of listening to the radio or bringing along their own tapes.[18]

Eight-track tapes were designed to have four different sets of left and right tracks of music on a looped tape. A piece of foil joined the ends of the tape creating the loop. When the tape reached the foil, the playback heads on the player would move to the next two tracks. One often heard the audible *click* of the heads moving. This could result in a song's interruption, which started again on the next track. In addition, songs might be in a different sequence than on the album. This was necessary to fit them on the tape. While usually not a problem, some albums were "concept albums" requiring that songs be played in a certain order. Leaving out a song entirely was also an option.

Another company was developing the cassette tape at the same time. The Phillips Company patented the cassette tape in 1964. Norelco and Sony were two of the earliest companies to become involved with the new technology. The cases that cassettes come in are "Norelco cases." Car cassette players started to make progress, but record labels were slow to release prerecorded tapes. Two events that may be the turning points for cassettes were the introductions of high-quality tape and portable cassette players.[19]

The Sony Walkman, first introduced in 1979, gave people the ability to take their music with them anywhere. Originally only a cassette tape player, models with AM/FM stereo soon hit the market.[20] As with most music technology, younger people embraced it first. Teens were walking around while listening on individual headsets. Many adults at the time saw this as an antisocial gesture. People were not supposed to be isolating themselves in public. Almost as if to play extrovert to the introverted Walkman, the boom box was born. AM/FM/cassette players with external speakers were showing up everywhere. While Walkman owners listened quietly, owners of a box played the music so all could hear. By this time the eight-track was dead.

Around the time that the eight-track became popular, FM stations began to dominate the airwaves. The clear stereo sound drew people in, slowly at first, to classical stations and then to alternative rock stations. Most members of the radio community and audience considered FM a novelty. From the mid-1960s to the mid-1970s, one jazz station in Chicago used the gimmick that it only had female DJs. Once again, radio had a new savior.

Other stations countered with the morning zoo format. Said to have been begun by radio personality Scott Shannon, no longer was one DJ enough. Stations battled to outdo each other. Often there were on-air teams of at least two DJs, a newsperson, traffic reporters, guests, and more. It was not the solitary passive listening of the past, but a more upbeat, entertaining format designed to get the audience member laughing. The perfect morning program would have people talking around the water cooler at work. As they progressed, these morning shows became more and more outrageous, until the shock jock was born.

Many claim to be the original shock jock. The shock jock programs, while using a large morning crew, did not target the same audience as the morning zoo programs. While the earlier programs were aimed at a demographic of adults, the shock jock program was targeted to adolescent boys and sometimes girls. Pushing the envelope of good taste and FCC rules, the shock jock built a loyal following that often led them beyond the radio station. Among the first shock jocks, if not *the* first, was Don Imus. Imitators in most major cities followed him.

Of course, radio once again held its breath when Music Television (MTV) began its first cablecast, leading with the Buggles's "Video Killed the Radio Star." Would people, especially the younger audience, continue to listen to radio when they could turn on MTV and see the artists as well as hear them? In the beginning, MTV operated very much like a radio station. Instead of DJs, they had VJs (video jockeys). In essence they were performing the same role as a DJ, but without the local feel. At first many in the radio industry did not know what to make of the new twenty-four-hour-a-day video format. There had been programs in the past that played music videos. *The Midnight Special* and *Rock Concert* had relied on a mix of in-studio performances (usually lip-synched) and videotapes. However, the videos on this provider were different. Where most of the early videos were just performances, these began to evolve into another type of art. It is still debatable how much of an impact MTV had on the radio industry, but one thing is certain: on MTV a song could get exposure even if radio stations were not playing it. Entire formats of music, such as new wave, gained popularity on MTV before the radio stations began playing the music. Following MTV's success, there were many followers, including VH1 (Video Hits One), BET (Black Entertainment Television), CMT (Country Music Television), and Canada's MuchMusic, yet the radio listening audience remained fairly consistent.

The compact disc (CD), an entirely new format, was introduced in 1983. All recorded matter, from Edison's recording of *Mary Had a Little Lamb* to the soundtrack to *Footloose*, had been analog. This new medium was digital and offered a clearer sound. CDs soon took the place of both records and tapes, and had a very good chance of siphoning more listeners from radio.[21]

While some see the Internet as a threat to radio, radio has welcomed the new technology. Many stations now have an online website where listeners from around the world can tune in. Chapter 7 will look at this area in more detail.

Why Radio Is a Great Choice

While radio has faced many competitors—television, movies, the Internet, and satellite-delivered subscription radio—it remains a viable business. How can a product that has changed very little in the past fifty years still compete with today's younger and more technologically advanced media?

There are several correct answers to the above question.

- Radio is for the most part a local medium, with local news, sports, weather, and audience members.
- Radio is a personal experience. It is one person talking to the audience member. The audience feels a relationship to that person.
- Radio is portable. It is the one medium commuters usually take with them on their way to work or school. It is easier to listen to the radio than read the newspaper while driving a car.
- Most of all, radio is inexpensive.

Everyone loves a good bargain. While some people may be rich enough to purchase goods at high-end retail stores, most shop for a better deal. The cost to reach the audience is where radio excels.

If we look back at the reason why many of the early radio programs didn't make the move to television, the answer was cost. Radio drama was much cheaper. There were no sets, no props, and no costumes. Theater of the mind meant that the audience member supplied all of those. Today, radio is still much more affordable than television.

Imagine an advertising agency that has written the following copy:

EXT: (Daytime)

Circus parade with thousands of onlookers.

The parade is led down the street by marching band.

Following are acrobats, clowns, etc.

Next are the elephants.

The parade stops . . .

(Cut to close-ups): Various audience members are cringing and holding their noses.

Looking upward, they see a squadron of fighter jets in tight formation flying low over the parade releasing a spray.

Smiling, they release their noses, taking deep breaths of relief. The elephants trumpet, and the parade starts again.

VO: Carnival Deodorant for Men . . . just think what it can do for you!

To produce this commercial for television requires a film crew, extras for the onlookers, a band, performers, elephants, a squadron of fighter jets, and a voiceover announcer. Such a commercial could easily run hundreds of thousands of dollars. The cost of producing a commercial for the Super Bowl has reached $2 million—not including the $2.4 million it costs to air it one time.[22]

Now look at the cost of producing the same commercial for radio. Commercials aired on radio, even on a network program, will not reach the large audience or receive the publicity of a commercial aired during a network television program, but the difference in cost can be astounding.

Sound effects (SFX) CDs or computer files can supply the sounds of the crowd, the circus performers, and the marching band. There are two different ways of creating sound effects for radio: live or by using a prerecorded CD. In the case of live sound effects, one must sometimes get very creative. For example, the engineer and producer of a radio commercial wanting to have the sound of a snack chip crunching found that the sound really didn't reproduce well on radio. So instead they snap a stalk of celery to achieve the desired sound. Most stations or production companies will turn to a CD sound effects library, however. One may access these libraries, with hundreds or thousands of sound effects, in two different ways. A studio can purchase the library for a fee and use the sounds as often as it likes, or it can make an arrangement by which it only pays when it uses the CDs. Before CDs, this was known as a "needle drop fee" because placing a needle or stylus down played the LP. The term *needle drop* is still in use today, although "laser drop" may be a more accurate name.

The audience cannot hear the onlookers cringe or hold their noses, but some creativity with voiceover talent and processors can make it work. We can have someone, usually a female, play the voice of a child. "Mommy, the elephants stink!" The same voiceover talent can usually then play the voice of the mother, or the producers can hire someone else. "I know, Dear," she says, holding her nose. "Hey look, those planes are spraying something."

The sound of the jets, once again thanks to CD.

"Wow, they smell great now," says the child as the elephants trumpet and the parade starts again.

Male voiceover: "Carnival Deodorant for Men . . . just think what it can do for you!"

One might produce this spot, using union talent, for less than $4,000. In smaller markets the talent are often nonunion. There are two main unions for radio, television, and film talent: the American Federation of Television and Radio Artists (AFTRA) and the Screen Actors Guild (SAG). For radio spots AFTRA talent is generally used.

AFTRA has different rates for television and radio spots. It also has a sliding scale depending on how large the city is that will air the spot. The talent receives a higher pay rate if the spot will be broadcast in New York, Chicago, or Los Angeles. The talent also may receive a higher rate depending on how long the commercial will air, or the "run."

For the example, assume that this is a network spot that is going to air for thirteen weeks. Each of the two actors/announcers will receive $1,277.20 for their work, for a total of $2,554.40 for talent.[23] Time for a recording studio and engineer (unless the station produces it in-house) may run another $500. Additionally, there is a fee for a copywriter to create the spot. This can vary in price from a freelance writer to the price a large agency would bill. If the writer gets $500 for the copy, this still totals just $3,554.40 for a national radio spot. Most stations write and produce their own spots, using local talent or DJs, who command a lesser rate. Using the station does not require hiring a recording studio, and a salesperson often writes the copy. For big clients the station usually pays for producing the spots.

Another way that advertisers save money is by using nationally produced spots. If a client is part of a chain or sells national brands (like appliances) they usually have access to very professionally produced spots. These spots leave openings at the beginning, middle, or end for local tags.

It is common for many advertisers to use radio in addition to television. If a listener is familiar with the television spot, the cheaper radio spot will support the television message and help him or her to recall the visual images.

Radio Today says that despite the slight drop in listeners, radio is still heard by 94 percent of Americans each week, remaining consistent across 2003 and 2004.

Some key findings that are contrary to what one may believe:

- Of those who listen to radio, men and women thirty-five to forty-four spend the most time listening to radio, while male and female teens spend the least. The sixty-five-plus set is least likely to listen to radio.
- Men below the age of sixty-five tend to listen to the radio more away from home, while women of all ages listen more at home.[24]

Drawbacks to Radio

Radio advertising has its drawbacks as well. The audience perceives that there are generally too many commercials on radio. Clear Channel Communications has addressed this clutter by announcing that its stations will be playing fewer commercials.[25] Other broadcasters will more than likely have to follow suit.

Radio can only build a mental picture. Other media can actually show the product and, in the case of print media, the reader has the ability to return to the ad.

Newspaper, magazine, and Web pages have no word limits in an ad. If the client is willing to spend, adding more pages is always an option. Radio is very limited. There are only twenty-four hours in a day. It is also a difficult task to get a message out to the audience in just thirty seconds and make it memorable.

Three of the most important words in advertising are *attention, retention,* and *action.* A good commercial should get the audience's attention, give them a message that they remember, and then move them to purchase or do whatever the ad is designed to promote. One cannot even give a firm rule as to how many words go into a spot. In counting broadcast copy, one counts syllables instead of words. Things like telephone numbers and addresses take a lot of time. While the average person will read a phone number as one word, the radio professional realizes that each number is a word with one or two syllables.

Copywriters must be master wordsmiths in order to convey a message in such a short time. Many people advise to not even include a phone number unless it is an easy-to-remember one, such as 1–800–555–SHOP. Usually stations will offer fifteen-second spots (more for name recognition, multiple spots without a lot of content), thirty-second spots (a standard length), or even sixty-second spots (more information, but more expensive and a greater chance of the audience tuning out).

Because radio is a narrowcast medium, one set of ads will not reach the entire population and the audience will need to hear a commercial multiple times for it to have an effect. People tend to tune out commercials, either subconsciously or by choice, hitting the scan button on the radio. All of these negatives make selling advertising a challenge.

 ## Questions for Further Thought

1 Is it better to have a large audience with less disposable income, or a small audience with a large disposable income?

2 If you wanted to advertise a new car, what questions might you ask before buying ad time?

3 Do you see the PPM as a better tool for measurement or another invasion of privacy?

4 Why is it important to keep listeners for at least five minutes at a time?

Shop Talk

Copy: A written script for a commercial.

Cost per thousand: (CPM): The estimated cost for an advertiser to reach one thousand listeners (gross impressions) with a commercial.

Daypart: Divisions of the broadcast day into segments to easily report ratings.

Market: An area served by a radio station. May also be a portion of the audience that has been selected from the larger mass audience (target demographic).

Morning drive: Time slot with the most listeners and most expensive advertising time, 6 A.M. to 10 A.M.

Navigauge: New ratings company that uses a global positioning system to measure when and where in-car listening occurs. It also measures where a car stops and for how long.

Portable people meter (PPM): New technology developed by Arbitron and Nielsen companies to measure exposure to radio and television automatically.

Run of schedule (ROS): A strategy for buying radio time at a reduced price, but with less control of when it will air.

Shock jock: Radio host whose program is designed to target the young male audience through the use of what many would consider indecent or profane humor, interviews, and so on. Currently the most well known shock jock is Howard Stern.

Spots: Another term for radio commercials. Usually thirty seconds long but may be fifteen seconds to one minute in length.

Tag: Ending piece of a commercial that gives a piece of information. Often, in a nationally produced spot the tag is left open for local store information.

5

Commercial versus Noncommercial Radio

In its early years radio broadcasting, by today's standards, was all noncommercial. While manufacturers or department stores owned many of the stations like KDKA, churches, high schools, and colleges and universities owned many more. Yet even the school radio stations were often parts of the physics departments, more concerned with increasing the power and range of the stations than the programming itself. The University of Wisconsin's WHA, which started in 1902, is an example of one of the earliest of these stations.

Noncommercial broadcasting had a slow evolution, partially because of the development of commercial broadcasting and partially because of the cost of owning and maintaining such a venture. At the time, noncommercial stations received funding from individuals, organizations, or in the rare instance a municipality. Noncommercial radio was not deemed to be a serious player in the industry for most of the 1920s through the 1940s.

In 1930 the Association of College and University Broadcast Stations petitioned Congress to receive assurance that some frequencies be reserved for use by noncommercial, educational stations. Although many groups, including the Federal Radio Commission (FRC) were pushing for such an amendment, the frequency reservation never passed.

However, even though this was a defeat, it did put the issue of noncommercial educational radio in front of Congress and the people.

In 1938 the commission did agree to set aside some high-frequency AM channels for broadcasting to classrooms. Substantial frequency allocations for noncommercial use didn't occur until 1941.

With the number of commercial stations growing and the number of noncommercial stations dropping, the National Association for Educational Broadcasters (NAEB) was successful in getting the FCC to set aside 20 percent of the new FM band for noncommercial use. This solution helped both the FCC and the NAEB. While the educational broadcasters would rather have had the AM band, it gave them a place to broadcast. Little did they realize that in future years FM would become the most popular band. For the FCC it helped to expose people to FM as space on the newly introduced band began to fill up.

Yet in the short term there was still a problem. There were few commercial FM stations on the air, and many of those on the air were simulcasting their AM signal. Therefore there was little impetus for the average listener to purchase a new, more expensive radio receiver. Without listeners, there was little reason for stations to provide new content on the FM band. Adding to this catch-22 was the fact that the cost of operating an FM station was prohibitive for many who would like a noncommercial license due to the high professional standards set by the FCC. Once again the NAEB approached them with a proposal, asking for the lowering of the standards for operating educational stations.

The FCC agreed and created a new class of license in 1948—class D. Unlike commercial stations, class D stations were licensed at just ten watts of power. While this meant that the signal would only reach a mile or two, it made radio more affordable to many more potential licensees. This gave stations the lower end of the FM band, from 88.1 to 91.9.

This class D category brought an increase in the number of noncommercial radio stations throughout the 1950s and '60s. Stations became laboratories for schools teaching broadcasting and journalism (a change from the early days of physics departments using radio), pulpits for religious groups, classrooms of the air for some colleges and universities, and even outlets for the disenfranchised and dissenters of the Vietnam war.

The Educational Television Facilities Act created and funded noncommercial television in 1962. Yet private money was still funding noncommercial radio stations. A report on public television from the Carnegie Foundation outlined what the future of the new public television should be. The result of the report was the creation of what was supposed to be the Public Television Act of 1967.

NAEB reacted quickly when they realized that the educational television stations were leaving them out of the new act. With monetary support from the Ford Foundation, the NAEB conducted another study. The report, *The Hidden Medium*, was released just in time for Congress to consider it before enacting the television bill. Congress held a series of hearings resulting from that report. However, the accounts of the hearings differ at this point. One source believes that Dean Costen, deputy undersecretary of health, education, and welfare, made sure that the words "and radio" were slipped into President Johnson's Public Television Act of 1967.[1] Another source claims that the result of the hearings was that the name of the act was changed to the Public Broadcasting Act of 1967.[2]

President Johnson signed the law that he compared with the Morrill Act, which set aside land in each state for a "land grant" college. He stressed that the Public Broadcasting Act would set aside airwaves for education. But even more interesting, he makes note of what may very well have been the beginnings of the Internet in his speech, excerpted below.

The Corporation
for Public Broadcasting (CPB)

One of the original appointees to the board of the CPB was Dr. James Killian, a past president of the Massachusetts Institute of Technology. Near the end of his speech, President Johnson said that he had been talking with Killian about the following:

> I believe the time has come to stake another claim in the name of all the people, stake a claim based upon the combined resources of communications. I believe the time has come to enlist the computer and the satellite, as well as television and radio, and to enlist them in the cause of education. . . . Yes, the student in a small college tapping the resources of the greatest university in the hemisphere.
>
> —the country doctor getting help from a distant laboratory or a teaching hospital;
>
> —a scholar in Atlanta might draw instantly on a library in New York;
>
> —a famous teacher could reach with ideas and inspirations into some far-off classroom, so that no child need be neglected.
>
> Eventually, I think this electronic knowledge bank could be as valuable as the Federal Reserve Bank.
>
> And such a system could involve other nations, too—it could involve them in a partnership to share knowledge and to thus enrich all mankind. A wild and visionary idea? Not at all. Yesterday's strangest dreams are today's headlines and change is getting swifter every moment. I have already asked my advisers to begin to explore the possibility of a network for knowledge—and then to draw up a suggested blueprint for it.[3]

In addition to serving as chair of the CPB, President Eisenhower had appointed Killian as the Presidential Assistant for Science. The launch of *Sputnik* concerned the U.S. military, which feared that a nuclear attack on the United States could make communications among various headquarters impossible. The government formed the Advanced Research Projects Agency (ARPA). The result was a series of steps that led to today's Internet.[4]

One of the problems facing public broadcasting was funding. The Carnegie report suggested that since this venture was noncommercial, it should be funded similarly to the British Broadcasting Corporation (BBC), which received benefits of a tax on television and radio receivers. This system was quickly rejected, and instead Congress decided to set up a separate corporation that would be funded by Congress and oversee the operation of public radio and television.

The Corporation for Public Broadcasting (CPB) was set up under Section 396 of the Public Broadcasting Act of 1967. Among its provisions were that:

(1) it is in the public interest to encourage the growth and development of public radio and television broadcasting, including the use of such media for instructional, educational, and cultural purposes; . . .

(10) a private corporation should be created to facilitate the development of public telecommunications and to afford maximum protection from extraneous interference and control.

The new organization was created in the act, which stated, "There is authorized to be established a nonprofit corporation, to be known as the 'Corporation for Public Broadcasting,' which will not be an agency or establishment of the United States Government."[5]

While the theory of a media free from government interference was laudable, it didn't work in practice. The CPB, with hat in hand, was going to Congress every term to make a case for its budget. Many politicians, including President Nixon, who vetoed the CPB's budget in 1972, felt that the CPB was not essential and wished to do away with it, or at least greatly curb its funding.

A look at the history of appropriations for the CPB shows no apparent pattern to its funding. Some years the corporation would receive far less than it asked for. Some years it would ask for a smaller amount and receive far more. Even though it is not "an agency or establishment of the United States Government," it is still subject to the whimsy of Congress and the federal budget.[6]

The battles between public broadcasting and the government continued. In 1979, at the bequest of the CPB, the Carnegie Foundation released the results of a second study. This study suggested, among other things, replacing the CPB with a trust separate from government control. It also suggested that stations no longer call themselves "educational" but instead adopt the word "public" to describe themselves. This document was largely ignored. The CPB has more and more trouble finding funding each year, requiring stations, NPR, and PBS to search for alternative funding.

One of the immediate results of the 1967 act was to fund noncommercial stations that met a minimum requirement, which was set at having at least three full-time employees, and broadcasting at least six days a week, forty-eight weeks a year. These standards have changed to five full-time employees, and broadcasting eighteen hours a day, 365 days a year. The act also created a center that could produce and distribute programming to stations. In the early days, NAEB stations would "bicycle" programs among member stations, allowing them to share station productions and costs.

National Public Radio (NPR)

Al Hulsen, the head of the radio division of the CPB, had to decide if the radio stations should follow the lead of the old radio and current television networks, all airing the same programming at the same time, or if they should follow the lead of the contemporary stations of individual formatting and programming. He decided there would be one national production center, National Public Radio (NPR). In 1970, board member William Siemering wrote an almost poetic mission statement for the new organization. In its opening paragraph Siemering wrote, "National Public Radio will serve the individual: it will promote personal growth; it will regard the individual differences among men with respect and joy rather than derision and hate; it will celebrate the human experience as infinitely varied rather than vacuous and banal; it will encourage a sense of active constructive participation, rather than apathetic helplessness."[7]

The *National Public Radio Purposes* went on to delineate seven priorities:

1   Provide an identifiable daily product which is consistent and reflects the highest standards of broadcast journalism.

2   Provide extended coverage of public events, issues and ideas, and acquire and produce special public affairs programs.

3   Acquire and produce cultural programs which can be scheduled individually by stations.

4   Provide access to the intellectual and cultural resources of cities, universities and rural districts through a system of cooperative program development with member public radio stations.

5   Develop and distribute programs to specific groups (adult education, instructional, modular units for local productions) which meet needs of individual regions or groups.

6   Establish liaison with foreign broadcasters for a program exchange service.

7   Produce materials specifically intended to develop the art and technical potential of radio.[8]

Programming

The first president of NPR was Donald Quail, and the first program director was William Siemering. The first program delivered by NPR was *All Things Considered*, a ninety-minute news-oriented program. The idea behind the program was to give listeners, especially those driving home, an update on the news, but also to include pieces on the arts, science, business, and just about anything the producers thought the audience might like. Different from other news programs, *All Things Considered* was more like a magazine on the air. It offered many different short segments, generally taking a lighter approach, including interviews with newsmakers and celebrities, and offered stations an opportunity to break for local news, weather, and other announcements. But *All Things Considered* did not tone down the news. The program evolved to offer up-to-the-minute news, including live reports from around the world as well as in-depth analysis of events by bringing in experts from all fields. While it took a while for the audience to build, it began winning awards just two years into its run.

With such a prestigious program on the air, stations began to see the benefit of becoming an NPR affiliate. Not only would they be eligible for the federal funds granted to the CPB, but also they would be able to offer audience members a show unlike any they could produce locally while at the same time giving themselves a favorable brand.

The number of NPR member stations continued to grow, even as funding for the CPB was slowly cut off. Some NPR stations formed the Association of Public Radio Stations (APRS) to lobby Congress. The organization's board included the heads of two of the largest public radio systems, Minnesota Public Radio and Wisconsin Public Radio, as members. APRS often clashed with NPR, and the infighting served to hurt the stations. In 1977 APRS merged with NPR, ousting Quale and replacing him with Frank Mankiewcz. Mankiewcz was in many ways exactly what NPR needed at the time. The one-time press secretary for Senator Robert Kennedy knew the workings of Congress and, as a lawyer, he knew the legal system. He had also worked as a journalist, giving him a strong news background.

His first action was to get Congress to set aside 25 percent of the money the CPB received for radio. Prior to this, public television had actually been allowed to allocate the money themselves, giving radio whatever percentage it liked. Using his Hollywood connections, Mankiewcz was able to get the rights to produce a serialized version of George Lucas's *Star Wars*, starring many of the original cast members. His skills as a press secretary came in handy in promoting NPR and making sure that it received news coverage. His journalism background helped make NPR the station many tuned to for their daily news and for breaking news coverage.

With the continued success of *All Things Considered* in the afternoon drive slot, NPR looked to develop another program to fill the morning drive time. Listeners first heard *Morning Edition* in 1979. Wanting to replicate the success of the afternoon program, *Morning Edition* had many of the same elements as *All Things Considered*. The two-hour program with host Bob Edwards was designed so that each segment was short enough that it could be heard in the car—nine minutes—even if it meant staying in the car for a few extra minutes after arriving home. This is something that NPR refers to as the *driveway moment* story; the story that is so intriguing the listener is willing to stay to finish it. The program also has spots where local stations can break in with news or can stay with the NPR feed.

The show had a rough beginning. Its sister program didn't have the resources to share, and *All Things Considered* had a very limited budget. The show owes its success to many people. Bob Edwards, who hosted the show from its beginning until he left in 2004, was one. His smooth baritone voice was more like a cup of coffee that listeners could sip while waking up. The newspeople and regular segment guests and commentators all seemed to take their lead from the host and producers, and realized that they were part of a morning program as different from a morning zoo as it was possible to be. When Edwards left the show after having been with it for just shy of twenty-five years, there were many rumors as to why he was leaving. Most people believed that NPR was looking for a younger sound and that Edwards did not fit the role. In response to more than 35,000 complaints the network received, NPR Ombudsman Jeffrey Dvorkin stated on the NPR website: "The suspicions of ageism were exacerbated when management said it wants to 'freshen up' the sound of *Morning Edition*. Some listeners assumed that 'freshen up' must automatically mean 'younger.'"[9]

During the Mankiewcz years, another development greatly helped NPR achieve success. The use of satellites, or "birds," to deliver programming to stations meant that they could not only get superior sound, but also simultaneously download multiple programs. This gave the stations some flexibility in which shows they selected and when they broadcast them.

Public Radio International (PRI)

Satellites, however, also gave stations the ability to send their signals out, provided they had access to an uplink, and totally bypass NPR. Mankiewcz did not like the fact that NPR would no longer have total control over content production and distribution. William Kling, of Minnesota Public Radio, who once had helped put Mankiewcz into power, approached him with an idea. Kling wished to offer MPR's *Prairie Home Companion* for distribution. When Mankiewcz turned him down, Kling responded by starting a rival programming and distribution company for NPR stations, American Public Radio, later to become Public Radio International (PRI).

Prairie Home Companion, hosted by Garrison Keillor and featuring his stories of the fictional Minnesota town of Lake Woebegon, harkens back to the days of early radio. It offered skits, stories, and musical guests. Broadcast before a live audience, usually from its home at the Fitzgerald Theater in St. Paul, Minnesota, it remains one of the top-rated program on NPR. It has even inspired a line of catalog products ranging from hats and T-shirts to tapes, books, and other paraphernalia.

PRI now offers a variety of programs, including news (*The World, Marketplace*, and *BBC World Service*), documentary (*This American Life*), entertainment (*Michael Feldman's Whad'Ya Know?, Ask Dr. Science, Brain Brew*), and music (*Classical 24, Mountain Stage, World Café*, and *AfroPop*).[10]

With more budget cuts during the Reagan years, Kling saw an opportunity to offer stations programming at a price even lower than NPR's. In a move often second-guessed, Mankiewcz tried to undercut the APR programming prices. In fact, his prices were so low that NPR began losing money. Kling and APR, on the other hand, backed off of their offer, leaving NPR vulnerable. NPR lost so much money that Mankiewcz, his staff, and roughly one quarter of the employees lost their jobs. Ron Bornstein, of Wisconsin Public Radio, the other person who had helped Mankiewcz become NPR president, became interim president at this point. With the help of loans made by the CPB, and member stations guaranteeing their repayment, NPR was able to climb out of debt. Because the stations had taken responsibility for the debt, the CPB decided that instead of paying money to NPR, it would pay the money directly to the stations, which could in turn purchase programming from NPR, APR, or another source.

At this time, some of the larger stations organized under the banner of the Station Resources Group (SRG). They contended that stations could no longer rely on federal funds and should start proactively seeking grants and donations. This changed the way public padio worked. Stations now needed to be more like their commercial counterparts. No longer could a station program what it felt people needed to hear. It needed, instead, to program what the people *wanted*, especially those who would help fund the station.

Stations had to turn to other methods of funding to augment the federal funds. Stations licensed to state-owned institutions of higher education might receive funding from the schools. This money may be from tuition and student activity fees but is usually from state tax dollars that help support the university. Some stations will look for grants from various local and national corporations. Stations may seek underwriting from a local business that wants to reach the typical NPR listener and have its name associated with the quality of its programming. Of course, the largest share of money comes from listener donations. In fact, most stations receive over half of their income from listeners. In essence, the percentage of the population that donates to the station is paying a fee in exchange for not listening to commercials. Unfortunately, only a small minority of listeners of public radio stations donates to them.

While in the past a corporation or business underwriting a program was only allowed a message stating, "This program is brought to you by the Smith Corporation," the new rules allow for a hybrid message that is half underwriting style and half commercial. The stations may now mention the underwriter of a program along with a brief slogan or mention of what the business does, "This program is brought to you by the Smith Corporation, located in Jonesboro, making quality widgets since 1895. Visit them on the web at www.smithwidgetcorp.com." This new style of message gives sponsors more incentive to associate with NPR stations.

A study of public radio listeners called *Audience 88* found that the primary predictor of listenership is education. The more years of schooling a person had, the more likely he or she listens to noncommercial radio or public radio. But the study found that this did not necessarily correlate with financial data. While many people with advanced degrees are wealthy, the biggest factor was education and not social status. In fact, if one were to use a combination of factors to determine the definitive listener of public radio he or she would be "the teacher rather than the doctor, the social worker rather than the investment banker. The ultimate public radio listener turned out to be the Ph.D. who drives a cab."[11]

Programmers like NPR and PRI charge stations by the size of their market and the number of audience members who tune in to the program each week. By the same token, member stations often judge whether to keep a show or not by how much money they raise during the pledge drives while that program is on the air. If a program has few listeners but they are large donors, it may be worthwhile to keep it on the air, while a program with a large base of listeners who do not contribute is costing the station money.

This in itself goes against the premise that the Public Broadcasting Act had set forth. As A. G. Stavlitsky points out, "In the founding ideology of public broadcasting the audience was characterized not as a market of consumers, to be captured for profit, but rather as a public of citizens, to be 'served.' As such the broadcaster's mission was to educate, inform, and uplift the audience."[12]

Now public radio stations must appeal to the broadest audience, possibly at the risk of forsaking their original mission. They have also begun to change their thinking about what "localism" and "community" mean. Instead of thinking of the community as located within geographic boundaries, they now think of them as being within social boundaries, people who have the same lifestyles, education, tastes, and so forth.[13]

In 2003 NPR reported income from station memberships of $2,115,535 and income from station programming fees of $52,696,842. It also reported: "For the 18th consecutive year, NPR programming set new records in 2003, capping audience growth of 64 percent in the last five years with an all-time high of more than 22 million average listeners per week."[14]

Programming

Today NPR has more than 760 noncommercial member stations. NPR produces and distributes more than one hundred hours of programming each week. Among its offerings are *Weekend Edition* (an offshoot of *Morning Edition*), *Wait . . . Wait . . . Don't Tell Me* (a current events quasi game show), the talk show *Fresh Air*, and the number one program on NPR, *Car Talk*. NPR is also carried on Sirius Satellite Radio.

Car Talk, with its hosts Tom and Ray Magliozzi, is an interesting program that can only be heard on NPR. The Brothers Magliozzi, or as they sometimes refer to themselves, "Click and Clack, the Tappet Brothers," did not start out as radio hosts. Both brothers both graduated from MIT, one with a degree in engineering, the other with a Ph.D. in marketing. During the 1970s they opened a do-it-yourself garage, which Ray still operates. Once popular in areas of the United States, these garages would rent stall space and lend tools to the shade-tree mechanic without a tree to work under. Today the garage is a more traditional garage with mechanics doing the work. The brothers accepted an invitation in 1977 to be on a local NPR station with other mechanics taking phone calls and discussing car problems. Quickly they received their own weekly show. Callers would call in with questions about how to replace a blown head gasket, or how to drop a transmission. Their knowledge combined with their sense of humor caught the attention of Susan Stamberg, who was hosting *Weekend Edition* at the time. The brothers became weekly guests and in 1987 started their own weekly show on NPR. As they often note, the program has gone from people who worked on their own cars to people with problems often only tangentially related to their cars.

The Magliozzis often laugh at themselves, and routinely invite past callers back on the program to "Stump the Chumps," a segment in which they see if the answer they gave the caller was correct. Sometimes they were right; sometimes they were wrong. When they are right, they act surprised and when they are wrong they blame each other. The "Puzzler," a riddle that is sometimes about cars, but often about physics, engineering, history, or other topics, is a segment appearing in what they humorously refer to as the, "third half" of the show. Almost 4 million people, listening on over 550 stations, regularly hear the show. Tuning in to any program will usually find an unexpectedly high percentage of graduate students and professors calling in, showing that they can reach every level of the population with a show about the once blue-collar topic of car repair.

There are more noncommercial stations on the air, however, than the NPR member stations.

Community Radio

Another type of noncommercial station is the community station, often operated by a community foundation or local government. They are very localized and specialize in the affairs of the community. While there may be one or two full-time staff members, most staff members are volunteers.

The FRC and until recently the FCC have encouraged such localism in broadcasting. The FCC used the "public interest" clause to show favoritism in granting licenses to community members over outsiders, and making public affairs part of the renewal of the local stations. With the adoption of the ruling creating the class D license, the FCC took another step toward the development of local broadcasting.

Pacifica Foundation

In 1949 a small group of pacifists and conscientious objectors to World War II received a license for a radio station in Berkley, California, KPFA. The Pacifica Foundation that they formed in 1946 was led by Lewis Hill. Hill's dream was to have a "pacific world in our time." The group accepted the station on the new FM band, although they originally wanted an AM station in another town.

The station was to be supported by subscribers, each paying ten dollars per year, quite a sum at the time, especially when the concept of noncommercial, listener-supported radio was new.

The station had a rocky start. The original plan called for the station to be in a blue-collar area where they would use the airwaves to win people over to their peaceful way of thinking. The new location, Berkley, home to the main campus of the University of California, didn't allow the station's strategy to work as planned. Facing bankruptcy, the KPFA changed strategy and programmed for the intelligentsia, who had more money. The new format appealed to the educated and elite with programs featuring famous authors and poets, while at the same time appealing to the growing underground by offering panel discussions on banned books.

Hill, a published poet, committed suicide in 1957, leaving behind a note that read, "Not for anger or despair/but for peace and a kind of home."[15] Hill's legacy KPFA lived on, continuing to be noncommercial while often being near the heart of controversy. When Native Americans took over the abandoned Alcatraz Island in 1969, KPFA brought a Marti Unit out to the island and broadcast their statements live over the air. This *Radio Free Alcatraz* was the way that many non–Native Americans heard about the demands of the Native Americans and their need for government attention.

The Pacifica Foundation also acquired licenses for stations in New York, Washington, D.C., Los Angeles, and Houston. In fact, one of the greatest controversies to hit broadcast radio started at the Pacifica station in New York, as detailed in chapter 9.

Native American Radio

Native Americans, seeing the effectiveness of *Radio Free Alcatraz* and the media coverage it received, began to think about starting Native American radio stations. Today there are fewer than thirty stations owned and operated by Native Americans. However, the FCC announced in February 2004 a new Memorandum of Understanding (MOU) with several American tribes. Native Americans usually staff the stations. Located on or near reservations, the stations provide entertainment, community service programming, and in many cases attempt to keep the culture of a people from becoming forever extinct. There are also several satellite services delivering programming and webcasts.

College Radio Stations

While some larger universities have NPR stations, many schools cannot afford the full-time staffing, or simply do not wish to have an NPR station. Stations at high schools, colleges, and universities can differ greatly. At schools where the station is an NPR member station, announcers tend to be paid and programming ranges from all NPR to a mix of classical music and news, or sometimes jazz. Some larger schools may even have more than one station. The University of Tennessee, for example, has an NPR station, an AM commercial news station, and a noncommercial student-run FM station.

If a station is not an NPR station, it generally falls under one or both of the following categories: a learning component of a broadcasting major, or a student-operated station charted by the student government association. With the latter, a paid faculty member or graduate student is the advisor. The format can be an eclectic mix of alternative, country, jazz—virtually anything. Stations may allow individual DJs to decide upon their show's format, while some stations may place certain formats at certain times, called block formatting.

For example, 6 A.M. to 9 A.M. may be CHR; 9 A.M. to 12 P.M., urban; 12 P.M. to 3 P.M., community service programming; and so forth. There is flexibility as long as the show fits within the genre. A freeform format is not uncommon at these stations, usually during the evenings or overnight shifts, allowing any type of music or show.

The Lean Years

In 1978 the FCC stopped issuing class D licenses (except in Alaska) and required stations to operate at one hundred to one thousand watts. While many small groups could afford the equipment and upkeep of a small ten-watt station, the new requirements were cost-prohibitive for many. The number of community noncommercial radio stations declined over the next two decades to a point where they became almost nonexistent. For the most part, only the largest universities, churches, and civic groups were able to keep a station on the air. Smaller voices became endangered.

Many radio broadcaster wannabes turned to alternative and sometimes illegal means in order to get on the air. One of these methods falls under the category of pirate radio.

Pirate Radio

Pirate radio is any radio broadcasting done without a license. While the occasional college student may set up a small transmitter in a residence hall, pirate radio was at its peak in the 1960s and '70s, more so in England and the Netherlands than in the United States. English radio was entirely state owned, at the time, essentially blocking the alternative or counterculture programming that many wished to hear. Radio London is perhaps the most famous of all pirate radio stations.

Many of these stations were aboard ships in international waters, where they were free to broadcast without fear of reproach. As long as the stations remained at sea, they were legal. Land based stations, however were strictly illegal. Government licensing bureaus can easily triangulate and locate stationary stations on land.

In the United States, pirate radio was generally the underground radio of the counterculture hippie movement or other fringe groups.

In the mid-1980s a resurgence of unlicensed broadcasting began in the United States in response to the FCC's actions. Many felt that the individual had lost his or her voice on the air, and that major corporations were controlling radio and forcing it to become homogenized.

A new type of broadcaster emerged: the microradio broadcaster. The driving force and ideology of microradio stations was Free Radio Berkley (FRB), whose plan was that the FCC would be overwhelmed by the sheer number of unlicensed radio stations and therefore powerless to shut them down. Unlike the original private radio broadcasters, the FRB wanted broadcasters to not go underground, to challenge the FCC's authority.

The FCC fined the founder of the FRB, Stephen Dunifer, $20,000 for operating an unlicensed radio station.[16] He appealed the decision to the Circuit Court, which ruled that the FCC did not prove that a low-power station caused harm to any commercial stations. However, the FCC once again fined Dunifer, in 1998, saying that he had never filed for a license or waiver and therefore had no legal standing to question their decisions. Dunifer once again appealed; in that case the court agreed with the FCC.[17]

Today, anyone caught broadcasting a pirate radio station is subject to a $10,000-per-day fine up to a maximum of $75,000. In addition, equipment used may be confiscated and criminal penalties may result if the person "willingly and knowingly" is operating without a license.[18]

Low-Power FM

Due mainly to the number of microstations being put on the air, the FCC began to seriously study a reinstitution of some type of low-power radio station license in 1999. Despite opposition from commercial broadcasters, the FCC announced in 2000 that it would begin accepting applications for low-power FM stations (LPFM) by regions. The "stations are available for non-commercial educational entities and public safety/travelers information entities, but not individuals or commercial operations."[19]

These new stations must operate at one hundred watts. While the cost of hundred-watt stations was prohibitive in the 1970s, new technology makes it far less expensive today.

Application Process

In order to obtain a broadcasting license, an applicant must fill out a series of forms (all downloadable at www.fcc.gov/mb/audio/lpfm/index.html). These forms require the name of the organization and its board members, and whether any board members have media holdings; the exact location of the antenna, including height above the ground and height above sea level (for this a contour map is generally used, and antennas within a certain distance from airports must have special approval); a proposed list of the type and amount of programming the station will do; and an engineering study that shows that the frequency selected from among those on the FCC's available list will not interfere with another station's signal. Following the filing of the application and the application fee, there may be a substantial wait time, depending on whether anyone else has applied for the same frequency.

The FCC eventually issues a construction permit (CP). The permit is not the license, but just FCC approval to begin building the station, erecting the antenna, and so on. A license is then issued if the station is built *exactly* as proposed. In rare instances eager permit holders have begun construction of stations prior to receiving the CP. This is a mistake. In these cases the FCC may require that the licensee destroy the previous work and begin anew.

The new ruling states that stations of this type must be available for public safety and travelers' information. Such stations are usually set up near highways, offering information about area attractions, road construction reports, weather information, and so on, and are licensed to a local government. These stations are usually unmanned and have a message repeated on a tape loop.[20]

Since 1970, the FCC has allowed two other types of low-power stations: FM translators and FM boosters. The booster or translator allows "supplementary service to areas in which direct reception of radio service is unsatisfactory due to distance or intervening terrain barriers (e.g., mountain)." These stations can be no more than 250 watts or 20 percent of the main station's power.[21]

A translator receives the signal from a station and simultaneously transmits it on another frequency. These transmitters, called fill-ins, literally fill in holes in the station's signal coverage.

A booster is essentially the same as a translator but is broadcasting on the same frequency as the main station. It is taking the signal and pushing it out a little farther than would normally be possible.

At the time of this writing, the FCC was not accepting applications for noncommercial LPFM stations, but had announced that it was going to revisit the LPFM rules.

Another type of station is not strictly a broadcast station, but uses the same technology. Many large cities have services that read daily newspapers, magazines, and other materials to those who are visually impaired. Some services read everything from news to advertisements, comics, and photo captions. Readers, generally volunteers, often come from the radio community. Special radio receivers decode these programs, which use a station's carrier wave to reach them.

For many, a small section of the FCC rules allows for certain types of very-low-power unlicensed stations. The FCC allows these stations to bypass the licensing process due to their very low power. Mostly used for colleges, universities, and high schools, these stations use technologies called carrier current or leaky line.

Carrier Current

Carrier current programming requires a station to inject the signals into the electrical power lines. Via the wires, the signal is sent around a building or entire campus. The signals, due to the technical and government limitations, are AM between the range of 535 and 1,700 kHz.

Leaky Line

Leaky line uses special coaxial cable designed to "leak" the audio signal. This signal may not travel more than two hundred feet from a building. It allows for on-campus broadcasts, but not broadcasts to the community at large. Another disadvantage of the system is that besides being limited in how far the signal carries, it can also block a signal on the same frequency from coming onto campus.[22]

Cable Radio

Another way of delivering a radio broadcast signal is cable. Cable radio operates much like cable television. The coaxial or fiber-optic cable carries the audio signal along with the video. This requires a station to send its signal to the cable head-end through a dedicated telephone line. The cable provider then sends the signal out to its subscribers. The main disadvantage of the cable radio system is that it relies on listeners using a splitter that sends the cable signal arriving in their home to the television set or monitor, and also to a stereo. Unfortunately, most radios do not have an RF connector like a television set.

But the emerging leader in the nonbroadcast, noncommercial radio race has to be the Internet. Internet radio use is at an all-time high, and just about anyone with access to a computer can put a station on the air. More about this will be discussed in chapter seven.

 ## Questions for Further Thought

1   With all of the alternatives to radio, is there still a need for NPR?

2   What can community radio offer that commercial radio stations can't?

3   Why are some illegal radio stations referred to as "pirate stations"?

4   Should the CPB allow advertising and scrap "underwriting"?

Shop Talk

Block format: A formatting strategy in which each show is independent of others, as opposed to having one station format for all shows.

Construction permit (CP): An OK from the FCC to build a radio station. This step comes before the official licensing.

Freeform: Without format. Any genre of music may be played during a freeform radio show.

Localism: Concept that radio stations should serve the public interest by featuring local content.

Low-power FM (LRFM): New category of noncommercial radio station licensed to schools, church groups, and for government safety and travelers' information.

Marti Unit: Remote transmission device that allowed reporters and DJs to go to a remote location live.

National Public Radio (NPR): Nonprofit supplier of programming to noncommercial "public" radio stations. Funded via radio station fees and the Corporation for Public Broadcasting (CPB).

Pledge drive: Period during which noncommercial radio stations set aside time to ask listeners to support the station through donations.

Public Broadcasting Act of 1967, Section 396: Legislation that established the Corporation for Public Broadcasting (CPB).

Underwriting: Method for corporations to sponsor a noncommercial station without violating advertising rules.

6

Is There Anybody out There?

So You Want to Work in Radio?

There is no "typical radio station." Radio stations today may have as many as one hundred employees or as few as three. Some stations have DJs, while others rely on satellite-delivered programming. Some are small independent stations, while others are owned by massive chains. But following are some of the careers available at small and large stations for those who want to make a career of broadcasting.

The DJ

When most people think of working at a radio station they immediately think of being a disc jockey. Perhaps you are lucky enough to work on-air at a college or university station or even a professional one.

The disc jockey (DJ) is a bit of a misnomer. In the early days, the DJ had more work to do to make a smooth program. Turntables take a few seconds to get up to speed. They do not start at $33^{1/3}$ rpms. This was not a problem for the person at home playing an album. The record usually had several seconds at the beginning of it that allowed for this. But in order to make a smooth segue the DJ needed to start a song at just the right spot. Also, not every song on the air was at the beginning of the disc, especially for AOR stations. Therefore, if a song was not the first on the record, the DJ would put the turntable in neutral and turn it back one to two revolutions. The turntable's needle was placed at that point. When the "play" button was hit, the turntable would already be up to speed by the time the music started. This was known as "cuing" a record.

In the course of cuing the records, DJs would hear the first bit of every song they cued up played backwards. Rumors spread that the Beatles had hidden messages in their music that could be heard when the records were played backwards. Some accusations claimed that the subconscious mind would hear and process these messages even when played forward. While the Beatles denied using this "back masking," other bands did use it to entertain DJs. Today's DJs, of course, can load one or several CDs into the players and hit a button to find the proper cut. Some stations have even gone to an all-digital format in which the music is preloaded onto a computer, taking a lot of the "jockeying" out of the job.

The DJ is also responsible for running the board, which is the audio mixer that controls all content going over the air. (This is examined further in chapter 7.) There is also the announcing. Depending on the station, format, and audience, the DJ may take an active part in the show, bantering, talking about the music, taking phone calls, or in the case of a morning drive show, be an all-round entertainer, part standup comedian, part newsperson, part talk show host. At other stations, the DJ will just give the names of songs, the time, temperature, and so on. Some stations have even gone so far as to replace the DJ with prerecorded station messages giving the call letters and station's slogan. "You're listening to Cool Breeze, 98.6."

The disc jockey's position has its advantages and disadvantages. On the positive side, DJs, especially those in major markets, are well paid and sometimes accorded celebrity status. In addition, they get perks such as free concert tickets and opportunities to meet bands and celebrities on a daily basis.

There are also disadvantages, however. Radio often uses baseball terminology. The person waiting to go on the air is "on deck"; the room that most businesses would refer to as a break room is often known as the "bullpen." Before a DJ makes it to "the show" he or she has to pay their dues in the small-town, "minor league" stations. This is done by taking a low-paying job, putting in some time, and hoping to climb the ladder. Almost every DJ reads the industry classified ads in trade publications like *Broadcasting and Cable, Radio and Records,* and *Radio Inc.,* or on company websites, hoping to find a larger market or bigger station or maybe just a better time slot. It is common for a DJ to move across the country and back several times, each time to a slightly larger station, hoping that he or she will one day make it to a major-market station. But just as in baseball, for every one who becomes a major-league player, thousands never make it. Because the lives of DJs can be transient, it is sometimes difficult to make true friendships, knowing that they will be moving soon. The sit-com *WKRP in Cincinnati* (1978–82) expressed this well in the show's theme song: "Baby I got tired of unpacking, town to town, up and down the dial."[1]

Many programming services will provide radio programs via satellite to local stations. Some services design programming to coexist with a local DJ, including slots for news, sports, entertainment, or comedy segments. Other programmers design shows to replace the local talent. Some stations purchase programs through a service, while others get them directly from a station in a different market. In all of these cases, the station customarily receives exclusive rights to the service for that market. No other station may carry the same programming. In rare cases, a station may purchase the rights to air a program to keep other stations in the market from competing with their programming.

For example, if your station had the number-one morning show, you wouldn't want the competition to bring in a show that might draw listeners from your station. Instead, you purchase the show, continuing to air your local program while effectively having blocked the competition from bringing a threat to your ratings.

But stations have many more jobs vital to their daily operations. At the head of the ladder are the general manager and/or station owner. With recent trends toward group ownership, it is rare to find an owner-manager outside of small markets.

The General Manager (GM)

The GM oversees the entire operation of the station and is ultimately accountable if it prospers or fails. Reporting to the general manager may be several midlevel management personnel.

The Program Director (PD)

The PD is in charge of the overall sound of the station and oversees the on-air staff. All DJs report to the PD. The program director is responsible at most stations for developing a "hot clock," also known as the "format clock." The clock represents one hour of airtime and lets the on-air talent know what should be played and when. Unlike the freeform radio format, stations today are very structured. The clock dictates a standard that all shows must follow and can also affect the ratings.

A typical hot clock may look something as seen in Figure 5.1. It is not uncommon for stations to have a different clock for each of the dayparts. Those listening during morning drive tend to want more time, weather, and traffic reports, while these are not as important to audience members at 9 P.M.

Figure 6.1 Hot Clock

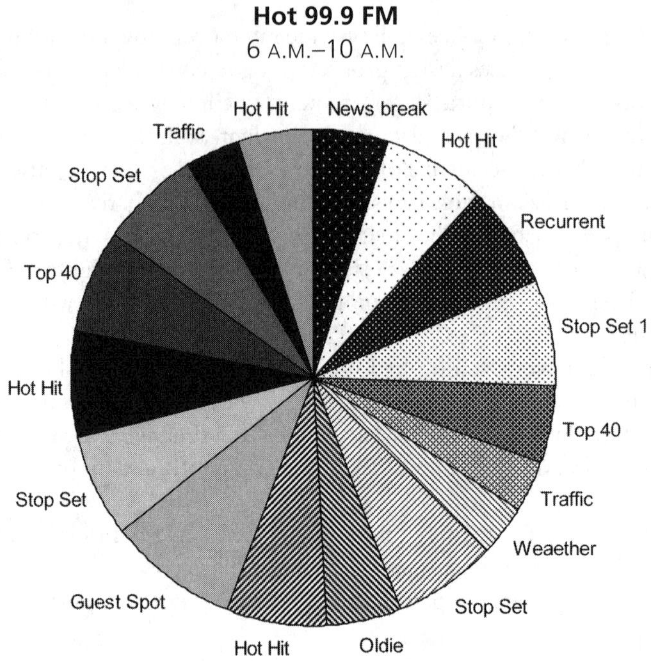

Hot 99.9 FM
6 A.M.–10 A.M.

Hot Hit
News break
Traffic
Hot Hit
Stop Set
Recurrent
Top 40
Stop Set 1
Hot Hit
Top 40
Stop Set
Traffic
Guest Spot
Weaether
Hot Hit
Stop Set
Oldie

The Sales Manager

The sales manager oversees all salespeople working for the radio station and is accountable to the GM for sales figures. This person sets weekly or monthly sales goals, trains new salespeople, assigns lists of potential clients to salespeople, and as an incentive gets a share of all sales that the staff make. The sales staff members usually work on commission, but some stations may also include a small guaranteed minimum salary as well. Using future commissions as a loan, this draw versus commission pays a salesperson who didn't have a good week or month. A salesperson who isn't bringing in money shouldn't expect to stay at a station for long. A good salesperson needs many traits. He or she needs to be well groomed, personable, and articulate, and should have a thick skin. Salespeople usually receive far fewer "Yes" responses than "No." It is not easy to face what can at times seem like a constant stream of rejection. But as Tom Hopkins teaches in the book *How to Master the Art of Selling,* every rejection brings you one step closer to a sale.[2] Sales is not for everyone, but a good salesperson usually makes more money than the on-air talent. At one point the highest-paid salesperson in Chicago worked for a news/talk radio station. At the time he had an entire staff, paid for out of his own earnings.

Some stations in major cities like New York complement the local salespeople with companies that court national advertisers for their clients. Most GMs were sales managers at one point.

Salespeople

The people who sell adverting time are either called sales reps, marketing consultants, or account executives, depending on the station. Regardless of the title, the salespeople generally have the same tasks and responsibilities:

1   place cold calls and follow leads to look for new potential advertisers;
2   develop presentations and/or ads on speculation;
3   close deals; and
4   service existing accounts.

A cold call is when a salesperson walks into a business or office and tries to sell a client who has never expressed an interest in advertising with the station in the past. Sometimes a good salesperson will try to develop leads before making such calls. He or she may listen to other stations to see if the client is buying airtime elsewhere, and look in the local newspaper and other publications and also watch local television to get an idea if the potential client realizes the value of advertising or if he or she seems averse to the idea. A business that is advertising on a rival station may be easier to sell than many people imagine. Obviously the advertiser is trying to reach a similar audience. If the potential client is advertising on television, in the newspaper, or on billboards the approach is generally that radio is an inexpensive yet effective way to reinforce the ads through repetition.

Sometimes, in order to secure a client a salesperson will write a script and ask a DJ or production person to cut a spot on speculation (spec). The hope here is that a person hearing his or her business in an advertisement will be more likely to buy. The salesperson takes a tape or CD to the client to hear the spot. Some stations will even arrange to air the spot while the salesperson is meeting with the client.

Some stations have people known as closers, but salespeople at most stations are their own closers. Many salespeople forget the most important part of selling: asking for the sale. They do a great job of "schmoozing" the client, but never get around to sealing the deal.

Servicing accounts can range from visiting the client to make sure he or she is happy, to seeing if they wish to renew or increase their contract. Sometimes it means ensuring that the spots have aired, bringing the client the affidavit, and, at small stations, even collecting from those clients who are in arrears. Sometimes a salesperson may have to return his or her commission, a charge back, if the client does not pay. Therefore it is in the salesperson's best interest to make sure the accounts are up to date.

There seems to always be a good-natured rivalry at most stations—the on-air staff claiming that if it weren't for them the sales staff would have nothing to sell, the sales staff claiming that without them there would be no money to pay the on-air staff.

News Directors

Some stations will have a news director, who may be a one-person newsroom or may oversee several reporters. News/talk stations are more likely to have larger news staffs. The news director has the responsibility of looking at all of the thousands of possible news stories for that day and then deciding which should be assigned, and who should cover them.

Music Directors

A music director develops the playlist for the station. At many smaller stations the program director and music director is often the same person. Record labels send thousands of free CDs to stations in hopes that their songs will receive airtime. Some music directors give a quick listen to those that seem promising and select a song based on their knowledge of music, the station's audience, and their own intuition. Of course, if the CD is from a band or artist who has a following already, there is more of a chance a song will make it on the air. Most labels will prerelease a single of the song they believe will be the hit song from the album.

Music directors determine what receives airtime in other ways, too. They may use a variety of sources, such as *Billboard* magazine, which not only lists what songs are getting play but which CDs are being purchased, call-out research, requests, or even other stations, by listening to what their competitors are playing. Music directors wish to stay ahead of the game when it comes to picking music. David Dye, host of the PRI nationally syndicated program *The World Café*, is one of the best at identifying new artists. He had artists like John Mayer and Los Lonely Boys on the air months before most stations had heard of them.

Traffic Director

Despite the title, the traffic director is not the person responsible for the daily traffic reports. Instead this person schedules all commercials. If a client purchases ten spots during tomorrow's morning drive, there had better be ten spots aired. Many stations adhere to a policy that complicates matters even more for a traffic director. They make an effort to ensure that competitors' ads are not aired during the same commercial break. So an ad for Joe's Used Car Heaven shouldn't follow one for Bob's Home for Auto Savings.

Radio stations are selling time, something that is intangible. Therefore stations sign affidavits to assure the clients, who cannot listen to a station twenty-four hours a day, that they received what they purchased. If a commercial does not air as planned, or only part of it is aired due to technical difficulties, the station airs what is known as a "make good" spot. Some stations will even give the broadcast equivalent of a baker's dozen without telling the advertiser. If a client, especially a new one, buys ten spots, the station may actually air twelve or fifteen, giving the client more of a chance of hearing one, and also raising the chance that the commercial has a positive effect on the client's sales. This also falls under the traffic department.

Radio stations also air public service announcements (PSAs). These free commercials promote various community events or nonprofit organizations. Stations air them for many reasons. They air them because, as we will see in chapter 8, broadcasters must prove that they have operated in the public interest when they apply to renew their station license. They air PSAs because it creates goodwill and a positive public image, therefore helping in identifying the station as one that cares about the community. Finally, a station may air a PSA because the management and staff believe in the cause or event. Most organizations have one or more charity event that they are involved with. Some may work closely with the United Way, some with the Boys and Girls Club of America, and others put together teams for the March of Dimes' Walk America.

Often the traffic department is in charge of the production of commercials as well. All commercials have a date when they are to begin (start date) and a date they are to end (kill date). If a sale ends on the fifteenth, a spot should not run on the sixteenth. By the same token, if a client's contract states that a spot should begin on a certain day someone must make sure it doesn't begin beforehand. This also falls under the traffic department.

Promotions Director/Marketing Director

The promotions director and/or marketing director are responsible for getting the name of the station and its image out to the public. Radio stations promote themselves in many different ways. They may purchase television and radio ads, actually giving money to what one may see as the competition. They may purchase space on billboards, sides of buses, or just about anywhere else a business would advertise. But they also promote more than their name.

Often a stations will cosponsor a concert or event. The station may give free advertising to sponsors to compensate them. So if a there is a community health fair, and the station is a cosponsor, they give free advertising to the event. But in exchange, they receive their name on all of the advertising in other media, have their names on signs and banners, and will usually either have DJs or other station personnel there at the fair to hand out paraphernalia or even do a live broadcast. In this way they are not only getting the station's name out, but showing that they care for the community.

In addition, almost every station does on-air promotions or contests. Stations design these to make listeners tune in at certain times or for certain lengths. At one point, before caller ID, a popular contest was to make a random phone call and if the person answered with a certain catch phrase about the station—"WMAQ is going to make me rich"—he or she would win a prize. Soon, this phrase could replace the simple "Hello" in that market among listeners and nonlisteners alike.

Another contest asks people put a bumper sticker on their cars. If the station's van known as the Party Wagon or Prize Mobile or some other name spots a car during a certain period announced on the air, they follow it and give the driver a prize.

Some larger stations employ a production manager or assign the duty to another staff member. The production manager oversees the recording of commercials at the station. While many commercial spots, especially for national brands, come prerecorded, local business owners commonly have the station write and produce their commercials.

Engineer

Every station needs an engineer, either full-time or part-time. Due to the complexity of the electronic equipment, especially the transmission equipment, a highly trained engineer can be invaluable. "Dead air" is any time a station does not have a sound going out. One reason DJs segue one song over another is so listeners scanning around the dial will always hear something playing. Many engineers, especially ones that serve more than one station, receive higher pay than the DJs. However, if you are afraid of heights, this is probably not the job for you, as most engineers also have to service the broadcast towers. A warning light on top of a tower that burns out must be immediately replaced. Some freelance engineers charge by the foot. The higher they climb, the more the station pays. It is not uncommon for a station to pay someone hundreds of dollars to change a lightbulb.

There are also many other positions that may be part of a station, such as office staff, receptionists, interns, accountants, and so on.

Interviews with Industry Professionals

Carol Hughes, Music Director/Middays
KFDI FM 101.3, Wichita, Kansas

How long have you been in radio?

Fourteen years.

How long have you been at this job?

Five years.

How many stations have you worked for and what did you do at them?

This is my third radio station, but all in the same market. Each station was owned by the same company. At my first job out of college, I actually started as receptionist and moved on to copywriting and continuity and eventually did promotions, on-air, production, and whatever else needed done. My second job was mornings as well as copywriting. And now, I'm the music director and middays.

What are your responsibilities?

I schedule all of the music as well as work with the program director on adding new music to the station. Since we're a reporting station I need to make sure all of the songs are played properly. I talk with all of the record reps regarding their new music during music calls once a week. I also work with the labels to coordinate any artist visits and interviews. And then . . . I am on air ten to three each day so there's not a lot of extra time.

What do you like the best about your job? Why?

I really wanted a job that wasn't the same each day . . . a job that I would enjoy going to every day, and I really found that in radio. I loved the variety, from music director, to on-air, to remotes, concerts, and all of the various events I am asked to attend. I particularly like helping nonprofit agencies get the word out about their services and events. Of course, I love the music and the listeners. I spend my entire air shift answering the phones and talking with people about so many different things . . . our station is very active in the community, so many people really feel like they're your friend.

In your opinion, what is the most pressing issue facing the radio industry today?

Certainly it can be said it's satellite radio, but I think the biggest issue is voice tracking—there's way too much of it![3] It's gotten so corporate that they're really worried about the bottom line and forgetting that what separates us from satellite is our ability to be locally involved in the community and actually talking to the listeners. Many jocks voice track shifts in entirely different cities and it's hard to be part of a community you really don't know anything about. I know it's cheaper to pay someone for one hour as opposed to an entire shift—but I think the benefit of having someone playing local phoners and getting immediate, pertinent information on the air outweighs the cost savings.[4]

Milt McConnell
VP/Market Manager, Citadel Broadcasting

How long have you been in radio?

Since 1970.

How many stations have you worked for and what did you do at them?

I oversee the operation of KKOB-AM, KKOB-FM, KBZU-FM, KDRF-FM, KRST-FM, KMGA-FM, KNML-AM, KTBL-AM, and the Joint Sales Agreement with KHFM-FM (Albuquerque, New Mexico).

I have been in Albuquerque for nineteen years. I used to run what are now the Clear Channel stations across the street prior to Citadel. I originally came here in 1986, taking over KRKE-AM and -FM. As duopoly happened, we acquired KLSK . . . and then when deregulation occurred with the telecom act of 1996, we then acquired KHTZ and KTEG. I ran WFBQ and WNDE in Indianapolis prior to coming here . . . also worked for WIFE News Radio, WIKS-FM (all Indy). My first station was WEDM-FM, Warren Central High School, Indy . . . then on to WFIU during my Indiana University broadcast journalism years. First commercial job was 1976 with Brewer Broadcasting with WTCJ-AM, Tell City, Indiana . . . and then on to their Richmond, Indiana, property WQLK . . . before going to Indy.

When did you decide you wanted to work in radio?

During high school when I had the opportunity to sign on a new educational radio station and handled news and play-by-play sports duties.

What are your responsibilities?

I am responsible for delivering cash flow targets by generating increasing revenues through about ten different income streams while holding down operating expenses. We are charged with producing double-digit broadcast cash flow year over year.

What do you like best about your job? Why?

I enjoy the challenge of developing new properties within our cluster and redirecting our operation to increase ratings (and therefore revenue). Also, it is all about leading the 150 people here to be the best they can be in a very challenging media environment.

Where do you see yourself going from here?

I am hoping to live long enough to convert some of the newspaper dollars to electronic media. In our market, for example, the newspaper does more revenue than *all* of TV and radio combined. We have many opportunities ahead of us with HD radio and having three additional channels for each of our licenses. Also, our ability to package our content for podcasting will be another key to our continued growth.

In your opinion, what is the most pressing issue facing the radio industry today? Why?

Our ability to answer the fabulous PR that both satellite radio and Internet radio are getting nationally. Wall Street is missing the fact that there are 290 million terrestrial listeners . . . and at this point 4 million satellite subscribers . . . and some 20 million Internet listeners. Local business depends on local content delivered by local radio stations. It remains a *great* business to be in due to the nice margins. We need a better concerted voice to get our positive points across to meet these seemingly endless articles about all of the "new" competition out there. Apple is doing very well with iPod . . . and XM and Sirius are getting way too much press considering they are losing $600 million a quarter. Our industry "leaders" are not answering the call.[5]

Sheri Lynch
Cohost, *The Bob and Sheri Show,* Nationally Syndicated from
WLNK-FM (Charlotte, North Carolina)

Tell me about your show.

Our show is more like a television magazine show than a traditional morning radio show. We're more like a cross between *Entertainment Tonight* and *Primetime Live* . . . with a lot of heavy phone interaction. It's comic; it's humorous, but it's really "lifestyle talk." Everything crosses into our territory: during election season we have political content, during Hollywood awards season we have heavy content revolving around Hollywood. . . . We're two people talking about the way we live, and that includes television, movies, food, sex, marriage, kids, the workplace, all of it.

That's an ever shifting and ever moving beast that we follow, but because of that we're a little harder to pigeonhole in the industry. Because we're not political, we're not sports, we're not hard news, we're not a morning zoo with a lot of silly characters and skits. We're a lifestyle show and our show follows the zeitgeist. After September 11 things got really serious for a while because that's where our audience was. And so we follow . . . we're like nomads hunting the buffalo and the audience is our buffalo and we follow that . . . we follow that as it makes its slow way across the plains. It makes the show a joy to do. It gives us so many places to evolve to. We're never stuck or static . . . but it does make us a little hard to quantify in the industry.

How did your program become a syndicated show?

Well, when the FCC deregulated the radio industry . . . a lot of people on the ground did not imagine that one of the side effects of consolidation would be that as companies gobbled up radio stations and were ever more focused on increasing their bottom-line profits . . . ultimately the way to do that—the only way to do that—became to cut expenses, because you can only increase revenue up to a certain point and then the market won't bear it anymore. But Wall Street was hungry for profits and profits and profits at an escalating level and the next place to get those profits was to cut expenses. And the first expense to go was talent on small and medium and even large radio stations all over the country.

So consolidation created a huge opportunity for syndicated programming, and we were a strictly local-only show at the time that all of this began to break, and we saw this as a potential opportunity. We saw there are a lot of operators in a lot of markets that are going to have to cut costs but they're still going to have to put something around those commercials. And, you know, something that students don't realize, they're really naïve, they think they're getting into radio to play their favorite songs and you're getting into radio to play commercials. So, we packaged our program and took it out on the road and "What the heck, let's see, can we sell this?" It turned out that, yeah, there was a pretty big market for syndicated programming.

Unfortunately, in the radio industry the bulk of the programming that they put on the air is really targeted to males. We have a show that is about 60 percent female in our audience breakout. We have a show that targets women. So we succeeded but it was a much slower uphill climb than we anticipated it would be. Even though the most coveted demographic in radio for advertising purposes are females twenty-five to fifty-four, the programmers in radio produce programming aimed at males eighteen to thirty-four. So there was a real disconnect there for us but we persevered and we slogged through and we gave to radio station owners and operators a more cost-effective way of getting quality programming on the air, much cheaper. So that was the first impetus to syndication, and the second was, as radio performers it's really a nomadic business and your career grows market to market. You have to move around a lot, you have to be willing to pull up stakes, and we had built something here, we had families, and we didn't want to be nomads. So we had to make a business decision: Is there a way to stay here and bring those markets to us? Syndication was the answer to that. So ego wasn't really on the short list of why we did this. It was really a business decision and a gamble; frankly, we're just lucky that it paid off.

So much of the programming on the dial around the United States that is allegedly pointed toward women is delivered by men. The thing that makes our show different and significant is that here we have a radio show targeted toward women and it's delivered by a woman. And the sensibility is just the complete opposite. In talk radio when you are a talk radio personality it is very different from being a television actor or a television anchor. What you need in order to be a successful radio personality . . . is to have the ability to drink in the world, filter it, and present it back to your audience in a way that is simultaneously uniquely you and universally them. And here is a genius analogy—and my partner Bob came up with this. There was a period of time on daytime television when Phil Donahue was the preeminent performer talking to women; no one could touch him. He was king of the world; he had it all. Phil Donahue's talk career ended the day Oprah Winfrey's began. Because as great as Phil was, when it came time to talk the talk to women, to meet them where they live, and be empathetic, he did not have the one thing that Oprah did . . . the right set of chromosomes.

On radio you are in so many ways a surrogate for that listener. I've seen a lot of people come into radio from television and from stand-up comedy and from film and these backgrounds and they can't cut it as a radio personality because I believe you either have the ability to turn yourself inside out to the microphone or you don't. Some do and some don't. And you know the great ones when I mention their names; whether you like him or hate him, Rush Limbaugh is a great radio personality.

He is a surrogate for so many listeners. When Rush Limbaugh came on the scene there was a nascent or conservative male radio listener that felt nobody was speaking for him. And Rush became his voice. You may hate the guy but he is a great radio personality.

It's why I believe the delivery system may change; antennas may go to satellites to iPods to chips they plant right in our heads, but there will always be a human compelling need for radio because it comes back to sitting around the campfire and swapping stories. It's potent, it's the oral tradition, and I think it's hardwired into us as a species. That need to talk and share stories and relate. And on radio you find our "Hey, I'm not the only one here in the tribe who thinks this way."

How much preparation do you do for each show?

Every hour on the air is probably three to four hours of prep. But again it goes back to what we do is lifestyle radio. In order to meet the people who listen to us where they live, we have to live there too. We have to go to the soccer games, we have to be in the community, at our kids' schools, we have to have fights with our spouses and go to the movies and we have to fantasize and be disappointed and struggle financially. Every morning you have a four-hour shared experience where we're all sitting around the cubicle BS'ing about what's going on.

The show is live six to ten, then we put in about an hour after that doing production, commercials, promotional announcements, and voicing stuff for all of our affiliate stations. The joke about being syndicated is you have as many bosses as you have affiliates and nobody wants 60 to 280 bosses.

Then you break for lunch, and I'm also a writer so I try to log two to three hours in the afternoon where I'm writing my own stuff, answering e-mail for the show, researching stuff, booking guests, hunting my producers down and saying, "This is on the *New York Times* bestsellers list, let's see if we can get this person. . .The Trout Festival is happening right now in Nebraska; let's go out there and see if we can talk to somebody there . . . I think it would be a hoot." And so you know you do put in probably a ten-plus-hour day, it's just not conventional hours or office settings. And at night you've got a DVR or a VCR, and you're scanning through and recording what is relevant, and where it's time sensitive you get up early the next morning . . . and you watch the last hour of the Oscars, and you scan through the big interview on *Primetime Live* or the *MTV* music awards or the hot new show that comes on after you have to be in bed because you have to have a knowledge about some things and at least familiarity on a whole lot of stuff.

If you were honest with yourself at the end of your life you'd say to yourself, "Why was I an expert on Paris Hilton?" It's the job, right? You spend time with your kids and your family and try to get in bed by nine. So it's a job. When people say to me, "What does it take to be in radio?"—well, if you're not disciplined, keep going. I don't care if you have an amazing voice and you know the lyrics to every song, if you are not disciplined, don't bother. There is no room left in our industry because of consolidation.

What do you see as the main issue facing radio today?

Right now radio is really confused by the FCC. Radio is terrified of the FCC because legislation has been passed that if a guest comes on or a caller comes on the show and uses an obscenity and I don't hit the dump . . . (we're on a seven-second delay, like any talk radio show is) . . . if I let an obscenity get on the air, I'm fined, Bob is fined, our boss is fined, and then every single one of our affiliates is fined and one single obscenity could bankrupt me and bankrupt my kids. It's tough.

I think right now the industry is reeling from what to do with the FCC. It doesn't help that we're reeling from the FCC at a time when we're looking at satellite coming in. They'll be encroaching on the broadcast market share . . . it's *Jetsons* time. . . . The dinosaurs of radio didn't anticipate iPods and podcasting and the Internet. I think everyone kind of knew that one day that there would be something in the sky that would make broadcasting redundant, but the acceleration on technology now is so fast that you don't even have time to figure out what it is before it's up and running.

We launched beta testing on podcasting our show a couple of days ago. The marketplace is different and consumers weaned on this technology are different too . . . shorter attention spans and a very high expectation of having hundreds of options at their fingertips. So radio has to figure out how do we fit into that, how do we respond to that, and how do we remain competitive, and what can we say without being destroyed by the FCC? Satellite has free rein and not only are they not going to regulate satellite . . . content, it really puts broadcasters at a disadvantage because we are on a playing field that is shifting beneath our feet minute by minute and no one will tell us the rules.

See, you can't dig your heels in as a broadcaster and say, "We're doing it the old way," because the consumer will leave you behind. You get no mad "props" for doing it the old way, not in this world . . . you don't have the brand loyalty that you even had thirty years ago. . . . Radio is not immune to that, but the answer here is not to throw up your hands and hide, and to say, "Oh my God, the sky is falling!" The answer is to look at the marketplace and figure out what it is that you do best.

And I submit to you that what radio does best is not playing music. From a song-to-song standpoint, we can't compete with satellite, we can't compete with the Internet, and we can't compete with iPod because all of those technologies give you better quality with fewer interruptions and more choice in music than terrestrial broadcasters can deliver right now. . . . I believe—and I'm biased because I'm in talk radio—I believe that person-to-person spoken talk radio is what we do best and you can't get that . . . you can't download that off of iTunes. When broadcasters figure out what they are best at delivering, that's what they'll deliver and that's where they will survive. But if you want to be a jukebox and go head to head with satellite or iPod, good luck. That's not one you're going to win, and yet a lot of folks in radio don't believe that and they're going to fight the good fight and we're going to find their fossilized dried-out bones by the watering hole.[6]

Radio Station Economics

Just as anyone or any business has money coming in and monthly expenses, the same is true for radio stations.

Income

The media differ from other businesses in that they can range from being totally supported by advertising to being totally supported by the end user. Imagine visiting your local grocery store and getting bags of groceries for free. In exchange you would see ads for cars, televisions, or other products printed on the bags and boxes.

This is essentially how the media works. On one extreme of the spectrum are the media of books and CDs. The consumer pays the full price for these media (although publishers did experiment with inserting advertising

Figure 6.2 2004 Advertising Money

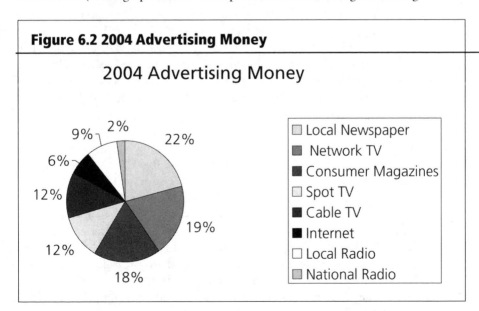

2004 Advertising Money

- Local Newspaper — 22%
- Network TV — 19%
- Consumer Magazines — 18%
- Spot TV — 12%
- Cable TV — 12%
- Internet — 6%
- Local Radio — 9%
- National Radio — 2%

in paperback books during the late 1970s).

A mix of advertisers and customers supports some of the other media. The sale of tickets supports part of movie costs, but as anyone who has been to a movie in the last ten years can attest, there are also commercials. In addition to the trailers for upcoming films, there are a series of commercials for soft drinks, video games, and the like. Magazines move even closer to being 50 percent advertising-supported and 50 percent customer-supported. Newspapers are supported mainly by advertising, as are broadcast television (with the exception of satellite or cable) and radio.

So the higher the ratings and the more desirable the audience, the more money the station has coming in as income. As mentioned earlier, radio did not begin as a commercial venture. It wasn't until 1922, when WEAF (New York), owned by AT&T, sold a fifteen-minute commercial to the Queensboro Corporation, that radio began to make money. Prior to this the idea was that by owning and financing a radio station manufacturers or stores could encourage the sales of radio receivers. AT&T didn't call this advertising but instead used the term *toll broadcasting.* The belief by AT&T that it had the sole ownership of this means of gaining income led to the breakup of its relationship with RCA.

Over the next several years, many things happened that made advertisers begin to think more seriously about radio as an advertising medium. Following its formation, the FRC was able to reduce interference on the spectrum. Advertisers received a better idea of what they were getting for their money with early audience research. The research also gave the networks assistance in their development.

Many countries, like England, decided to have their radio broadcasting systems set up as noncommercial. Taxes on radio receivers supported the medium in these countries. But Americans were used to newspapers and magazines, supported by advertising sales, and quickly accepted the use of sponsorships in radio. Of course, the advertising during that time did not resemble the advertising of today. Usually one company sponsored a show. The name of the company often became part of the show's title, as in the *Texaco Star Theater* or *The General Mills Adventure Theater.* Not only did companies sponsor programs, but some stations accepted program-length commercials, an early precursor to the infomercial. Ad agencies began the practice of selling time for the networks as station representatives during the late 1920s and early '30s. Some even began to produce programming for the sponsors. The main drawback to this system was that it gave the sponsor total control over the programming. Sponsors had script approval, final say in the hiring and firing of talent and crew, and even worked mention of the products into the shows.

This type of advertising continued until NBC executive Pat Weaver (father of actress Sigourney Weaver) developed what he called the magazine format for television. He noticed that magazines had multiple advertisers in every issue. This gave the magazines more freedom, as they didn't have to fear their one sponsor pulling out.

Remarkably, World War I actually helped radio advertising. Many companies had money that would be taxed at 90 percent if it wasn't spent. Instead of losing it to the government, they purchased advertising time with what they called "ten-cent dollars."[8] Even companies that had turned their efforts to the war effort continued to purchase ad time to keep their names before the American people.

By the 1970s, as the FM market began to slowly grow, so did the advertising support. While the amount spent on advertising in 2004 was over $20 billion, some industry leaders fear that advertising revenue may decline in the coming years due to increased competition from the Internet, satellite radio, CDs, and MP3s.

An AP newswire article noted that advertising revenue, while growing, is not growing at the levels enjoyed during the heyday of the 1990s. Meanwhile, the loss in listeners has turned off investors. In 2004 earnings rose 2 percent and in 2003 only 1 percent, although Clear Channel predicts an increase of over 3 percent for 2005. Even so, when looking at the entire amount of money spent on advertising, radio accounts for very little.

Expenses

Radio is one of the cheapest media to own and operate, yet it has many expenses. First there are the salaries. The size of the station and the size of the market will determine the amount of money the station pays in salaries each month. While it is not unheard of for star on-air talent in the major markets to draw six- or seven-figure salaries, the average on-air host is making closer to ten dollars per hour.[9] The average salesperson, however, earns quite a bit more. A survey conducted by Warner and Spencer found:

> In markets 1–99, the middle radio salesperson earns 143% more than a typical news reporter in similar size markets ($39,000 vs. $16,000) and 85% more in markets 100+($24,000 vs. $13,000). There is even a higher differential between radio sales managers and radio news directors in similar size markets. Sales managers in markets 1–99 earn 219% more than news directors ($83,000 vs. $26,000) and 200% more in markets 100+ ($45,000 vs. $15,000).[10]

Some larger stations also offer benefits such as insurance to their employees, although a trend in the radio industry as in all others is to use part-time employees wherever they can. These benefits average 29 percent of the employees' total compensation package.[11] Another way of looking at this is if a person's salary is $20,000 per year, the employer is paying about an additional $8,000 toward health benefits, retirement savings, and so on.

Then there are equipment expenses. As mentioned earlier, station engineers are important. One of their jobs is often to keep old equipment running as long as possible. A good microphone can cost from $200 to over $1,000, while transmitters can cost from $2,000 to $3,000 for a low-power exciter to over $250,000 for a full-power one. It is easy to see that the main investment for a radio station is its equipment.

Station promotion is another expense that a station must factor into its budget. The cost of producing giveaway items like hats, T-shirts, and bumper stickers is included here, but there are also big promotions that give away trips or automobiles. A station often does a "trade-out" in this case. Every time the contest is mentioned the station includes a "tag," like, "And we want to thank our friends at Triple A Travel Agent and Dry Cleaners for sponsoring our contest."

Stations do trade-outs not only for promotional items, but for other items as well. A trade-out with a local chain of gas stations may supply salespeople with gas for their cars, or a trade-out with a car dealership may actually supply the leases on those cars.

Even though the record labels send free CDs to the stations in hopes of getting airplay, the stations must pay to air them. The licensing of music became headlines during the Napster file-sharing controversy, and then again when college radio stations started to air over the Internet.

Media Licensing

American Society of Authors, Composers and Publishers (ASCAP)

ASCAP began in 1913 as a way to ensure that songwriters received payment for the use of their music. Before 1909, there was little a songwriter could do if someone borrowed his or her music. But in 1909 the United States instituted a copyright law, discussed in chapter 9. ASCAP's concern was that songwriters receive compensation when their sheet music was sold. Not long after being established, recorded music was included as well. Composers received one cent per copy.

Today songwriters receive 5.7 cents per song. If one considers a CD that sells 1 million copies, this means that the person who wrote one of the songs receives $57,000. But with broadcasting came a new complication. At first the record industry saw records receiving airtime as free advertising. But songwriters wished to receive compensation for stations' playing their songs. Radio stations used songs to generate revenue, so why shouldn't the writers?

Broadcast Management Incorporated (BMI)

BMI started in 1940 as competition to ASCAP, partly because broadcasters didn't like the monopoly that ASCAP had, but also because ASCAP didn't license composers of country music or rhythm and blues. These two populations helped BMI grow so that today it represents over 300,000 artists. BMI licensed over half of the music played on radio in 1990.[12] ASCAP represents over 200,000 composers in the United States and thousands more worldwide.[13]

Music falls under intellectual property laws. This means that the person who writes a song, or who owns the copyright to that song, must be paid if someone uses it to make money. That applies whether it is in a film or a television program, performed on stage, or played on a radio station (broadcast or online). Today's composers usually register their work with one of the two organizations.

Society of European Stage Authors and Composers (SESAC)

A third organization, SESAC, was started in 1930 mainly to license European writers and also gospel music. For many years SESAC was primarily known for licensing gospel, but today the organization represents a diverse range of artists, such as the composers of songs performed by Christina Aguilera, Garth Brooks, Mariah Carey, Kenny Chesney, Eric Clapton, Destiny's Child, Neil Diamond, Bob Dylan, Alan Jackson, Jagged Edge, Ludacris, Luciano Pavarotti, LeAnn Rimes, U2, UB40, Usher, and Cassandra Wilson.[14]

A quick glance at a CD will usually tell with which of the licensing organizations the song is registered.

Stations may pay a blanket license fee to each organization that allows them to play any of the songs that are registered with it. For instance, ASCAP has two different license agreements; one for large stations and one for smaller ones. If a station has over $150,000 gross revenue, the fee is 1.615 percent of that revenue. The organization offers a sliding scale that offers a flat fee for stations making less than this amount.

Gross Income	Fee
$125,001–$150,000	$1,800
$100,001–$125,000	$1,450
$75,001–$100,000	$1,150
$50,001–$ 75,000	$800
<$50,000	$450[15]

If a station—such as a news, talk, or sports station—does not use much copyrighted music they may apply for a per-program license that offers an even lower rate.

Stations must fill out program logs listing what music has been played. In addition, the organizations randomly record programming off the air. BMI states that their surveys include over 450,000 hours of airtime. Using these numbers, they generate an estimate of how many times a song has been played and issues the composer and publisher of the song a royalty check.

Presently the royalty rate that a composer receives from BMI is six cents for larger stations and a minimum of three cents for smaller ones.[16] ASCAP, on the other hand, has a very complicated method of determining the amount of money a composer receives for airplay of a song that includes when it is played, how popular the song is, how it is used, and so on.[17]

A radio station can play music of ASCAP members by purchasing a license. Music licensed by over sixty foreign licensing bodies that are affiliated with ASCAP is also included. Additionally, the station can use the music in commercials or as part of a jingle. A license does not allow a station to change the words of a song for a jingle or commercial.

Until the Fairness in Music Licensing Act of 1998 these rules applied to most restaurants, bars, clubs, and stores that played music either from a radio, television, CD player, or other source. However, the new law made wide sweeping revisions stating that bars and restaurants smaller than 3,750 square feet and all nonfood or beverage businesses of less than 2,000 square feet are exempt. Those that are larger are still exempt as long as they use no more than six speakers with no more than four in one room and as long as there are no more than four video/television monitors fifty-five inches or less, with no more than one in each room.[18]

Future of the Job Market

Each year the U.S. Department of Labor issues the *Career Guide to Industries* and the *Occupational Outlook Handbook*. These reports examine what jobs are available, the skills needed, average salaries, and the projection for future job growth. With deregulation, the trend is for fewer large corporations owning more of the stations. This means that there are fewer local mom-and-pop radio stations left.

The latest indexes indicate that the radio market will probably continue to feel the effect of this consolidation, with large companies owning more than one station in a market. Thus, smaller staffs are needed. One large sales team can sell airtime on three stations as opposed to three separate teams. These teams may even offer package deals for airing on all the stations under the group umbrella. One newsroom can do the reporting for all three stations. A group owner might not see the need for a music director or program director at each station. One person may oversee a handful of stations across the country all playing the same music. Stations from coast to coast may replicate a successful format and sound.

The outlook is not very bright for DJs, either. According to the *Occupational Outlook*,

> Competition for jobs as announcers will be keen because the broadcasting field attracts many more jobseekers than there are jobs. . . . Applicants who have completed internships or have related work experience usually receive preference for available positions. . . . Announcers who are knowledgeable in

business, consumer, and health news may have an advantage over others. . . . Employment of announcers is expected to decline through 2012.[19]

Getting an accurate estimate of industry salaries is difficult at best. Depending upon the source consulted, the average salary for on-air talent can range from $9.91 per hour for a DJ to $14 per hour for a news anchor.[20]

Of course, station management and salespeople tend to be the highest-paid members of a radio station. For station managers in the top fifty markets, the median salary is just under $60,000, and for those in the bottom fifty the salary tends to be around $40,000.[21] The same is true for engineers. The average salary for engineers in larger markets is $65,333, while engineers in smaller markets can expect around $44,000 per year.[22] According to the latest figures published by the National Association of Broadcasters (NAB), a morning drive DJ can average $120,136 while a station manager's salary averages $252,191. It should be noted that the data from this study only included the 200 largest markets and may be skewed.

The question that remains in the forefront is whether owners who are not local understand the issues that are important to the local audience. How invested are they in the community? Will they cover news in an objective manner or do they have an agenda that reaches outside of the local town? Studies indicate that media owned by larger corporations all tend to have the same biases, political and otherwise. As mentioned earlier, the trend of multiple station ownership also means that fewer jobs will be available for those seeking work in the industry.

Yet, the consolidation trend means that salespeople and station reps have the ability to make more money than ever. In general, group owners are able to offer more resources than a single station owner can—health benefits, access to a network of stations, syndication of programming, and the ability to draw on research and other resources available to a large corporation to name a few.

The radio industry is in a time of flux. New ownership rules, competition from new sources, and federal regulation make this one of history's most challenging times to be a radio broadcaster.

 ## Questions for Further Thought

1   With the increase of chain owners, satellite radio, and programming choices, what can radio station owners do to keep revenue high?

2   How will new media affect the job outlook?

3   Is there an untapped segment of the market that broadcasters should be looking at?

4   In your opinion, should radio stations be required to pay fees to licensing organizations? How is this related to downloading music illegally from the Internet?

Shop Talk

American Society of Authors, Composers, and Publishers (ASCAP): Music licensing organization that collects and distributes royalties to those who write and/or publish music.

Back masking: A popular myth that bands insert messages in a song by recording them backwards and adding them as a track. This is similar to subliminal advertising. While some bands have done this, there is no proof that it is perceived at the subconscious level.

Blanket license: A fee to purchase the rights to use the music of one of the licensing organizations as opposed to paying a percentage of the station's revenue.

Broadcast Management Incorporated (BMI): Music licensing organization that collects and distributes royalties to those who write and/or publish music.

Dead air: Anytime there is nothing to hear on a radio station, either due to technical problems or DJ error.

Hot clock: A visual representation of an hour's programming. The hot clock may be different for each daypart or even hours within a daypart.

Segue: Seamless transition between two components, usually music or music and a commercial.

Society of European Stage Authors and Composers (SESAC): Music licensing organization that collects and distributes royalties to those who write and/or publish music.

7

Analog to Digital and Back

This chapter will take a closer look at the technology that has affected the radio industry in both positive and negative ways. It also examines new technology as well as future technology.

The equipment needed to broadcast during the early days of radio was minimal, and included a microphone, transmitter, audio board, and antenna. Standing before a microphone, the actors, announcers, or band had their programs sent to the transmitter. At the transmitter site, the signal was encoded into electronic waves, amplified, and broadcast using the antenna. In fact, the radio studio over the last fifty years has changed very little. The basic setup of a microphone, headphones, board, turntables, and sound-processing equipment still exists in one form or another.

The Typical Radio Station

The Studio

A good place to start is the basic setup of a studio. Most studios have a countertop or table that has a microphone, sound mixing board, speakers, headphones, and a source of music. Of course, there is also a chair, although while most DJs prefer to sit down while doing a show, some prefer to stand because sitting can compress the diaphragm, not allowing the voice its full potential. There is also a theory among some that a sitting DJ sounds like he or she is sitting and, therefore, talks with less energy.

Many studios or booths have a large window facing into a hallway or lobby. This makes the booth seem larger than it is and less like a closet, but it also allows potential advertisers and others to see the DJs while they broadcast. Many of the studios configured this way have the DJ facing the window. But sound reacts to walls much in the same way that a ball acts on a pool table. If a ball is shot directly at a cushion of the table, it will bounce right back, but if it is shot at an angle, it will bounce off at an angle. One will notice that there are usually a lot of odd angles in a studio. Similarly, if a person speaks directly into a wall, the sound will bounce back. Windows with a downward tilt keep the DJ's voice from echoing back into the microphone. Booths will also usually have some type of sound-deadening material on the walls. This baffling can come in many forms but often is a foam with angles cut into it resembling an egg carton. The sound is deadened by the material, while the angles reflect what is left in many different directions.

Headphones

Headphones, or "cans," are a necessity for the radio announcer. When the microphone is turned on, or "hot," the speakers in the studio are automatically turned off. Shutting off the speakers eliminates feedback. Signals that are amplified and played through speakers, then picked up by a microphone, cause feedback. The microphones pick up the signals after they have gone through the process again. This all happens within milliseconds, resulting in a high squealing noise. By wearing headphones, the DJ is able to hear the music and his or her voice as they sound going out over the air. The microphone operates much in the same way that the human ear does, picking up sound waves directed toward it. Try placing your hand in front of your mouth and saying, "Peter Piper picked a peck of pickled peppers." You exhale wind through you larynx and out of your mouth, creating sound waves. These waves are much like the waves Maxwell, Hertz, Marconi, and others envisioned in the electric spectrum. Like dropping a pebble into a pool of water, waves will ripple outward. Your sound waves move to the microphone, which then interprets them into electronic impulses.

Headphones differ greatly in style, cost, and frequency response. While some more expensive headphones offer a frequency response of up to 30,000 or even 40,000 Hz, most humans can only hear in the range of 20 to 20,000 Hz at best.[1] In fact, the older one gets, the less one can hear in the upper and lower ranges. Prolonged exposure to loud noises, music, and so on damages the hearing so that few people can actually hear the full 20 to 20,000 Hz range after their teen years. The organization Hearing Education and Awareness for Rockers (HEAR) was founded with the help of the Who's Pete Townsend,[2] who lost most of his hearing while playing with what the *Guinness Book of World Records* once named the "loudest band" and after having played the "loudest concert."[3]

Some prefer headphones designed to be open-aired that allows exterior sound in, while some prefer to have headphones that cancel out all other noise. Many DJs will invest in their own headphones to avoid wearing those that others have used.

Monitors

The speakers or monitors usually hang near the ceiling, but in such a way that they are facing down at the DJ, enabling him or her to hear them better. The speakers act like the microphone, but in reverse. They receive the electrical signals and translate them back into sounds. In fact, one may hear a faint signal by plugging a microphone into certain headphone jacks.

One problem with relying solely on the studio monitors is that they are usually high-quality, expensive speakers and the DJ is hearing the programming before it is transmitted. For this reason most stations also have an on-air monitor, or radio set up to hear what the signal sounds like to the audience member listening in the car or at home.

CD Players, Turntables, and Computers

Most radio stations have music as their primary format. Therefore it is important that some type of playback system be available. Some stations rely on CDs, some on vinyl records, and others on computer-encoded MP3 files. Radio stations will have CD players and turntables that are essentially the same as those consumers may purchase, but due to the increased usage they receive they must be more durable (and are more costly).

The Audio Board

The audio board or mixer is another essential piece of equipment. Imagine you are an artist painting a great masterpiece. You look down at your palette and see eight colors. As the artist you must chose whether you are going to put one color or a mixture of colors on your canvas with your next brush stroke. In many ways, this is what the audio board or mixer does. At any given time, a DJ or engineer has many possible sources of audio. There is the microphone or in some cases multiple microphones, music sources, telephones, and so on. The board allows a person to select which "color" to choose. Sometimes red is the best color, just as sometimes music is the best sound. But sometimes an artist will slowly move from red to pink on the canvas. In the same way, a DJ can segue between two songs, letting one song fade out as the next song fades in. This keeps the station from experiencing dead air. Maybe an artist wants to layer one color atop another. A DJ may add his or her voice over the top of the first few seconds or last few seconds of a song, using a technique called a voiceover. Sometimes an artist wants bold or soft colors. The DJ controls the modulation of the sound by increasing or decreasing it with the board while reading the volume unit (VU) meter. If it is undermodulated the song sounds muffled or "in the mud." Overmodulated music sounds distorted. Each board has a series of controls called busses. Each buss controls a particular source or number of sources. For example, buss number one may control the microphone, buss number two the telephone, buss three a music source such as a CD player, and so on. Some boards offer an option of assigning more than one input to each buss. In this case, buss one may control a CD player and a tape player. A simple A/B switch allows the DJ to determine which of the inputs is being controlled. It is not advisable, however, to assign two sources to the same buss if they may be needed at the same time—say, a microphone and a CD player: each of the sources should be one that does not interfere with the other.

One of the main jobs of the DJ is to "ride the gain" or adjust the levels of modulation. Older boards had knobs called pots, short for potentiometers. Today's board will more than likely have sliders, much like a dimmer switch on home lighting. The DJ slides the control up or back to control the modulation levels. In addition to adjusting modulation, most busses also offer the option of shaping the sound by adjusting various elements such as the bass, midrange, and so forth, much like the stereo in your car or home. A basic board may offer three or four options, while more expensive boards may offer up to ten different knobs. Most boards are almost identical, with the biggest differences being in the number of levels of adjustments and the number of busses. Television stations and recording studios often have the same basic types of sound equipment, and many people who have worked in radio find the transition from one industry to the other quite easy.

Another feature that boards usually have (depending on their age) is an automatic start button. A DJ or engineer may start a cued CD by pushing a button on the board instead of reaching for the player. This allows a DJ to continue talking, monitoring the VU meters, and doing an intro or voiceover while the song begins. Many stations prefer DJs to perform segues. These may take the form of relating one song to another by announcing— or more often slowly fading out—the first song while bringing in the second. DJs usually separate two songs differing greatly in tempo or feel by a jingle, bumper, or stop set.

The board will also have a cue function. The cue function allows the DJ to preview a piece before it airs while the regular show is being broadcast. This is useful for unfamiliar pieces or if there are two songs that run together on the CD without a denoted break. When the DJ is "spinning vinyl," he or she needs to listen to the record in cue. This allows him or her to back up the song just enough between tracks to allow it to get up to speed before putting it on air.

Air-Check Recorder

Stations will also usually have a tape recorder or computer set up that will begin recording whenever the DJ turns on the microphone. This allows the DJ to listen to an air check of his or her show. There is no need to record the entire program; they, their boss, and potential bosses want to hear them, not the music. When one applies for an on-air job, an air-check tape or some type of audition reel is required. "Reel" is a bit of a misnomer, since most are CDs at this point. A good DJ will take his or her air checks and assemble a montage of the best, including commercial voiceovers as well as program elements.

Sound Processors

In addition to the simple sound-shaping devices on the board, stations usually have some additional sound processors. These can arrange from limiters that automatically push a signal downward if it is overmodulated, to signal boosters that push a low signal higher, to compressors that keep sounds in a specified range, to devices that allow for all types of effects such as echo, reverberation, and so on. At one point WLS-AM (Chicago) added a hint of echo to all of their broadcasts so that a listener scanning the dial would immediately be able to identify their sound.

Some people swear by compressors and limiters, while others say that they make the music sound clipped. Some stations preset a sound and then lock the controls to keep DJs from altering them. DJs, especially male DJs, tend to like to boost the bass on their microphones to get a deeper sound.

The average person hearing his or her recorded voice will respond with "I don't sound like that!" or something similar. This is because we hear our voices from inside of our bodies as well as outside with our ears. Our bones, especially the collarbone and skull, act as resonators, making our voices sound richer and deeper in tone than in actuality. This becomes quite apparent when using headphones. You can try a trick that old radio and television announcers used to use. They would cup a hand behind their ear, making a larger cup shape, or a cheap headphone!

Microphones

A microphone is classified either by its element, pickup pattern, or the nature of its use.

Element. The earliest microphones used by radio stations were adapted from the old candlestick telephones. These microphones used carbon granules and a diaphragm that would vibrate when sound hit it. A problem with the design was that the carbon and diaphragm would also hit each other. Microphone revisions kept this from happening. The microphones were circular, held in place by springs attached to an outer circle. Broadcasters throughout the 1920s used these microphones. Today's shock-mounted microphones still employ a version of this method. In the modern version, springs absorb the shock if a microphone is bumped, which keeps it from making noise over the air.[4]

Changes to the design and technology of microphones became more important as the quality of the broadcast signal and recording equipment improved. During the 1920s a new generation of microphones was invented for use in motion pictures with sound. These condenser microphones used a vacuum tube that needed to be located close to the element (diaphragm) that in turn amplified the sound. Today's condenser microphones use a capacitor instead of a tube, and may run off a battery or phantom power, coming from the board or another source.

Another major innovation came with the invention of the ribbon microphone. The most famous of the ribbon-style microphone was the 44A, developed by RCA. You may have seen such a microphone in old movies or pictures. The distinctive diamond shape makes the microphone easily recognizable. Singers of the era often used the RCA 44A. Inside the ribbon microphone is a thin piece of metal film or ribbon. The ribbon is stretched between two pieces of metal and suspended in a magnetic field. The sound waves vibrating off the ribbon created differences in the electrical current. While these microphones are extremely sensitive and are still valued today, they are very heavy (eight pounds) and extremely fragile. A loud noise or even a puff of breath could break the ribbon. Over the years, microphones have gone through many refinements. Newer ribbon microphones exist that are not as bulky and a little more durable.

Another microphone type is the dynamic microphone. It has a coil of wire like the condenser microphone but does not need a separate power supply. It has a diaphragm that vibrates as noise hits it. The coil moves in response to the diaphragm's vibrations, creating electrical signals. The dynamic microphone is the most commonly used microphone in radio stations.

Pickup patterns. The early microphones had an omnidirectional pattern, meaning that sounds from anywhere in the vicinity were picked up. The ribbon microphone eliminated the pickup from the sides, resulting in a pattern that approximated a figure eight, with the microphone at the center of the two loops. The ribbon microphone picked up sounds from the front and back of the microphone. This was a great advantage, especially for crooners like Bing Crosby and Frank Sinatra and for radio show announcers. These people would usually work close to the microphone so the sensitivity, along with the deadening of extraneous noise, worked well.

Late in the 1930s engineers at RCA developed another type of microphone. Wishing to eliminate the "figure eight" pickup pattern and focus the microphone in one direction, the RCA 77A ribbon microphone was introduced. It was unidirectional with a pattern that resembled an upside-down heart shape, hence its nickname, the cardioid mic. Many other manufacturers replicated and produced this new design, and the subsequent smaller 77B. The Electro-Voice 635A was a staple in the broadcast industry right into the 1980s and '90s. One salesperson would take the microphone during demonstrations, hammer nails into a board with it, and then use it to talk. This represented a far cry from the sensitive ribbon microphone. In addition to being sturdy, this microphone resists wind and loud noises. Today the newer RE 20 has replaced the 635A.

But engineers and companies kept refining the unidirectional microphones. Eventually the industry was introduced to the supercardioid with a much more directional pickup pattern and the hypercardioid with an even more directional pattern, and there is even an ultracardioid

Switchable microphones became popular during the 1940s and '50s. These microphones were able to be switched between different pickup patterns. An engineer no longer needed a variety of microphones, but could rely on one and, if necessary, switch the pattern to suit the room or occasion.

An additional refinement came with the invention of the windscreen. This device, originally designed for outdoor recording, made its way into the radio studio. It keeps the popping of *P* sounds and other plosives to a minimum. Some microphones have internal windscreens, while some use external.

A general rule of thumb for those beginning in the industry is to work with the microphone approximately the distance between the thumb and pinkie finger extended, about four inches from the mouth. The microphone should point slightly to the side of the mouth. Speaking directly into a microphone will increase the likelihood of popping *P*s and hissing *S*s. *Never* test a microphone by blowing into it, as spit can build up inside the microphone and affect its performance and lifespan. Instead, gently tap it, snap your fingers, or talk into the microphone to test it.

Further refinements have continued to make microphones sensitive yet durable. A typical on-air microphone may cost as much as $1,000, while a microphone that reporters take out in the field, where durability is more important than sound quality, may be as cheap as $100. While these microphones offer great sound quality and are fairly inexpensive, some stations or DJs may invest in microphones that are usually found only in recording studios and run into the thousands of dollars.

Nature of use. A shotgun microphone is a version of a very directional pickup pattern. These types of microphones are very thin and resemble the barrel of a shotgun. They can be pointed at a source somewhat away from the microphone without picking up sounds from the left or right of the pattern. Reporters usually have a microphone or tape recorder on the speaker's stand during a press conference. In events where the reporter cannot get close to the action, however, a shotgun may be a valid option.

For sporting events, stations use parabolic microphones on the field. A parabolic microphone resembles a microwave dish. It has a dish shape often made of clear plastic with a shotgun microphone pointing into the dish. The dish focuses the sounds coming toward it into the center and reflects them into the microphone. Used from the sidelines of sporting events, they capture the sound of players hitting each other, a batter connecting with a pitch, or other natural sounds.

Occasionally a DJ or talk show host may do a program on stage in front of an audience. Instead of tying the talent down behind a microphone, a wireless microphone can be used. Wireless microphones have a small transmitter that sends a signal to a receiver. The receiver sends a feed into the audio board. Good-quality wireless microphones have different frequencies, allowing the board operator to control each one separately. The wireless may be a handheld or a lavaliere (often referred to as a "lav"), a tiny microphone, which can be smaller than a pencil eraser, that can clip to a lapel or other inconspicuous place and go virtually unseen.

Transmitters

Early transmitters were not reliable and were prone to many technical problems. Often an engineer or staff member was kept standing by to make constant adjustments. Key innovations to transmitters include the ability to generate a stronger signal while using less energy, the introduction of a transistor to replace costly tubes, which often burned out, and the computer technology that brought the size and cost of transmitters down. While an early radio transmitter could be the size of a small building, today's transmitters range from the size of a home stereo system to a home entertainment center depending on the power requirements.

Antenna

Often a station's transmitter is located near the antenna. The antenna can be miles from the station. While it may not seem like a major concern, the tower is one of the things that the FCC and FAA tightly regulate. The tower's height, where it is placed, and its upkeep all fall under the FCC's jurisdiction. The FCC dictates certain rules stating that an antenna may not interfere with the path of airplanes, that they must be illuminated at night in certain areas, and they must be painted according to the commission's standards.

Broadcasters seek ways that will maximize their tower's height and minimize cost. A station with a taller antenna will usually reach more people. In major cities, the highest spots are atop the tallest buildings, which often house transmitters and antennas for several radio and television stations. In suburban and rural areas the highest point may be atop a hill or mountain. Astute businesspeople often purchase this piece of land and open "tower fields," where they lease tower space to radio stations. Some stations may also lease space on their tower to other broadcasters or cell phone companies in an effort to recoup their costs. With transmitters located so far from the station, an engineer often had to be sent to take readings as per FCC regulations and make adjustments to the signal. However, with new computer technology, a DJ can monitor and make adjustments to the station's transmitter remotely, regardless of its location.

For taller towers, especially those within an airport's flight path, lights are required so that pilots can spot the tower at night. FCC regulations state that someone must inspect the tower at least once every twenty-four hours to ensure that the lights are in working order. Some stations employ a camera to remotely look at the lights, some an alarm system, and others have the tower close enough that someone looking out the window can inspect it. Stations using an automatic monitoring system still have to inspect towers physically at least once every three months. If the lights are malfunctioning, it is imperative that the local airport be notified to warn pilots and reroute flights if necessary.

Because of the necessity of the lights many stations hire a freelance engineer or other specialist to climb the tower and replace the bulbs once a year. This can be a dangerous job. Even though a tower may look stable and the towers are anchored to the ground with heavy cables, they are built to sway in the wind, to reduce the likelihood that they will snap in storms or heavy wind gusts. Some of these people charge by the foot, the taller the tower the higher the fee, so many stations find it economical to have all the lights changed at one time instead of repeatedly paying for this service.

Towers are also directional. When the FCC grants a license, it requires that a station follow a very strict broadcast pattern to avoid interfering or "walking on" another station's signal. For that reason it is common for a local station to broadcast only a mile or two in one direction but twenty-five or thirty miles in another.

Recorded Media

Early radio was live. While the technology to make recordings have been around since the early 1900s, two variables kept it from making progress into radio: sound quality and the audience's bias toward live radio.

In the beginning, the audience didn't want to hear records on the radio. They wanted to hear something else. Why, they asked, should we listen to a recording of a song when radio was offering live bands and performing artists? As chapter 2 illustrated, plenty of live programming didn't rely on records.

This wouldn't change until the late 1940s and early 1950s. Making a move to the typical DJ program of today at that time would have been the equivalent of taking all television programs off the air and replacing them with music programming. Today's audience has become accustomed to drama, sit-coms, soap operas, and so on, just as the radio audiences of the 1930s and '40s had.

At first the sound reproduction was not good. The early Edison phonograph played cylinders made of paraffin wax. Sound vibrations were etched directly into the soft wax, which made a record. Placing a needle into the groove while the disc rotated translated the vibrations back into sound waves.

If you have an old LP, a simple experiment will illustrate this point. Roll a piece of poster board or other thick paper into a cone shape. Put a

Figure 7.1. Edison Phonograph Co. recording of The Star Spangled Banner (1905).

Photo W. Richter

sewing needle through the tip of the cone. Next place a pencil in the hole of the LP and, while spinning the record, bring the needle into contact with the groove. Properly done, you'll hear sound. The experiment works better with old 78-rpm records, but will also work with newer 33⅓s even though they rely more on amplification.

Here's an interesting piece of trivia. Each side of an LP, no matter how many songs, has only one groove running from the outside edge to the middle. One notable example was *Monty Python's Flying Circus' Matching Tie and Handkerchief* album, which had three sides. The record has two tracks running parallel to each other on one side. Dropping the needle in the second track resulted in a whole different set of cuts than the ones on the first track.

Giant funnels, or horns, were used to gather sound before the development of electronic microphones and amplification. Crowding tightly around the funnel, an entire band or orchestra would play. (This is completely different from today's recording sessions, where each instrument has its own microphone.) The vibrations of their music created a paraffin or clay master. Companies used the masters to produce records. Since these records were tubes, there was only one playable side, the outside. Therefore the maximum amount of time was two to four minutes per record.

The record that took the tube and flattened it out into the platter or disc shape was the 78 rpm. This record set the standard for decades and was a giant step in the technology of recorded sound. In addition to offering a superior sound, it also allowed more recording time on the disc, three to five minutes per side.

The 78. In 1889 Emile Berliner marketed five-inch hard rubber records for a gramophone, sold in Germany as a toy or novelty. In 1900 he introduced the seven-inch record in Montreal, Canada. The following year he introduced the standard ten-inch record. These offered a longer recording time as well as superior quality. His Berliner Gram-o-phone Company and RCA Victor marketed the Berliner records. However, the 78 could still only hold three to five minutes on a side. Books resembling photo albums often held the series of discs needed for a concert. The name stuck, and records became known as albums. There really wasn't any great research done in choosing the record speed. The reason for the speed was that the most commonly available motor at that time had a gear ratio that resulted in the record revolving at 78 rpm.[5]

The 33⅓. In 1945 the next great innovation came, from Peter Goldmark, an engineer for Columbia Records, who developed the CBS color television system. Despite not being adopted as the industry standard, it was used to transmit video from the Lunar Orbiter in 1966. Goldmark liked listening to operas and concerts on his Victrola, but was tired of having to get up from his chair and change the LP whenever a side was finished. Setting to work, he used his engineering skills to devise a better method. He was finally able to get more music on a side of a disc by slowing the speed to 33⅓ rpm. These new records were called long-playing (LP) records and could play about twenty-five minutes per side.[6] Goldmark later would help the United States in developing the first spy satellite used over the Soviet Union.[7]

But there was a problem with the LP that no one could have anticipated. While Goldmark was working on his project, RCA engineers were working on a secret project as well: the 45.

The 45. The next step in recording history was the invention of the 45-rpm single. These records held one or two songs per side. Many bars, saloons, and "juke joints" reopened following the repeal of Prohibition. But the Depression meant that most places could not afford live music, hence the newfound popularity of the jukebox. Jukeboxes originally used cylinders and 78s, but the 45 seemed to be an ideal size for the coin-operated device. It allowed for many songs by different artists instead of just a few from the larger LPs.

A huge fight occurred between David Sarnoff of RCA/NBC and William Paley of CBS, one often referred to as the Battle of the Speeds. Having just committed to production of record players playing both 78s and 45s, Sarnoff did not wish to retool his factories to accommodate the 33⅓ rpm. CBS/Columbia Records gave its technology to anyone who wished to use it, and the 33⅓ rpm started to become popular. Still RCA refused to support or manufacture the new format, and CBS/Columbia refused to recognize the 45. Eventually, at the urging of the NBC Symphony Orchestra's conductor, Arturo Toscanini, they decided that the 45 format would be used for popular music while the long-play format would be used mainly for classical and opera. This solution allowed both men to save face.[8]

Reel-to-reel tape. Another invention that revolutionized the radio and recording industries was the reel-to-reel magnetic tape. During World War II the U.S. Navy wished to have a better method of recording intercepted U-boat messages. It contracted with the Brush Development Company in Cleveland to work on a superior recorder. The United States knew that Germany was already using a magnetic tape recorder. In fact, Jack Mullin, a technician assigned to the Signal Corps, had the assignment of picking up any useful parts he might find as the Germans retreated. Among other odds and ends, he found two working recorders and various tapes.

The Brush Company contacted the Minnesota Mineral and Mining Company (3M), the manufacturer of adhesive tape, and asked if they could apply a metallic powder coating to tape. While the results were not immediately great, they did set the scene for postwar advancements. Brush kept experimenting with tape recorders on its own, and 3M continued to perfect the audiotape. Even though the companies had yet to see any money, they felt that this technology had a great future.

Then in 1946 Mullin demonstrated the German tape recorders at a conference in New York. As fate would have it, Bing Crosby had just received a contract allowing him to prerecord his radio programs, as long as his ratings did not slip. No other artist had been allowed to do this. A staff member heard about the tape recorders and immediately thought they could be used for the shows. This was the break that introduced the audiotape to radio, a relationship that would last for years to come.[9]

The 3M Company perfected the magnetic tape, while a new company, Ampex, created a superior machine. Unlike the phonograph, the reel-to-reel recorder didn't have any uncertainty about speeds. Most players had speeds measured in inches per second (ips) as opposed to rpm. Tapes could be recorded at either $7^1/_2$ ips or 15 ips. Those recorded at the faster speed had a better quality, but one could record only half as much content on a tape. Using the slower speed meant doubling the time, but at a reduced quality.

Carts

Another sound storage system was the cartridge, or "cart." In the late 1950s two radio stations were attempting to find a better way to play commercials.[10] Based on the same looping tape as the eight-track, the cart had only two tracks and did not require the playback head to move. Stations used carts in many ways. Carts came in various lengths, generally ranging from ten seconds to ten minutes. A station could put a jingle or liner on the cart, and then when the hot clock called for one, the DJ reached to the cart rack, pulled one down, and placed it in the machine. A simple hit of the "play" button would result in the cart playing. But there were problems with the system.

On longer tapes, one could record a primary tone (this was the start of the tape), a secondary tone (for a second cut), and a tertiary tone (for a third cut). All of these tones were inaudible to the human ear. Sometimes a instead of playing the cut that was due, another cut would be played when the DJ hit the button. Hurried DJs often pulled a cart out of the machine after a song played, not waiting for it to recue. The next DJ who put the cart into the machine and hit the "start" button but got dead air for seconds, even minutes before the start/stop tone was reached. The cart machine caused more than one heated argument.

CDs

Sony, CBS/Sony, Philips, and Polygram introduced American consumers to music's next generation in 1983. They had announced in 1982 the development of the compact disc (CD). They demonstrated the CDP-101, the first player, that year. *CDP* stood for *compact disc player*, and the number was because in binary code *0101* is equal to 5; the player's engineer, realizing that this was only a moderate system and that improvements were needed, gave it a rating of five.[11]

Recording music in a digital instead of an analog format opened the door for a technology revolution. This new format took all sounds and translated them into binary code using zeros and ones. Even though the disc is less than five inches across, it holds over three miles of playing track and, unlike the LP, the music starts at the inside and works its way outward. A series of microscopic pits and level areas encode the surface with zeros and ones. These pits and levels affect the laser's reflections inside the player. A photodiode reads the reflected light, converting the code into an electrical signal. Finally, the electrical signal is decoded back into sound.

At first, many CDs were released that were either already available as LPs or cassettes or had been originally recorded to tape. These masters were in an analog format and therefore not as precise as the new digital system. A computer could analyze recordings and check them against sounds preprogrammed into its memory. If the sound was not registered, it could delete it, as in the case of static, pops, and crackles. Another system had a program that could take older works, and, using an algorithm, guess at a missing note and replace it.

Early CDs had three letters on the back, identifying "A" for analog and "D" for digital. The first letter was how the music was recorded (all older music was A); the sound was recorded onto a master reel-to-reel tape, sometimes up to thirty-two tracks or more and two inches wide. The second letter was for how the music was mixed, and the third (always a D) how the music was mastered.

Artists and music lovers immediately fell into two camps, one supporting and one opposing the CD. Those embracing the technology liked the new cleaner sound. They enjoyed the fact that CDs could hold more music on one small disc than an entire LP could hold, and that the CD was a format that could theoretically last a lifetime. Each playing of all previous recorded material resulted in a loss in quality. Older records such as the 78 rpm used needles that were as large as if not larger than a sewing machine needle. With each playing, the needle scraped away a miniscule part of the record's groove. Over time the record became hard to hear.

Even the LPs of the 1980s, with their sophisticated technology and the turntables' tiny stylus and needles, were subject to wear, causing the needle to glide across the record or skip. In addition, the records scratched easily, causing the needle to stick in one place. Many DJs devised tricks to keep their favorite records going. Placing a nickel or two on the stylus would put more pressure on the needle, allowing a record to be played, but at the same time cutting deeper into it. Some DJs would put a little isopropyl alcohol, a standard maintenance item for cleaning the heads on tape decks, on the record to help the needle ride over the scratches.

Tapes are more vulnerable to erosion than records. Tape—whether cassette tape, reel-to-reel, or video—is magnetic. The tapes have microscopic iron filings embedded in them. Inside the recorder there are usually two heads. One is to record and one is to play back. Some professional models have a third head for erasing. The record head magnetically lines up the filings into a pattern. The playback head can read the pattern and translate it back into sound. Each time the tape crosses over the head, a tiny bit of the tape comes off. Many engineers recommend cleaning heads with isoprophol alcohol at least once a week to take away the buildup that affects the sound. Over time, tapes lose their original sound quality. As tapes wear they become prone to stretching and breaking.

But those who opposed the CD then still do today. Many artists and DJs are returning to vinyl LPs. Many still feel that the music on a CD doesn't replicate the music as it was recorded. They feel that the music from a CD is a computer recreation of sound, that the subtle nuances that older records offered are now gone, that CDs have no "soul."

As Sony began selling the new CD player in the United States, CBS/Sony released the first catalog of fifty CD titles, including the first popular CD, Billy Joel's *52nd Street*. Sony introduced the CD player for the car and the second generation of CD players in 1984. The following year, the third-generation players hit the market. In 1988, CD sales surpassed those of LPs for the first time. In 1990 sales of CDs reached 288 million in the United States, with sales of players reaching 9.2 million. Worldwide sales of CDs neared 1 billion that year.[12]

Live Remotes

Another advancement in the technology of radio was the ability to do "live remotes" on location. Alternate studios were often set up in hotel ballrooms, opera houses, fairs, or department stores for early remote broadcasts. The equipment was cumbersome, however. Sending a program via telephone lines back to the main studio and then relaying it to the transmitter site was also costly. Often these early broadcasts were for demonstration purposes. The signal only aired in the immediate venue. Most were little more than traveling shows, novelties.

The FRC shut down these broadcasting gypsies as part of its effort to clear up the airwaves. While some of the portable broadcasters tried to fight the decision, ultimately they lost.

Today when we think of portable radio, we most often think of on-location segments that are part of a permanent station's programming. Sometimes this may be on-the-spot news coverage or sometimes it may be a remote broadcast in which a DJ is at a store or event to give the station publicity while at the same time bringing people in. It wasn't until the invention of remote pickup (RPU) technology that remote broadcasts became practical.

Dedicated phone lines were another technique. Harkening back to the original days of the networks, stations with regular broadcasts from a sports stadium or other venue paid the phone company to run a phone connection between the two venues. These lines couldn't make or receive calls, since they were not on the grid. One may compare these lines to a hotline phone between world leaders, the old-fashioned stock ticker-tape machines, or the newswire services before the widespread use of computers. Of course, the phone company still charged for using these lines and the sound quality was never the best.

Today, with the use of satellites and cell phones, broadcasts may be done from anywhere in the world. It has become almost routine for one to turn on a radio and hear a reporter live in a city that is under attack. As technology advanced, so did radio.

The Future of Radio

Technological advances in most fields have historically taken place slowly at first and then picked up momentum. Media, like technology, usually evolve in three stages:

1 the novelty or development stage;
2 the entrepreneurial stage; and
3 the breakthrough to the wider market.

Take computers as an example. The first electronic computer as we would define it today was ENIAC, introduced in 1946.[13] This computer filled an entire room. If you have a scientific calculator it is more powerful than that technological marvel. In 1943 Thomas Watson, president of IBM, predicted, "I think there is a world market for maybe five computers."[14] This was still the developmental stage. Computers went through years of refinements before they reached the entrepreneurial stage. Computers were made smaller and faster. The first home computers were sold in the mid-1970s. This was the entrepreneurial stage. Men such as Steve Jobs, Steve Wozniak, and Bill Gates began making the PC more affordable. They found a way to make money using the technology and marketing it to a new population. The computer was still expensive, but by the late 1990s home computers had reached the breakthrough phase and were the norm. During this phase the prices fall as more consumers accept the new technology. More than 60 percent of U.S. households have a computer today.[15] Moore's Law, postulated by Gordon Moore, cofounder of Intel in 1965, states that the number of transistors able to be placed on a circuit would grow exponentially, thereby making the next, better generation of computers available every eighteen to twenty-four months. Since that time the numbers have remained somewhat constant. In fact, as recently as March 1, 2005, Intel's CEO Craig Barrett announced that the technology is in place to create parts that are sixty-five nanometers (65 millionths of a meter) across.[16]

The technology in radio broadcasting has picked up speed over the years. Most stations have either made changes to their existing equipment or are in the process of upgrading. Those who don't may not survive over the next few years.

Digital Music Files

Future technology is either here or being installed at most radio stations. Instead of playing music on turntables, or even a CD player, stations are making the move to digitizing their music libraries. The program director or DJ can preprogram a playlist of all songs, spots, and PSAs. Not only that, but the digital files can be put into the computer so that they automatically play. One advantage of the system is that a program director can listen to a song in his or her office, put it into rotation, and have it on the air instantly.

In days past, phoned-in requests required a DJ or intern to go to the music library in search of an album or CD. With an entire library at one's fingertips, a song can be brought up as simply as using an MP3 player. Newer versions of this technology even allow the DJ to prerecord segments of the show and enter them into the computer.

Digital music also offers a huge advantage over tapes and film when it comes to editing. Prior to the ability to store music digitally, if one wanted to edit out a segment from a piece of tape there were four basic tools, a razor blade, grease pencil, adhesive tape, and a cutting block. At one industry conference a company announcing the arrival of its new digital editing system advertised "Free Analog Editing Systems." They handed out boxes with the four above-mentioned supplies.

Editing tapes for the news or commercial spots before the digital revolution was often time-consuming. One first found the edit point on the tape. Next the editor slowly rolled the tape back and forth across the playback head. He or she listened for a place that sounded as if a break in the voice, music, or other content occurred. The tape was marked at this point with the grease pencil. The endpoint of the edit was found in the same way and marked as before. Finally, the tricky part was attempted. One had to gently remove the tape from the heads to place each edit point in the metal cutting block. The block, designed like a miter box, had a guide for making angle cuts. Each mark was cut, the piece disposed of, and the two remaining ends were spliced together by putting a small piece of adhesive tape on the back of the tape, so as not to interfere with the playback.

Today a few simple clicks of a mouse, makes the edits, allows for previews and corrects mistakes. Even the most basic music editing software has a feature allowing one to see readout of the sound waves represented. Users may even enlarge the readouts on the screen, ensuring that accurate edits are made before saving them.

Voice Tracking

In major markets, it is not unusual for the overnight DJ to have recorded his or her portions or voice tracks sometime earlier that day, thus being able to keep daytime work hours. While versions of this automated assisted radio originated the late 1950s, today's computers have taken it to an advanced level of sophistication.

This technology is a mixed blessing for DJs and radio stations. While some on-air talent love the idea of tracking, a process that can take less than thirty minutes for an entire show, others may find the job less exciting. Most college DJs who program their own shows often find the job of a DJ at a commercial station to be mundane, and they find that they do not have a lot of creative input.

A plus for radio-station owners is that they may be able to cut costs by using automation at their stations. As discussed in chapter 2, services have existed since the 1970s that allow a station to pay for music and DJs delivered via satellite. Often these new advanced services are indistinguishable from a live, local DJ. The owner of a small station can pay half to one quarter of the salary of a local DJ and get a major talent instead. For group owners wishing to maximize profits and minimize costs, this is attractive too. From their corporate headquarters they can send the same program out to hundreds of markets, saving hundreds of thousands of dollars each year.

Digital Audio Broadcasting (DAB)

One innovation attracting a lot of attention is digital audio broadcasting. In 1992 the World Administrative Radio Conference approved a new frequency known as L-band for digital radio transmission. The new system offers sound quality that has a clear sound with almost no interference. Canadian broadcasters and consumers jumped on the idea, and stations are presently making a transition from AM and FM to the new L-band. The plan is to complete the transition by 2010.

In-Band, On-Channel (IBOC)

On the U.S. side of the border, the FCC and stations have been slower to react to the new system. In 2002 the FCC selected the in-band, on-channel (IBOC) system as the method to use in the transition from traditional broadcast to digital radio. This system allows stations to broadcast a traditional analog system and a digital system on the same channel simultaneously, the advantage being that everyone will not have to purchase new radio receivers in order to listen to radio. However, those who do will receive the added benefits of the enhanced digital signal.

So how is a digital signal different from the analog signals that we are accustomed to? Today's AM stations send out signals that are ground wave and sky wave. Station programming and carrier waves joined together are emitted over the antenna. AM radio towers emit a wave that follows the curvature of the earth, the ground wave, which is subject to interference from the terrain, the type of soil, even buildings, and another one that bounces off of the ionosphere, the sky wave. During the daytime the AM carrier tends to penetrate the ionosphere. AM signals often reach hundreds, even thousands of miles on certain evenings when the conditions are just right due to the sky wave. A 50,000-watt AM station can reach a distance of hundreds of miles because of the sky wave. People in California or Maine may suddenly hear a Midwestern station. The signal may have bounced off the ionosphere, hit the ground, bounced back up, and bounced back down again.

This is why most AM stations either cut back on their power or go off the air from sundown to sunrise. Of course, not all AM stations are that powerful. The distance also depends on factors such as time of day and even the station's frequency. Often you will lose an AM signal while driving through a tunnel. This is because the sky wave is being blocked by the mountain or whatever obstacle you are driving under. AM is also more prone to electrical interference. Thunderstorms, sunspot activity, even someone operating a kitchen appliance can interfere with the broadcast signal. The ground wave follows the curvature of the terrain, slowly degrading the farther it gets from the transmitting tower.

FM stations are basically line of sight. The signal from an FM station is a straight line that runs from the top of the tower to the horizon plus or minus a few miles. For this reason stations try to put their towers as high as legally possible. Due to the higher frequency, the FM signal does not bounce off the ionosphere. This means that at best a 100,000-watt station can expect to reach only sixty-five miles. Broadcasters are willing to accept that it takes twice as much power to run an FM station that doesn't travel as far as an AM station because it offers a superior sound. Again, this is all determined by the frequency, power, and tower of the station.[17]

Since new digital processes encode music into a series of zeros and ones, stations can send out signals that are unaffected by interference or obstacles. The digital AM signal should sound comparable to today's FM signal, while the digital FM stations will have CD-quality sound. This may mean a resurgence of music on AM radio if stations can broadcast in stereo. This should help broadcast stations compete against satellite radio and the use of CDs while allowing AM stations the opportunity to gain better footing against FM in the competitive market.

Digital radio also offers other unique features. Stations may be able to program more than one format on each frequency, giving them more stations. The idea of getting more data from a limited medium is not new. Western Union developed a system called multiplexing in 1913 that allowed eight messages (four in each direction) to be sent at one time, and 1936 they were able to send seventy-two messages).[18] Used for most cable television and telephone systems, fiber-optic cable transmits hundreds of signals simultaneously via light beams.

Radio Data Broadcasting Systems (RDBS)

In addition, digital radios can receive encoded messages sent by the station. By using a system known as radio data broadcast systems (RDBS), a radio station can send messages of up to eight characters to the receivers. These messages can display the name of a song, the artist, background information, weather, traffic, or a host of other data.

Some luxury cars have digital radios as standard features. Wondering if anyone in their audience was aware of the text option, Tom McGinley, director of engineering at KISS-FM (Seattle), along with the station's staff, put a text-only message saying that the tenth caller would win a DVD player. In this way, only those reading the radio—not those listening with standard analog radios—would know of the giveaway. He anticipated only a few phone calls, but listeners inundated the station with calls.

Enhanced Other Network (EON)

A radio equipped with a RDBS receiver can also allow a listener to pre-program the stations by call letters or even by genre, whichever he or she prefers. Another feature included is the enhanced other network (EON). The radio is programmable to interrupt a radio broadcast or even a CD if a weather alert is being broadcast, or just a traffic or weather report on another station. While this appears to be a great system, one should ask two questions: How quickly will this system be offered to advertisers so that a version of pop-up ads begins to appear on digital radio receivers, and how safe is it for drivers to read the radio while driving?

In 2004 Clear Channel Communications, the largest owner of radio stations with twelve hundred stations, announced that it was adopting digital radio for one thousand stations located in the larger markets. Clear Channel estimates the cost to convert each station to digital to be around $100,000. While large corporations like Clear Channel can afford such a price, many of today's smaller stations cannot. Some industry analysts predict an end to the independently owned station as more and more stations convert and as the price of digital receivers, now available only for cars, comes down in price.

Internet Radio

The Internet has added yet another ingredient into the radio broadcasting mix. Originally designed as a medium for data exchange among the military in time of nuclear war, it developed into a tool for the government and universities, and now has become the home to countless websites covering almost every topic imaginable.

Evan Harrison, head of Internet business for Clear Channel Communications, believes that a profitable strategy is to use the Web as a complement to local radio stations. Radio stations have long augmented their radio stations with companion websites. These sites often have been used as a promotion and marketing tools, offering audience members additional information about the on-air personalities, bands, songs, and contests. Some innovative stations began using their websites to offer broadcasts to distant listeners around the world. Yet slow modem speeds limited the streaming audio and proved to be more irritating than entertaining. Clear Channel envisions bringing video to their sites. In essence, as MTV brought radio to television, radio may now bring television to the Web.[19]

Internet radio has become more feasible with the availability of faster DSL and broadband connections. Companies willing to host radio sites made it possible for almost anyone to have a radio station without having to worry about obtaining an FCC license, as mentioned in chapter 5.

Live365.com, a website that offers users a proprietary software system and space for radio stations, announced in late 2004 that they had over 17,000 radio stations being hosted on their site, surpassing the 13,525 terrestrial stations. However, while 95 percent of Americans listen to traditional radio on a weekly basis, only 10 percent are listening on the Internet. Yet the number of those tuning in on the Web seems to be climbing.

The new rating system, comScore Arbitron Online Radio Ratings service, completed the first Internet radio ratings, for fall 2004, using their three charter members, America Online's AOL Radio Network, Microsoft's MSN Radio, and WindowsMedia.com and Yahoo's LAUNCHcast. Based on their findings, the service estimated that these three Internet radio services have a 4.1 cume twelve-and-older audience per week. A newer survey, completed in March 2005, estimates over 5.5 million cume listeners (Monday through Sunday, 6 A.M.- midnight).[20] It is still unknown whether the Internet will become the delivery method for radio in the future. Internet radio companies will face barriers just like any other industry. While vastly improved over the last several years, streaming audio still does not sound as good as a true radio signal. Internet audio for cars is another problem. Autos would need to access the Net with a cell phone or some type of wireless technology, or rely on satellite radio.

Podcasting

Podcasting is a relatively new technological advancement that is changing the way we think of radio. This blending of the words *iPod* and *broadcasting* gives a hint as to what this new medium is. Instead of streaming audio or having to download massive files to a computer, podcasting allows a person to sign on to a podcasting portal site. Audience members can automatically download, often directly to an iPod or MP3 player, new programs. They may then listen to them at their leisure. The podcast is possible due to Really Simple Syndication (RSS), a process that allows the automatic downloading of text files from multiple Internet sources on a regular basis. The brainchild of Adam Curry, a former MTV VJ, who wrote the first software program (available at www.ipodder.org/), individuals as well as stations and conglomerates like Clear Channel Communications are quickly adopting it. One-time presidential hopeful John Edwards has added a podcast to his website. Several NPR stations have podcasts available as well, showing commercial radio stations that this may be another opportunity instead of a challenge. Many proponents of the podcast feel that the opportunity for a listener to download a program to listen to while jogging, doing homework, or participating in another activity is akin to TiVo for radio. It will allow the audience to time shift a program and is as easily measurable as any website hit.[21]

In a *USA Today* article Steve Rubel, vice president of a prominent public relations firm predicts that "not only will podcasting become a popular tool for corporations, but also for celebrities and musicians who want to stay in regular touch with their fans."[22] Another person put it this way: "PODcasting will shift much of our time away from an old medium where we wait for what we *might* want to hear to a new medium where we choose *what* we want to hear, *when* we want to hear it, and *how* we want to give everybody else the option to listen to it as well."[23]

Podcasting is a relatively inexpensive alternative for anyone who wishes to have a radio show. All that one needs are the basic programs now included with most computers, a microphone, headphones, and maybe some music. If music is used it may be original, no copyright fees, or prerecorded. A license to use BMI music for one year of podcasting costs $283 for 2005. This is the minimum amount. If the podcast is making money it could eventually fall under the higher rates mentioned above regarding radio station licensing.[24]

Satellite Radio

In the United States the FCC put two frequencies in the S-band (digital audio radio service) up for auction in 1997. The two frequencies for satellite use sold for more than $173 million to two different firms, CD Radio, which became Sirius Satellite Radio, and American Mobile Radio Corporation, now known as XM Radio and owned by the Hearst Corporation.

In 2000 a Russian rocket carried the satellite *Sirius-1* into orbit. The company launched *Sirius 2* and *Sirius 3* later that same year. This gave the provider three satellites in an elliptical orbit rather than the more standard geosynchronous orbit. Engineers at Sirius feel that this better ensures seamless coverage.[25] In 2001 XM put two satellites into geosynchronous orbit, *XM-1* (dubbed *Roll*) and *XM-2* (*Rock*). Boeing Aeronautics built the satellites, and the company Sea Launch put them into space. Sea Launch specializes in private payloads. Its launch pad, moved to the equator for the launch, resembles a cross between an oil-drilling platform and something from a James Bond movie.[26] In 2005 *XM-3* was launched due to failing solar systems aboard *Rock* and *Roll*.[27] The company has scheduled *XM-4* to lift off in 2007.

Figure 7.2. XM-3 Liftoff

Photo courtesy Sea Launch

Sirius offers 120 channels, 65 channels of commercial-free music plus additional channels that are advertising-supported. The headquarters in Rockefeller Center in New York has thirty-three digital recording areas covering more than fifty thousand square feet and a library of over 2 million music titles and programs.[28] The Washington, D.C.–based XM Radio has 3 million listeners with over 150 channels, 60 music channels that are commercial-free plus an addition 30 channels of news, talk, sports, and so on.[29]

The satellite radio companies are very similar to satellite or cable television in that they are subscriber-based. They also offer a plethora of stations carried simultaneously across the country. A person driving across the country may stop in a motel anywhere in the United States and see the same program on HBO or ESPN. The same is true for the satellite music services. A driver may go from coast to coast listening to the same station without losing the signal.

Only 2 percent of drivers have satellite radio today, but the figure is predicted to rise to 10 percent by 2008. Both companies have arranged to have satellite-ready receivers installed in new cars and trucks. GM, a partner with XM, will be installing XM receivers. Ford and Daimler/Chrysler have announced plans to install Sirius radios, and Toyota has signed deals with both providers.[30]

Communities in mountainous areas that could not get television originally adopted cable television as a means of getting signals over the mountains. When it started to become a big business, it was the smaller towns that were quicker to adopt the new delivery system. Major cities were carrying up to twelve stations of broadcast television for free. Many—especially older viewers—did not see the need to pay for something that they could already get free. Slowly cable began to penetrate the larger markets until it finally reached over 50 percent of homes in 1987.[31] As of 2003 it was in almost 70 percent.[32] But today it has competition from satellite-delivered programming. Recent numbers indicate that cable has remained somewhat flat while satellite television has been able to sign up 20 percent of homes.[33] It appears that instead of taking viewers away from cable, satellite encouraged more of the population to pay for television.

So what do all of these changes mean for today's radio-station owners, employees, and advertisers? Radio advertising sales broke an all-time high in 2004. Advertisers spent $21.4 billion with radio stations in 2004, which was 2 percent more than the year before. However, this increase did not match the percentage increase of the previous year.[34] While some analysts were projecting an even higher percentage for 2005, many predict the economic market to flatten out at best, if not decline. Combining national and local radio advertising money, radio accounted for slightly more than 7 percent of all advertising expenditures. Looking at just local markets, radio ad sales revenue equaled 30 percent of local newspaper ad sales and 42 percent of local television.[35]

There is an increase in competition among all stations for listeners. If one thinks of the market as a lake, there are only a certain number of fish in it. Today, as more listening options are made available, there are more and more fishing lines being tossed into the lake. Some boats may use more tempting lures (programming strategies) to catch the fish, while others (group owners) are using more boats.

Traditional radio stations are facing more competition in the form of CDs and iPods, satellite radio, and the Internet, but the trends over the past few years have seemed quite stable. For the period of spring 2003 through spring 2004 the percent of Americans age twelve and older who listened to the radio at least once a week was steady at over 94 percent, while the amount of time people spent listening to radio dipped just slightly, from twenty hours per week to nineteen hours and forty-five minutes.

This doesn't mean that the numbers will continue to remain steady. Already many small stations are facing the reality that stations owned by large groups are better capable of weathering out any storm on the horizon. With millions of dollars and teams of experts, major groups such as Clear Channel Communications can afford to lose money in the short term better than a station that is barely paying its bills.

Many stations, especially those in the Clear Channel group, are already altering business practices in an attempt to stave off some of the threat hanging overhead via satellite radio. While the FCC only puts a cap on the amount of advertising that may be broadcast during children's television content and puts none on radio advertising, at one point the National Association of Broadcasters had a code that recommended only eighteen minutes of commercials per hour. This code was struck down by the justice department in 1984, however, as violating antitrust laws. With the voluntary limits removed, many stations began increasing the number of spots they aired per hour. After all, more spots equal more money.

Today they are reversing that trend. Clear Channel announced that in an effort to clear up the clutter the company has begun reducing the number of spots per hour, cutting the number of sixty-second spots in order to air more thirties—and charging more for the spots. These actions are in response to research the company conducted that said that shorter breaks improve listener involvement. Navigauge also released a study that found that a thirty-second spot in the beginning of a commercial set will retain more listeners than a sixty-second one. It also found that during shorter commercial breaks, 80 percent of the listeners were still listening after the second spot and 70 percent after the third. Other stations are also following suit.

Another strategy is to increase a station's brand. Most listeners are loyal to their radio stations. Much like most people who are Coke drinkers stick to Coke, and those who are Pepsi drinkers stick to Pepsi, a station with a strong brand and community presence may be able to hold on to its listeners.

If history tells us anything about the radio industry, it is that the medium has always been adaptable. It has survived by meeting challenges of new technology and competition and metamorphosing into something stronger. No one is certain what radio will sound like or how it will be delivered ten years from now, but one can be certain that it will survive in one form or another.

 ## Questions for Further Thought

1   If you were an advertiser, would you be willing to pay more money to advertise on a Clear Channel station that is running fewer commercials?

2   Will podcasting replace traditional radio?

3 Will digital audio broadcasting save traditional radio, or is it too late?

4 What can local radio offer that the two satellite companies do not?

Shop Talk

Air check: A tape of a radio show used for review purposes. Sometimes a DJ or host will make a personal air check, or a program director may make a copy to review.

Bumper: Type of prerecorded device used to separate components of a show and/or to promote the show. Sometimes a theme song is used before going to a commercial break.

Buss: One column of control buttons and/or knobs on an audio board.

Ground wave: AM and FM radio signals that are limited by the contours of the earth, also called line of sight.

Line of sight: Stations that only can be received within sight of the transmitting tower, give or take a few miles. All FM stations qualify as line of sight.

Long playing (LP): Phonograph records that are 331/3 rpm.

Podcasting: Combination of the words *iPod* and *broadcasting,* a new way to download radio programs or Internet programming. Seen as a way to time shift listening for some.

Segue: Seamless transition between two components, usually music, or music and a commercial.

Sky wave: AM radio signals that bounce off the ionosphere, reappearing many miles away.

Stop set: A pause in a program to play spots.

Voiceover: Any announcing over a music bed, or, in television, over video.

Voice tracking: Through computer technology, a method that allows a DJ to record inserts to be added between songs, commercials, and so on. This method allows large chains to use one DJ for several markets.

Volume unit (VU): The measurement of audio expressed on the mixing board. May also be expressed in decibels (db).

8

The FCC

Exactly What Does It Do?

The communications industry works the same way as other industries. Its main purpose is to offer goods and services in exchange for money in order to earn a profit. However, the communications industry is subject to certain rules and regulations that do not often apply to others. Radio and television are subject to even more special laws and regulations than other media industries.

Why do these laws exist and where did they come from? This chapter will examine the history of broadcast law and present regulations and discuss laws that may be enacted in the future.

The Wireless Ship Acts of 1910 and 1912

Perhaps the first time the government stepped into a regulatory role was in 1910 when it issued the first law regarding the use of wireless aboard ships. The U.S. Constitution gave Congress the right to regulate wireless signals because the wireless was a tool of commercial shipping. The Wireless Ship Act of 1910 (Article 1, Section 8) required all ships carrying fifty or more passengers and traveling more than two hundred miles to have at least two Marconi wireless operators and wireless equipment that could reach at least one hundred miles on board. The operators worked in shifts so that one was on duty at all times. This rule did not apply to strictly commercial freighters, but Congress felt that it had the authority to protect citizens aboard the ships. At this time it was common for cargo ships known as tramp steamers to also have limited space to carry passengers. Following the sinking of the *Titanic*, it was discovered that there had been vessels nearby in the shipping lanes, but they did not have a Marconi operator on duty at the time. Spurred on by these events and also by the Berlin International Radiotelegraphic Convention in London, Congress enacted the Wireless Act of 1912. The 1912 act set aside certain frequencies for government use, set up administrative rules regarding the use of distress signals, mandated that all transmitting equipment that was being used for commercial purposes (for example, conducting business with ships) had to be licensed by the secretary of commerce, and said that operators had to be licensed. This licensing requirement was in effect, in one form or another, until 1995. After this time, DJs no longer needed to be licensed to be on the air.[1]

The first action to have a direct effect on the broadcast radio industry happened when the navy took control of all patents and took all stations off the air. Newspapers and magazines did not have to stop publishing, but the navy felt that radio was unique and that the resources it possessed where better used for the war effort. The secretary of commerce singled out radio as unique among media, even though it was the navy that undertook this action.

So many stations took to the airwaves following the war that they began blocking each other's signals. Secretary of Commerce Herbert Hoover faced a dilemma. Those who wrote and adopted the Wireless Ship Act of 1912 did not have broadcasting in mind. Broadcast radio was evolving faster than the law. The act didn't set aside any specific frequencies for radio broadcasting, so Hoover selected two, 750 and 833 kHz, allowing stations to operate on whichever frequency they preferred. Another problem was that while his office was charged with overseeing the licensing and operation of stations, he had no real authority to make rules, modify existing rules, or even enforce them. In many ways he was in a position that had no authority.

Quickly it became evident that two frequencies were not going to be enough. The secretary took the whole spectrum and divided it into station frequencies, separated by ten kHz. At the time the AM band was 550 to 1,500 kHz.

It is rare for any industry to ask the government to intervene in a regulatory role. But by 1922, even broadcasters knew that regulation of the industry was badly needed and long overdue.

Hoover called a meeting of industry personnel, the National Radio Conference, hoping that the broadcasters would be able to develop their own system of voluntary self-regulation. This may have been due in part to a reaction of the strict regulations that World War I had imposed on the industry, an aversion to stronger government oversight, or because his office lacked any substantial power. The meeting's results were disappointing at best, yet the conference met annually for the next three years. The broadcasters still asked for tighter control by the government. Each year, the conference submitted legislation to Congress, and each year the legislation never made it out of committee. Stations were ignoring suggestions that they voluntarily share frequencies by splitting the day. The interference caused by several stations broadcasting at the same time on the same frequency in the same city made it impossible to hear many stations.

The one thing that did come out of the meeting was the new standard for amplitude modulation or AM radio. Stations could broadcast between 500 and 1,000 watts on either 750 or 833 kHz.

In 1923 Hoover denied the renewal of a station's license due to overcrowding of the spectrum. The owner, Intercity Radio, appealed the decision and won. In the decision handed down by the court it was pointed out that while the secretary of commerce had the power to issue licenses, the Wireless Act of 1912 did not give him authority to deny or revoke a license.[2]

In an attempt to ease the congested airwaves, Hoover allocated more space on the spectrum for AM radio. Yet station owners were free to operate whenever they wished at whatever power they wished.

At the National Radio Conference of 1925, Hoover brought two important things before the group. First he reiterated his stance on self-regulation: "as I have said, the more the industry can solve for itself the less will be the burden on the Government and the greater will be the freedom of the industry in its own development."[3] Second he laid out four issues for the committee to consider at the meeting: "To sum up, the major problems for consideration are, to my mind: (*a*) Is public interest paramount? (*b*) Shall we limit the total number of stations in each zone pending further development of the art? (*c*) What basis shall be established for determining who shall use the radio channels? (*d*) What administrative machinery shall we create to make the determination?"[4]

The assembled group agreed that radio stations should be required to operate in the public interest and that there should be a temporary freeze placed on station licensing.

The freeze was overturned in 1926 when a federal court ruled that the Wireless Act of 1912 did not give the secretary the right to do impose a freeze on licensing. The court also ruled in the same case, *U.S. v. Zenith Radio Corp. et al.*, that he did not have the power to fine stations in violation of regulations.[5] Finally, Congress decided that there needed to be major revisions to the early act, and in 1927 issued a new one.

The Radio Act of 1927

The Federal Radio Commissions (FRC)

The Radio Act of 1927 accomplished several things. First it established the Federal Radio Commission (FRC). The act gave the FRC authority to regulate the industry by enforcing rules, making regulations, and modifying existing ones, the very things that had created a problem for the secretary of commerce's office. While the commerce office had many other issues to contend with, the FRC had only one charge: radio. This agency was independent of any existing government office, something that was uncommon.

The act also gave the FRC powers due to the scarcity of the spectrum, and because the airwaves belonged to all the people. Station owners were not getting a piece of the spectrum, but only permission to use it and as such should act as a trustee. It expressly stated that the powers given to the FRC were not limited to technical and engineering decisions. The rulings that it could make had a broader scope.

Something else it did, seemingly mundane, turned out to be the heart of communication law. The act stated that the FRC should conduct itself in the "public interest, convenience and necessity," as should the radio stations. These five words are easy to understand, yet hard to nail down because the wording isn't specific. In fact the wording "public convenience and necessity" was becoming a standard phrase in government agencies, having first been used in the Transportation Act of 1920, regarding railroads and whether new construction should be given approval, another duplicate railroad line built, or even if an old line should be discontinued.[6] What did Congress mean by this phrase as it applied to broadcasting? What qualified and didn't qualify under this provision? While this echoed what the National Radio Conference meetings had decided, by not giving examples the phrase was left open for interpretation by others.

Broadcasters and courts have been arguing the meaning of these words since they were first put down on paper. On the surface they mean that broadcasters should operate in such a way as to keep the public's best interests in mind. However, as we shall see, this isn't always a black-and-white issue.

Four Theories of the Press

There are many different ideas about what role the media should play in society. Countries adopted styles as each began using the mass medium. The four most common theories originated in a 1963 book *Theories of the Press*.[7]

Soviet Theory

Government-owned and -operated media follow the Soviet theory. The leadership uses the media to propagate its messages in this model.

Authoritarian Theory

The authoritarian theory allows private ownership but says the government has control over content. Some estimates say that up to 60 percent of the media in the world operate under this system, although these numbers can quickly change in today's environment of shifting governments.

Libertarian Theory

The libertarian theory permits privately owned media, without any government intervention. This theory assumes that a well-informed public can make well-informed decisions. It assumes that the main job of the media is to get information to the people.

Social Responsibility Theory

Social responsibility theory also allows private ownership, believing that a well-informed public is good for everyone. However, it notes that sometimes the media need to be reminded of the their mission in serving the public, so laws exist.

The First Amendment

After World War I, the government rejected the idea of the navy or any arm of the government owning the radio stations. Just as newspapers and other media were privately owned, so too radio must be a private enterprise. The First Amendment to the U.S. Constitution states that "Congress shall make no law respecting an establishment of religion, or prohibiting the free exercise thereof; or abridging the *freedom of speech, or of the press;* or the right of the people peaceably to assemble, and to petition the Government for a redress of grievances."[8]

The Marketplace of Ideas

One can trace this "marketplace of ideas" approach back to the writings of John Milton in 1644. Later, in the 1800s, John Stuart Mill further developed the concept in his arguments that freedom of speech outweighs government intervention. He said that if an idea is right and a person drops a wrong idea, they have benefited by hearing the idea. If the idea is wrong, it is almost as valuable because the person with the right idea will see even more clearly that their idea is correct.[9]

The marketplace of ideas philosophy imagines that there are local marketplaces, something that is not common in the United States today. One can think of the marketplace as being similar to a farmer's market. In today's times, it is most likely a mall. Inside this mall there are many stores, each store owner trying to sell you on his or her way of thinking. You are free to go into the store, examine the idea, and then decide to buy or continue looking. The founding fathers felt that if people could hear many different opinions they would make educated decisions.

So by operating under the U.S. system, which is basically social responsibility, a radio station should present many viewpoints to its listening audience. But from time to time, the government may need to step in and remind the station about its responsibilities. Over the years the FCC, government, and courts have issued various rulings limiting what may be said by broadcasters, imposing certain types of content on them and even punishing broadcasters for violating stricter rules than the other media must abide by. As we shall see, this is still an issue today.

The Federal Radio Commission 1927–34

The five members of the FRC were appointed by the president, pending approval by the Senate. Each commissioner represented a wide geographic area. In this manner, no one area should have more influence in getting stations, and stations from a particular area should not have more influence than others.

Congress initially envisioned the FRC as a group that would clean up the airwaves in about a year, and then serve more or less as an appeals group for the secretary of commerce's decisions. Because of this, they did not allocate any funds for the new commission and the commissioners had to do their own clerical work.[10] By comparison, today's FCC has around two thousand employees with a budget of almost $300 million in 2005.[11]

The FRC enacted new rules with the power given to them. As a commission appointed by the Senate, they were acting under the constitutional provisions that gave power to the commerce department but were also given the ability to make regulations, to license stations, to allocate the spectrum based on time, frequency, and location, to conduct hearings, and to deny a license.

The first thing the FRC did was to commence the task of cleaning up the airwaves. In looking at what had been described as a "cacophony of noise" present on the airwaves, the FRC noted that there are three important variables that must be considered in order for broadcasting to work: time, location, and frequency. One or two of the variables can be common to more than one station, but not all three.

Two stations can operate on the same frequency at the same time, as long as they are not close to each other. If a station in Nebraska is on the same frequency as a station in Georgia, it doesn't really matter if they are on the air at the same time. They are far enough apart to not interfere with each other's signals. If two stations are both in Boston, but on different frequencies, they can broadcast at the same time without the risk of interference. Similarly, if two stations are in Seattle, but are broadcasting at different times, it is fine if their frequencies are the same.

As a result, the commission set to work to clear the airwaves of clutter. Many unsatisfied broadcasters challenged its decisions. When it denied one station's renewal because there were too many stations on the air in its area, the court upheld its decision.[12]

Another station owner who was denied renewal came to court with a plausible argument that might have seriously jeopardized the FRC's powers. Gregg and two others were operating an unlicensed station in Houston under the name "The Voice of Labor." When the FRC sought to take him off the air, Gregg made a case that the FRC's authority was granted under the same provision as the commerce department, and therefore only gave the FRC legal authority over interstate broadcasting. Since his radio station did not carry over state boundary lines, he was only intrastate broadcasting. The FRC argued that they must have the leeway to regulate all stations since a station like Gregg's, while intrastate, could interfere with other interstate stations. The court agreed, giving more power to the committee.[13]

Border Blaster Stations

In 1931 the FRC denied Dr. John Brinkley a renewal because he was using his station to prescribe and sell his own medicines. Brinkley, who had attended medical school but never graduated, had purchased a diploma and had a long history of quackery. He had opened a clinic that dispensed shots of colored water, charging customers twenty-five dollars for the potions. He moved to Kansas, one of the few states that recognized his credentials, and started a practice. While there, he began a practice of implanting goat testicles in men to enhance their libido. He eventually even used human glands obtained from death row prisoners. His practice made him extremely wealthy. He owned several homes, luxury cars, yachts, and even airplanes. He also owned the radio station in question.[14] Brinkley claimed that the FRC, in denying his renewal, was engaging in censorship. The court ruled that the FRC was not censoring him, but using his past record to determine if he had acted in the public interest. The court made an important distinction: "There has been no attempt on the part of the commission to subject any part of the appellant's broadcasting matter to scrutiny prior to its release."[15] Had the FRC tried to stop Brinkley before he said something, then it would have been censorship. Because it was using his past performance, it was not censorship. Using past performance as a basis for the decision was fair when determining if Brinkley met the stated necessary criteria of a licensee.

Brinkley later moved his operation to Mexico, where he established a string of stations along the border. These border stations became known as "border blasters" because of their high power and ability to reach most of the United States and even into Canada. Brinkley operated the stations in various forms until the United States and Mexico signed a treaty in 1986.[16] At his first station, XER-AM, he continued his broadcasting, offering patent medicines. He also added the sale of Mexican lottery tickets, many years before lotteries were legal in the United States. The sales also ensured that listeners would tune in to hear the weekly winners. Brinkley continued opening his stations along the border, and continued to make them more powerful. Mexican authorities, feeling that the United States was hogging the most powerful frequencies, especially the clear channel ones, kept granting his requests.[17]

Telephone lines to a studio in Texas linked the station to the Mexican transmitter. Listeners tuning in might hear an announcement that they were listening to "Del Rioooooooooooooo Texas," and then some "hillbilly" music. Brinkley finally got the transmitter to 1 million watts, which made it the most powerful radio station in the world. Shortly thereafter, by an agreement between the Mexican and U.S. authorities, the station was shut down—although by this time the hillbilly music of the Carter family and others had been heard around most of the United States. In a way, what had started out as a punishment for Brinkley and retaliation against the government kept country music alive.[18]

In 1928, the FRC expressed its confusion over the ambiguity of the public interest, convenience, and necessity clause of the 1927 act and tried to define what it saw as operating in the public interest. The FRC stated that it was the interest of the audience that took precedence over that of the broadcaster. Consequently, the commission decided that it needed to expand the bandwidth and reduce interference, even if it meant denying stations' renewal applications. It also established different classifications of stations that were to operate at different levels of power.

Congress passed the Davis Amendment later that year, renewing the FRC and telling the commission to get rid of the interference problem and to get radio coverage equally to each of the five geographical areas they had divided the country into.

General Order 40

The commission established a new classification of stations in response to the Davis Amendment's charge. General Order 40 gave each of the areas an equal number of station frequencies, for local, regional, and clear channels. Local channels could cover just a small area consisting of the town of license. The regional channel hoped to get coverage out to areas surrounding bigger cities. A regional station broadcasting at a higher power might be more likely to be a network station and/or have resources that a small local station did not. Clear channel stations were superstations. These clear channel radio stations, of which there were only twenty-five, broadcast at 50,000 watts of power on frequencies that either had no or at the most a few stations sharing the same frequency across the country. At sundown, all stations that shared this frequency had to go off the air, or "go black." This meant that this handful of stations could effectively reach most of the country. The idea was that many rural areas still did not have any radio stations at all. These clear channel stations would be available to this market. Some of the stations and their programs became well known. WSM (Nashville) broadcast *The Grand Ole Opry*, making it available to most of the United States.

It was estimated that in 1940 there were still at least 20 million people who could not receive radio stations at night. By 1980 that number had decreased to 4 million. The FCC announced the elimination of traditional clear channel stations. Instead of ending their coverage completely, however, the commission allowed 125 new stations to stay on their frequency as long as they did not interfere with any signals within a 750-mile range.[19]

The FRC—a commission of five people without a budget and designed to last for only one year—lasted until 1934. By that time, the commission had accomplished the main goal of cleaning up the clutter of the airwaves, established the three classifications of radio stations, set up an infrastructure for the broadcasting industry, and paved the way for the new commission to replace it.

In 1933 President Roosevelt was concerned that different offices were regulating different communication industries. The U.S. Postal Service was overseeing telegraph communications; telephone service, due to its interstate nature, still fell under the commerce department; while radio was under the FRC.[20] He asked the chairman of the commerce department to undertake a study examining the communication industry. The committee suggested that one office be set up to oversee all types of communication. This finding may have been in part a reflection of the political climate of the time. The New Deal as articulated by Roosevelt called for a consolidation of government offices wherever possible, the goal being to cut down on the amount of bureaucracy. While this would set up a new office, it would eliminate areas of overlap and allow for better oversight of the burgeoning industry.

The Communications Act of 1934

No other document has had such an important effect on the broadcasting industry as the Communications Act of 1934. The Communications Act faced challenges, amendments, and alterations from 1934 until 1996, remaining mostly intact. The Communication Act has set the framework for government licensing and regulation of broadcasting for over seventy years.

Federal Communications Commission (FCC)

Several things happening in the United States at the time brought about the new radio act. The act of 1934 established the Federal Communications Commission (FCC) to oversee all electronic media, including wired (telegraph and telephone). Congress took the majority of the act directly from the earlier act of 1927. The concept of radio serving the public interest, convenience, and necessity remained exactly the same. Congress had established the FRC as a temporary, one-year commission, never meaning it to run as long as it did. Instead of having to renew the commission, the new act made the body permanent.

The act itself is divided into six sections:

Title I - Explains the purposes and applications of the Act, the terms and duties of the Commissioners, and confers general powers.

Title II - Covers communications common carriers that are subject to Commission regulation.

Title III - Relates to radio and is divided into four parts: radio licensing and regulation, radio equipment, radio operators on board ship, radio installations on vessels carrying passengers for hire, assistance for public telecommunications facilities.

Title IV - Clarifies procedural and administrative provisions.

Title V - Prescribes penalties and forfeitures for violators.

Title VI - Prohibits unauthorized interception and publication of communications by wire or radio and gives the President certain powers to deal with communication matters in the event of war or other national emergency and provision of telephone service for the disabled.[21]

The Beginning. The Communications Act of 1934 called for increasing the number of commissioners, appointed and approved in the same process as described in the 1927 act, from five to seven. The first commissioners of the FCC were Chairman Eugene Sykes, Thad Brown, Paul Walker, Norman Case, Irvin Stewart, George Henry Payne, and Hampson Gary. Sykes was chairman for only eight months. Anning Prall replaced him in March 1935 even though he continued on as a commissioner.

The new FCC set about tackling many duties upon its start. The act said that the FCC must operate in the public interest, convenience, and necessity, and the commission in turn felt that stations should also continue to meet this requirement. Since both the old FRC and broadcasters had wanted a better explanation of what meeting these goals meant, defining the statement was to be a goal.

The FCC decided that in order to better determine if a station was meeting the above goals, it needed more data when a station applied for renewal. In order to help accomplish the task of deciding which stations were to be renewed and which ones didn't meet the criteria, it started a process of requiring more paperwork from broadcasters. Over the decades, the amount of paperwork required continued to grow, to a point where it was almost impossible for a small station to keep up with it.

Traffic Officer of the Airwaves. The FCC's first job was to find the best use of spectrum space, and decide how many licenses should be assigned and where those licenses should go. This frequency allocation became another priority and a major cornerstone of what the FCC does. After all, the original plan for the FRC was to clean up the airwaves. A phrase often used and repeated by the courts was that the commission was a "traffic officer" of the airwaves, referring to its role in trying to keep everything running smoothly. There was no control over the traffic. Stations were operating on any frequency, at any time, and from any location when the Radio Act of 1927 had been enacted. Prior to the Radio Act of 1927, there was no one to police the airwaves. Stations were operating at any frequency, power, or time that they wished. Imagine a city that had no traffic laws, no traffic lights, no speed limits, and no rules concerning what side of the street one could drive on. This was the airwaves pre-1927, and the FRC (now the FCC) was there to direct the traffic and fine those who did not obey the laws.

Unlike the federal government, which was set up with one branch as the legislative, one as the judiciary, and one as the executive, the FCC is all three in one. The FCC makes the rules and regulations, has the ability to penalize infractions of those rules, and even has its own judiciary branch.

If one feels a law is unconstitutional (or that he or she has been treated unfairly), that person may appeal the case to an administrative law judge. This person is an employee of the FCC and is supposed to be an impartial party. The option of appealing to the court system is still available if the person is not satisfied with the judge's ruling. The FCC is headquartered in Washington, D.C., and is a federal body. Therefore it usually falls upon the Circuit Court of Appeals in Washington, D.C., to hear such appeals. If one wishes to appeal the decision of the circuit court, the only court of appeals is the Supreme Court of the United States. At the Supreme Court level, justices have the option of deciding whether a case is important enough to hear. If the court agrees to hear the case it grants *certiorari;* denying *certiorari* means that the court refused to hear the case and it is dead.

The FCC's history can at times seem contradictory. Sometimes it will rule in one way and the next time in a seemingly opposite way. At times the FCC restricted the number of stations any one person or group could own. Today there are few limits. At one time it said that stations could *not* editorialize; then it said that they *must* editorialize.

If decisions and rulings appear contradictory, one may look to the political, social, and economic forces operating at the time for clues as to why the commission ruled a certain way. At times the FCC has favored heavy regulation of content. At other times it has been more concerned with the economic impact a station would have on a market. Still other times the commission seems to be more concerned about the technical aspects of the media. The government eased antimonopoly laws during the Depression, for instance, as part of the New Deal. Following the Depression, these rules were more heavily enforced. During this time the government forced NBC to divest itself of one of its networks. The makeup of the FCC can also have an impact on its rules and decisions. From the very beginning, the commission has been comprised mostly of lawyers and broadcast executives.

As of 2005, with the stepping down of Michael Powell, Kevin J. Martin chairs the commission. Martin is a lawyer who has worked for President Bush as special assistant to the president for economic policy and deputy general counsel for the Bush campaign.

Michael J. Copps was most recently assistant secretary of commerce for trade development at the U.S. Department of Commerce and has worked as chief of staff for Senator Ernest Hollings and was a professor of American history.

John S. Adelstein has worked with numerous senators, most recently as senior legislative aide to Senate majority leader Tom Daschle. Adelstein also has taught history at Harvard and Stanford.[22]

Deborah Taylor Tate, an attorney, was the director of the Tennessee Valley Authority when she was asked to fill the position left open when Martin was named chair.

The commission is still awaiting appointment of a fifth member as of this writing.

The selection process for commissioners can also be directly related to some of the changes. The president appoints the commissioners, who then go before the Senate for approval. In an effort to keep some balance, no more than three of the five commissioners may be from the same political party. Congress at one point raised the number of commissioners to seven, but since has lowered it back to five. Commissioners receive five-year, staggered appointments. In this way all of the commissioners do not come up for reappointment or replacement at the same time.

Given this information, one can see that the president would likely appoint members who agree with his agenda and that the Senate would likely give approval to members who follow its present thinking. As we shall see later in this section, certain rules concerning broadcasting favor politicians who have no interest in seeing them changed.

The FCC has tackled many issues since its inception. The following are some of the rulings it has made, challenges to them, and in some cases the evolution of them.

To most, a ruling is generally not important unless it has elicited a challenge in the courts. Broadcasters, Congress, and other groups pay particular attention to these cases.

This section will begin with the licensing process, since the FCC did receive a charge to develop an equitable way of distributing them across the country.

As mentioned earlier, the spectrum is a unique resource belonging to all the people, like a national park or museum. The FCC only gives broadcasters a license to use the airwaves on behalf of the public. The commissioners had to decide the criteria by which a station would receive a license or renewal. The spectrum allocation had given AM broadcasters the spectrum space from 550 kHz to 1,350 kHz at first, until it was expanded to 535 kHz to 1,605 kHz and then to 535 kHz to 1,705 kHz in 1990. Technical requirements for modulating the amplitude dictated that AM stations be separated by 10 kHz. Stations are located in the middle of the space with 5 kHz on either side. Stations any closer will cause interference with each other. So while there appears to be many frequencies available on the AM band, there are only 116 available frequencies: 540, 550, 560, and so on up to 1,700. FM stations need even more space than AM.

The FM band is from 88.0 MHz to 108.0 MHz. The FCC divided this space into one hundred channels, each one being 200 kHz wide (.2 MHz). The video portion of television's channel six ends at 88.0. Video uses the FM band, while audio uses AM. Like AM, FM stations are at the center of the bandwidth. This means that while all AM stations end in a zero and are divisible by ten, FM stations end in an odd decimal, as in 88.9, 104.7, and so on.

In the beginning, the FCC decided that anyone who could find an area without an assigned radio frequency could apply for the license. If they were the first qualified applicant, the license was theirs. If they still wanted a station but there was not a frequency allocated, they could still apply if they could show that their station would not cause interference with stations already in existence.

But throughout the years, the FCC set several criteria that a person, group of people, or a business had to meet in order to receive a license. The commission also used these criteria in cases where two or more parties were competing for a license.

The FCC announced preferential status for applicants who, according to Section 308(b) of the act, met the requirement of citizenship, character, and financial, technical, and other qualifications. Once again, it is a case where Congress was not being clear when it worded the legislation. This left the FCC much room for interpreting the requirements.[23]

The qualification criteria as understood by the FCC have changed over the years. The commission originally preferred applicants who lived in the community and were knowledgeable about community issues and had a stake in the community. In recent years the FCC has often licensed group owners who not only do not live in the community but may have never even been to the town.

The FCC thought that one person owning more than one station in a market would be detrimental in that it would have a negative effect on the diversity of viewpoints. Today group owners often own multiple stations in the same city.

In 1953 the commissioners decided that no licensee should own more than seven AM radio stations, seven FM radio stations, and seven television stations. This was an attempt to bring a diversity of voices to the air. It also ruled that a single owner could not reach more than 25 percent of the national audience. This was often referred to as the 7–7–7 rule.

In 1970 the FCC issued a statement saying it would rather see sixty owners in a market than fifty. Fifty-one owners was preferable to fifty because, "It may be the 51st licensee that would become the communication channel for a solution to a severe social crisis."[24]

By 1984, a time of deregulation, the commission decided to raise the limits to twelve-twelve-twelve as long as no one person or group reached more than 25 percent of the country. But it did allow for fourteen of any one category if the station was at least 50 percent minority-owned with a reach of 30 percent of the national market.[25] This was an attempt to bring more diversity in station ownership. When looking at the 25 percent number, one must remember the distinction between an O&O station and a network affiliate. Most of the stations owned by the networks were in the largest, most profitable markets that didn't quite reach the 25 percent mark. The networks reach the rest of the country via affiliates. While the Communications Act of 1934 did not give the FCC the right to directly regulate the networks, it could regulate stations owned by the networks or those that had network affiliations.

Then with the Telecommunications Act of 1996, the FCC threw out limitations on the number of radio stations any one person or group may own. Later that year, the justice department put a limit on the number and type of stations any one person or company can own. There are presently no limits on the number of stations one person or company may own nationally, but there are limits per market. In an attempt to ensure that no one owner had more than half of the advertising revenue, they initiated the following limitations for the number of stations per market size:

- If there are fourteen stations or fewer in the market, the one entity may own up to five with no more than three being on one band (AM or FM).
- If there are fifteen to twenty-nine stations in the market, the limit is six stations with no more than four on the same band.
- In larger markets, with thirty to forty-four stations, up to seven stations may be owned by one party, with no more than four on the same band.
- In markets with forty-five stations or more, one party may own up to eight stations, with no more than five on one band.[26]

The FCC, which based earlier decisions on the limited spectrum argument, no longer sees this as a pressing issue. With new forms of media (satellite, cable, etc.), more than a select few have access to the American audience. While these are not "broadcast" outlets in the traditional sense and companies are charging a fee, the commission feels they give more opportunity for expression.

Citizenship and character still play a part in the granting of licenses. Originally, the FCC limited ownership of broadcast stations to American citizens. Today citizens of foreign countries may share in the ownership, as long as their share is no more than 20 percent. For parent companies the limit is 25 percent. As an example, media mogul Rupert Murdoch became an American citizen in 1985 so as to retain ownership of the Fox stations.[27]

Character is still an issue. Persons convicted of felonies or antitrust violations, or those who have lied to the FCC may not own a station or be part of station ownership. A current radio-station owner convicted of a felony must surrender his or her license.

While the rules once stated that a licensee had to prove financial soundness by showing enough resources to run the station for one year, even if no advertising revenue came in, the FCC now takes more of a free-market, capitalist approach. License applicants must only show enough capital to build the station and run it for three months without income. Under deregulation, the thinking is that stations providing a good product will survive. Those who don't will fail, just like any other business. Since there are so many media outlets available, having an individual station go off the air isn't a concern.

Today, with a very limited number of available spaces on the spectrum, most people do not start new stations, but purchase existing ones. Such transfers of licenses still must undergo FCC scrutiny.

Comparative Hearings

Competition for a license also used to take up a great deal of the FCC's resources. If a radio or television's license was up for renewal other individuals or companies could put in a bid for that license in an attempt to prove that they could do a better job if granted the license. Only in rare cases did the competition win. The FCC will not allow a license challenge today, unless the challenger can prove with hard data that the present license holder has done a grossly inadequate job.

However, in the case of new frequencies, the competition in the past could get quite fierce. It was not uncommon for four or more concerns to vie for the new frequency. In these cases the FCC would hold comparative hearings. All parties applying for a license had to go through a long process of presentations stating why they were the best candidate for the license.

At the same time, the FCC had instituted rules in order to promote the ownership of stations by women and minorities by giving them preference in the licensing procedure.

But the plan did not always work out as designed. Many times a license applicant would create a limited corporation with a minority member holding 20 percent of the stock. By FCC regulations, this qualified as a minority-owned company. Often unscrupulous individuals would put in a competing bid for a license never expecting to receive it. But entering a bid would slow the approval process down and usually cost the other applicant(s) money in preparing studies and paperwork. Since many of the minority and women applicants were first-time applicants with limited resources, the extra cost of the comparative process would put undue strain on them. The individual would then offer to drop his or her application for a price. This practice, akin to blackmail, was soon dubbed "greenmail." The FCC no longer uses the comparative hearing method for most license applications but instead has instituted an auction process.

Of the original Section 308(b) criteria, technical guidelines remain unchanged. Stations must still broadcast within strict technical guidelines. A station whose signal is too powerful or strays from its assigned frequency will face financial penalties, or as the FCC refers to them, forfeitures. There is a list of violations and fines ranging from hundreds to hundreds of thousands of dollars.[28]

Call Letters

Another of the duties of the FCC is to assign call letters to radio and television stations. Call letters have to be unique to each individual station. Each station must, under FCC regulations identify itself as close to the top of the hour as possible, giving the call letters followed by the city of license. The only things that may separate the two are the licensee's name and/or the frequency of the station. So while "WHAA, 107.5, Nashville" would be legal, "WHAA, The Power Station, Nashville" would not. The FCC does allow stations licensed to smaller outlying communitis but part of a larger metropolitan reporting areas to add the larger city at the end of the ID. "WHAA, Oak Park/Chicago" is fine, but "WHAA, Chicago/Oak Park" is not. As complicated as this seems, it still represents a relaxation of earlier rules.

The FCC is also part of an international agreement. The Berlin International Wireless Telegraph Convention of 1906 decided that all wireless aboard ships and on land must have a unique three-letter call sign. Prior to this, stations often chose their own call letters, often duplicating those of another operator. The United States did not sign this agreement until the 1912 convention that prompted the writing of the Wireless Ship Act of 1912.

Licensing both land and shipboard stations was under the jurisdiction of the Bureau of Navigation at that time. The bureau naturally decided that land stations should use the same system of call letters that ships were using.

"W" was for ships in the Pacific Ocean, and "K" was for ships in the Atlantic, and this system translated to the western and eastern parts of the United States. Because Texas is a gulf state, the original dividing line was the Texas border with New Mexico and ran north. The dividing line shifted to the Mississippi River in 1923. Sources differ on how it happened, but someone reversed the letters when assigning them to stations. So in 1913 the government decided to leave it as it was and give stations in the east the "W" prefix and stations in the west "K." Again for unknown reasons, someone began giving all stations "KD" as a prefix, as in KDKA.

Governments had to revisit these designations many times. The call letters "VAA" to "VGZ" were given to Canada. Eventually Canada would get call letters starting with "C," such as CHUM (Toronto) and CFOX (Vancouver), while "VOA" to "VOZ" are used only for Newfoundland.[29] In accordance with the agreement, stations in Mexico begin with the letter "X." The Texas rock band ZZ Top has a song, *I Heard It on the X*, honoring the border radio stations that at one time were heard across the United States.

There are still remnants of the original mixed-up assignment system. The country's first station, KDKA, still operates in Pittsburgh although it is an Eastern station, and WOW is in Omaha, Nebraska, and WACO-FM is in Texas. WACO-AM, the original station, is now known as KKTK.

Many stations try to either pick call letters from those available to reflect their ownership, format or location or a combination that is memorable for listeners. WLIT, plays lite rock, KKTY plays a country format. WIND is in Chicago (the Windy City), KFOG is in San Francisco, and then there is KALP in Alpine, California. Some may choose call letters that are just more memorable, such as WOW (Omaha), named for the Woodmen of the World Insurance Company, or WHEE (Martinsville, Virginia), and others may use their call letters to develop a mascot, like the WPZM Possum (Athens, Alabama). There are also WPIG (Olean, New York) and KATZ-FM (Yakima, Washington).

The first assigned stations had only three call letters, but the number was raised to four as more were assigned. Many of the older stations were able to get call letters that reflected their ownership. Some examples are:

- WGN, owned by the *Chicago Tribune*, for the "World's Greatest Newspaper";
- WLS, owned by Sears-Roebuck Co., for the "World's Largest Store"; and
- WCFL, owned by the Chicago Federation of Labor Unions.

The National Life and Accident Insurance Company in Nashville started WSM, which originated the Grand Ole Opry music program. The call letters came from the motto "We Shield Millions." WOR welcomed people to the "World of Radio."[30]

Time, location, or frequency separate stations in the United States.

The same is true for stations that are close to other countries. Just because a station is on the other side of a border doesn't mean that the signals can't cross over. In fact, over 90 percent of Canadians live within two hundred miles of the U.S. border.[31] U.S. stations routinely cross into Canada. So much so that in 1970 the government instituted the Canadian Content Rules (CAN-CON), applying them to Canadian television and radio stations. For radio, the rules ensure that at least 35 percent of the music aired each week is Canadian. To ensure that the Canadian music isn't hidden after midnight, it further states that at least 35 percent of the music played during the 6 A.M.–to–6 P.M., Monday through Friday, slot must be Canadian. French-language stations have higher standards to meet. The rules state that 65 percent of the vocal music broadcast per week and 55 percent of vocal music broadcast between 6 A.M. and 6 P.M., Monday through Friday, is in the French language. Further, ethnic stations must play at least 7 percent Canadian content. The Canadian Radio-Television and Telecommunications Commission (CRTC) says that a song must meet two of the following criteria to be considered Canadian:

M (music)—the music is composed entirely by a Canadian.

A (artist)—the music and/or the lyrics are performed principally by a Canadian.

P (production)—the musical selection consists of a live performance that is (i) recorded wholly in Canada, or (ii) performed wholly in Canada and broadcast live in Canada.

L (lyrics)—the lyrics are written entirely by a Canadian.[32]

As mentioned earlier, many stations were set up just on the Mexican side of the border of California and Texas. DJs like Wolfman Jack became famous by broadcasting at Mexican radio stations that could cover most of the United States.

In 1941 the United States, Canada, Mexico, and Cuba signed the North American Regional Broadcasting Agreement (NARBA), a treaty to run through 1949 as an effort to voluntarily regulate stations to reduce station interference between the neighboring countries. When the treaty expired, many problems caused the United States and Mexico to not sign the new agreement. Eventually the United States signed the agreement in 1960, joining Canada, Cuba, and new participants the Bahamas and the Dominican Republic. However, Mexico had also not signed the treaty. This accounted for the powerful radio stations throughout the 1950s and '60s. In 1969, and again in 1986 and 1992, the United States and Mexico signed agreements.

Under Castro, Cuba began to ignore the NARBA and withdrew from the agreement in 1982. To oppose the United States' plan to begin broadcasting what would become Radio Marti—a station broadcasting propaganda to Cuba—the Cuban government began constructing massive transmitters and towers directed at the United States. During 1982, the stations did a four-hour experimental broadcast that was able to "step on" the signals of stations in the United States as far north as Chicago. The broadcasts began with an announcer saying in English, "We are bringing you the news and some good Cuban music for your enjoyment." The FCC began allowing stations to increase their signal strength, but Cuba abandoned the broadcasts due to their high costs.[33] When the United States did begin broadcasting two years later, Cuba set up transmitters and towers to block out the signals.[34] Recently, the United States announced that it had broken though Cuba's jamming by broadcasting Radio and TV Marti from an airplane.[35]

The FCC as Regulatory Agency

In 1946 the FCC issued the *Blue Book*. The book contained the findings of random checks conducted by the commission. It had been randomly checking what stations were airing versus what they were reporting was aired. The FCC was showing that it was not going to be like many government agencies that were based in Washington but seldom ventured out. It was going to be a proactive regulatory body that was not afraid to challenge license holders. For decades, just the name of the FCC could bring fear into a license holder. The book also told broadcasters that the FCC was primarily concerned with the quantity of sustaining programs that the station aired, the broadcast of live, local programming, the creation of local programs that addressed matters of public concern, and what it called the elimination of advertising abuse.[36]

The FCC was also concerned about the fact that the networks held too much power over the local affiliates. Usually the agreements were for long periods, precluded a station from signing with more than one network, and gave the station little control over which network programs to air or not air, generally not allowing the station to preempt a network show for its own broadcast. The FCC especially didn't like the idea that NBC, with its two networks, had much more power and programmed to a greater number of stations than the fledgling CBS and Mutual networks.

Chain Broadcasting Regulations

As mentioned in chapter 1, the FCC began looking at chain broadcasting as early as 1938, trying to determine whether stations that were part of a network were serving the public interest, convenience, and necessity.[37] In a series of rules known as the Chain Broadcasting Regulations, the FCC slowly eroded the control that the networks (and especially NBC) held over the local stations. The 1941 *Report on Chain Broadcasting* stated, "No license shall be issued to a station affiliated with a network organization maintaining more than one network," obviously singling out NBC, the only company with two networks.

Soon after the United States entered World War II, on January 9, 1942, NBC brought suit in the case of *National Broadcasting Company et al. v.*

United States.

The case made its way to the Supreme Court, which ruled that the FCC acted within its authority when it regulated business agreements between stations and networks or program suppliers. In addition, it also ruled that the Communications Act of 1934 was constitutional and that the FCC had regulatory powers.

In writing the decision on behalf of the court, Justice Frankfurter referenced the fact that "In essence the Chain Broadcasting Regulations represent a particularization of the commission's conception of the 'public interest.'" He continued, "True enough the Act does not explicitly say that the Commission shall have power to deal with network practices. . . . It was given a comprehensive mandate to 'encourage the larger and more effective use of radio in the 'public interest,' if need be, by making, 'special regulations applicable to radio stations engaged in chain broadcasting.'"[38]

NBC also charged that the Chain Broadcasting Regulations were a violation of the First Amendment in that they inhibited freedom of speech. Again the court ruled in favor of the FCC, stating again that the spectrum is limited and not everyone who wants to use it can.

Another reason for this ruling was that the FCC and Congress were committed to stations serving the local markets. They wished for stations to carry local programming that would address the needs and concerns of the community residents. The commission kept the idea of localism in many of its rulings, but it wasn't until 1960, when the FCC issued its *Programming Policy Statement*, that it explicitly stated that broadcasters must determine the "tastes, needs and desires" of the community. This community ascertainment requirement caused a great deal of duress among broadcasters. Again, while this statement gave a list of things they should look for, it did not say what or how much programming was to be developed based on these needs.[39] Eventually, in 1970, the FCC amended the wording of this statement and replaced the tastes, needs, and desires language with the requirement that stations identify community needs and program accordingly. In 1976, stations added this extra paperwork to the pile they were already filing yearly.

Fairness Doctrine

The FRC and FCC have probably been the least consistent when it comes to editorializing and the right to reply. This has put broadcasters in a position that newspapers and magazines don't have to face. The print media have always had an option of running an editorial or not and of running replies to those editorials or not.

But the Communications Act, FCC regulations, and the rulings of the courts have sometimes told broadcasters they cannot editorialize, at other times told them they had to editorialize, and have had other content regulations that the print media are immune to.

Early on, the FRC said that there were not enough station frequencies for everyone to get every viewpoint across. The commissioners felt that important topics would always find a station willing to air them.

In 1940, however, the FCC renewed a station's license but issued a statement that most station owners read as being anti-editorializing. The ruling, called the Mayflower Decision, said the FCC was renewing the license but that "A truly free radio cannot be used to advocate the causes of the licensee."[40]

This had a chilling effect, in that stations afraid of not having their licenses renewed steered clear of controversial issues and editorials. But in 1949 the commission issued a report telling stations that they should "devote a reasonable percentage of their broadcast time to the presentation of news and programs devoted to the consideration and discussion of public issues of interest in the community served by the particular station."[41]

Now, after almost a decade, the FCC was telling stations that it was reversing the opinion outlined in Mayflower. The Fairness Doctrine was spawned from this report. The doctrine had two parts. The first said that stations must air issues that are so important to the community that it would be "unreasonable to ignore them completely." The second, and most controversial, part stated that stations airing such content had to make sure that "opposing views were given airtime," even if it had to give them airtime at no cost. For many years stations would give airtime to a spokesperson on behalf of a cause, and then at a later period or perhaps immediately following it, offer airtime to a spokesperson opposed to that view. A familiar phrase to audience members was "the views and opinions expressed are not necessarily those of this station, its owners, or management."

Section 315

Another section of the Communications Act that is similar to the Fairness Doctrine is Section 315. Originally part of the 1927 act (Section 18), it was included in the 1934 act verbatim: "If any licensee shall permit any person who is a legally qualified candidate for any public office to use a broadcasting station, he shall afford equal opportunities to all other such candidates."[42] The section went on to say that the licensee cannot censor the candidate but that there was no obligation to let any candidate on the air. So a broadcaster has a right to keep the gates shut and keep all candidates off the air, but if he or she opens the gate to allow one in, then they all can come in.

The FCC defines legally qualified candidates as those who have publicly announced their candidacies, are qualified to run under appropriate laws, and have qualified for the ballot, usually by petition in most elections or by being a strong write-in candidate.

As if it were not confusing enough, in 1959 Congress stepped forward and added an amendment to the section, Section 315(a). While the Fairness Doctrine was a set of rulings by the FCC, Section 315(a) was a law that told station owners, "A broadcast licensee shall afford reasonable opportunity for discussion of conflicting views on matters of public importance."[43] It also excluded candidate appearances that are on a bona fide newscast, bona fide news interview, or bona fide news documentary, if the appearance of the candidate is incidental to the presentation of the subject of the documentary, or on-the-spot news coverage of bona fide news events.

At the same time, a case before the Supreme Court, *Farmers Educational and Cooperative Union v. WDAY, Inc.*, resulted in the ruling that broadcasters could not be held liable for anything said by the candidates, nor could they censor anything that was said.[44]

While these instances are usually on television, there are cases where a candidate may be on radio. If a candidate for office is running for reelection and in his or her capacity as mayor or governor gives a press conference, a radio station covering it would not be obligated to supply equal time to the opponent. However, if the press conference was about the candidate's campaign and platform that would be a different story.

In 1967 Congress included advertising under Section 315(a). At the time, cigarette advertising on radio and especially television was prevalent. This ruling gave equal time to those organizations wishing to get the anti-smoking message across.

Personal Attack Rule

The personal attack rule, as the FCC applied it in a case against *Times-Mirror Broadcasting Co.*, said that if, "during the presentation of views on a controversial issue of public importance, an attack is made upon the honesty, character integrity or like personal qualities of an identified person or group" the station must contact the person under attack and supply either a tape, transcript, script, or summary of the show within a week and offer the person time on the air to respond.[45]

Red Lion Broadcasting Co. v. Federal Communications Commission, one of the biggest broadcast law cases, challenged this section. In 1964 a Pennsylvania radio station owned by Red Lion carried a fifteen-minute program featuring the Reverend Billy James Hargis. During his program the Reverend Hargis discussed a book, *Goldwater—Extremist on the Right*, by Fred Cook. Hargis said, among other things, that Cook had been fired from a job at a newspaper for making false charges against city officials, that he had worked for a publication that was affiliated with the Communist Party, that he had attacked J. Edgar Hoover, director of the Federal Bureau of Investigation, and the CIA, and that he had written his book to "smear and destroy Barry Goldwater." Someone contacted Cook and told him about the program. He demanded airtime according to the personal attack rule. The radio station refused. Eventually the FCC told the station that it had not met the rules it had set concerning personal attacks and that the station must allow Cook time on the air. Red Lion appealed to the Court of Appeals, which upheld the decision.[46]

At the same time, the Radio and Television News Directors Association (RTNDA) went to the Court of Appeals claiming that the Fairness Doctrine was unconstitutional. In this case the court ruled in favor of the RTNDA.

Red Lion appealed its case against the FCC to the Supreme Court, and the FCC likewise appealed the lower court's decision in *RTNDA v. Federal Communications Commission*. The Supreme Court decided that since both cases dealt with the same doctrine, it would hear both at the same time.

In its ruling the court said that "Believing that the specific application of the fairness doctrine in *Red Lion* and the promulgation of the regulations in *RTNDA*, are both authorized by Congress and enhance rather than abridge freedoms of speech and press protected by the First Amendment, we hold them valid and constitutional"[47] It continued, "Although broadcasting is clearly a medium affected by a First Amendment interest . . . differences in the characteristics of new media justify differences in the First Amendment standards applied to them."[48]

In 1974, partly due to the Supreme Court's ruling in *Miami Herald Publishing Co. v. Tornillo*,[49] the FCC stated that the Fairness Doctrine did not mean that a broadcaster must give exactly the same amount of time to opposing viewpoints. In fact, sometimes the opposing viewpoint deserved more time than the original, sometimes less. An attempt was also made to clarify what issues should be covered. The FCC said that this was up to the individual station to decide. The amount of coverage an issue was receiving in the news was only one factor; others were how much attention a topic was getting from the government and area leaders, and what type of impact the issue was likely to have in the community.[50]

To close what some broadcasters must have seen as a loophole, the FCC noted that a station couldn't develop a station policy that it would not air any opposing viewpoints: "the licensee must make a reasonable allowance for presentations by genuine partisans who actually believe in what they are saying."[51]

An additional amendment *§321(a)(7)* said that the FCC could revoke a license for

> "willful or repeated failure to allow reasonable access to or permit purchase of reasonable amounts of time for the use of a broadcasting station by a legally qualified candidate for Federal elective office on behalf of his candidacy."[52]

So although under Section 315 a station does not have to allow a candidate on the air, the section said that they must make reasonable access available to *federal* candidates. While the section covers candidates, it does not cover friends of the candidate or supporters, so the FCC developed the Zapple Doctrine, saying stations must treat the friends and supporters of one candidate the same as the friends and supporters of another.[53]

Other changes to Section 315 include the ruling in 1975 that debates were not *uses*, so that a station could cover a debate if only some of the candidates were invited, and not fear having to offer equal time. A third party, the League of Women Voters, had to present the debates at first, but the FCC decided in 1983, in the midst of deregulation, that stations could sponsor debates themselves.

As indicated above, candidates on the air because of bone fide news events do not trigger Section 315. But what about candidates on television shows, movies, records, radio hosts, and the like? Within recent memory, many performers became politicians. Professional wrestler Jesse "the Body" Ventura became governor of Minnesota. Actor Arnold Schwarzenegger became governor of California, and of course Ronald Reagan went from actor to president. While this is a hazy area, in a 1987 case, *Branch v. Federal Communications Commission*, the Supreme Court ruled that a newscaster who decided to run for office did not have the right to remain on the air during his candidacy. The court said in part that "nobody has ever thought that a candidate has the right to run for office and at the same time to avoid all personal sacrifice."[54]

The Fairness Doctrine remained part of the FCC rules until the mid-1980s, when a series of strange cases and judgments made their way through the commission and to the courts. First, the FCC issued a report in which it stated that the scarcity of the airwaves was no longer a problem and that the Fairness Doctrine did not assist freedom of speech but instead hindered it. Yet the FCC did not want to take action to eliminate it, claiming that it was up to the federal court system to interpret the Constitution. Then, in 1989 the Court of Appeals heard a case that once again changed the broadcast regulations.

Another portion of Section 315 seems almost absurd today. In 1980 the court was concerned that election campaigns could not afford a great deal of advertising time because they would be forced to pay the higher rate that anyone not buying a large number of spots would have to pay. Of course, Congress agreed, and Section 315(b) was born. Section 315(b) states that during the forty-five days before a primary election and sixty days before a general election candidates are to be charged the lowest rate that a station offers for that time period. In essence, broadcasters have to treat a candidate who only wants one or two spots the same as a car dealer buying one hundred or more. They must go to the lowest rate on their card. Stations cannot single out the candidates and make them pay more for a spot during other times, either. The section was eventually amended to only cover candidates running for federal office.[55]

In 1982 a station owned by the Meredith Corporation in Syracuse, New York, aired a series of commercials in favor of building the Nine Mile II nuclear plant. The Syracuse Peace Council, which opposed the nuclear plant, wanted equal airtime. When the station refused, the council took its case to the FCC. This time the FCC refused to enforce the Fairness Doctrine. The FCC ruled in favor of the group, but just a few months later issued a report saying that the Fairness Doctrine was no longer needed.[56] Later it announced that it would no longer enforce the rule.[57]

In the time between the filing of the suit and the ruling, the case of

Telecommunications Research and Action Center v. Federal Communication Commission decided, "There is nothing uniquely scarce about the broadcast spectrum," and that the Fairness Doctrine had not been codified by Congress, so the matter of whether or not the doctrine was a congressional law was no longer an issue.[58] Congress then passed the Fairness in Broadcasting Act of 1987, which "Expresses the findings of the Congress that the Fairness Doctrine: (1) fairly reflects the statutory obligations of broadcasters; (2) received statutory approval from the Congress in 1959; and (3) reasonably balances first amendment rights."[59] This bill was vetoed by President Reagan, effectively doing away with the Fairness Doctrine. The issue has arisen several times since then to meet the same fate.

The Telecommunications Act of 1996

Although the Communications Act of 1934 was amended in minor ways, the Telecommunications Act of 1996 was the first time the act faced major changes. Probably the biggest change was the lifting of the number of radio stations any one person or group could own. There was nothing keeping large media organizations from buying up radio stations across the country. The new version also lifted a previous ruling that stated that new owners had to hold a station for at least three years before selling it. Whereas the FCC once viewed stations shifting hands too often as detrimental to the community, they apparently no longer see it as a problem. The ruling also allowed the telephone companies to enter into the cable television market.

Safe Harbor

For many years broadcasters and the FCC discussed the concept of a safe harbor, hours in which broadcasters might air programming not appropriate for children. The Telecommunications Act set aside the hours between 10 P.M. and 6 A.M. as a time that children were unlikely to listen to radio.

Since the formation of the FCC the license renewal process had gone from a protracted process to a matter of literally mailing in a postcard. The new act made it even easier, in that renewal became almost automatic. The FCC would no longer allow competitive applications during the process.

The new act met with a great deal of controversy. Some people claimed that the mass consumption of smaller radio groups and independent stations equaled fewer voices and therefore was bad for free speech. Others, citing the fact that unlike the 1927 or 1934 acts, there were no longer only a handful of outlets, said that large groups could more effectively manage radio and provide much-needed resources to smaller markets. Over the next decade, the main impact of the Telecommunications Act has been the continued consolidation of radio ownership.

Emergency Alert System (EAS)

The FCC is also responsible for ensuring that the Emergency Broadcasting System (EBS), now known as the Emergency Alert System (EAS), remains in operation.

The original version of the alert system, Control of Electronic Radiation (CONELRAD), was a response to the mounting tensions of the Cold War. Established in 1951, it required that all stations except a few go off the air during an emergency. Those permitted to air had to broadcast on either 640 kHz or 1,240 kHz. Radio sets of the day even had special markings for those two frequencies. The U.S. government had a fear that incoming Soviet planes or missiles would use radio stations as navigational aids, as the Japanese had done at Pearl Harbor. With that in mind, local stations that were on the air were to keep switching among themselves.

The EBS debuted in 1963 as a means to alert people to emergencies and give the president a means of speaking to the entire country during such times. Stations when testing were supposed to:

1   turn their transmitters off for five seconds;
2   turn their transmitters on for five seconds;
3   turn their transmitters off for five seconds;
4   turn their transmitters on;
5   broadcast a 1,000 Hz tone for fifteen seconds to alert other stations; and
6   broadcast a "test" message so the public understood.[60]

If a station went off the air, the other stations would broadcast an emergency tone followed by an emergency message. But the original plan was flawed. If an EBS station lost power, it would trigger the sequence by alerting stations monitoring it.

One part of the EBS system seemed like something from an old spy movie. Somewhere next to the newswire machine, or later next to the speaker of the receiving unit at radio stations, hung a red envelope. The envelopes were clearly marked not to be opened unless an emergency message was transmitted. It is a safe bet to say more than one inquisitive DJ opened the envelope to see what was inside. This was hardly a top-secret code, and one can only guess that any enemy could have had access to it at any time. The envelope held inside it a list of dates and code words. In the event of a true emergency a message would come across starting with the code word assigned to that day. These were mostly two-syllable random words like *monkey* or *trouble*, but some were three or four syllables. If the message had the correct activation word, the message was genuine. There was also a termination word to sound the all-clear signal.[61]

The government altered the EBS in 1976 to include a two-tone signal. This system was more reliable. Every station had to run a weekly test of the EBS system. Stations broadcast the thirty-second tones when instructed at random times during the week. Local and state governments were given authority to use the system as a warning during times of natural disasters, like tornadoes or hurricanes, around the time of the transition to the EBS.

One flaw of the EBS system was that it still relied on each station relaying the message from station to station. In 1997 the new EAS went into effect. The new system has the advantage of remote triggering capability, eliminating the need for anyone to be at the stations.[62]

Under the EAS, not only the president, but also state and local governments are given access to the system in order to alert residents. The new system uses the same type of digital signal that the National Weather Service uses to activate the weather radio system. The EAS can automatically activate in the event of tornadoes, hurricanes, and the like. The most common uses for the system are presently to send out weather alerts and amber alerts for missing children. There is even talk about upgrading the system to connect to cell phones and to automatically turn on television and radio sets when an alert is sent.[63]

FCC Bureaus

The FCC also regulates broadcast television, cable television, cell phone, and satellite and telephone service in the United States. Obviously the chair and commissioners cannot perform these duties by themselves. The commission is divided into several divisions and subdivisions with separate heads and staffs, in order to efficiently regulate the industries. The Office of Engineering and Technology Bureau is dedicated to all technical aspects, from approving new equipment to managing the spectrum. The Field Operations Bureau is the police department of the airwaves. Members of this office are responsible for finding violators of FCC policy and enforcing the rules. The Common Carrier Bureau is the branch that regulates cell phones, satellite transmissions, and telephone. Common carriers are media offering services for a fee that is paid for and not accessible over free broadcast systems. The Private Radio Bureau regulates person-to-person radio services such as those found in emergency vehicles, in taxis, and on ships. The typical radio broadcaster should not have any dealings with this bureau except in the highly unlikely event that a technical malfunction of one user is interfering with another.

Television, radio, and cable TV all fall within the Media Bureau, formerly called the Mass Media Bureau. The Media Bureau is responsible for the licensing of all broadcast stations and enforcing rules pertaining to them. The Media Bureau is divided into seven smaller offices:

1   the Office of Broadcast License Policy;
2   the Video Division;
3   the Audio Division, for AM, FM, and digital;

4   the Policy Division;
5   the Industry Analysis Division;
6   the Engineering Division; and
7   the Office of Communications and Industry Information.

Day-to-day operations of the FCC are handled at the bureau level. Only when important matters of policy are involved do the commissioners step in.

FCC Notices to the Public

When contemplating any change to the rules or regulations, the FCC must by law take certain steps to ensure that the public is made aware of them. The FCC starts by posting a notice of inquiry (NOI) in the *Federal Register* and in the FCC's *Daily Digest*. The digest is available on the FCC's website or will be e-mailed to anyone who signs up for the free service. This is a process by which the commission is asking for input on an issue that it is studying. After a review of the NOI responses, the commission issues a notice of proposed rule making (NPRM). This is just a proposal asking for more feedback. Sometimes the FCC will issue both the NOI and NPRM at the same time. The next step in the process is the further notice of proposed rule making (FNPRM), if the FCC feels there are still issues and concerns. This is yet another chance for input from the industry and consumers. A report and order (R&O) is the result of the above processes. If it has enough information on the topic, the FCC can make a new rule, make changes to an existing rule, or do nothing. The commission posts its decision in the *Federal Register* with the date that it will begin enforcement. Broadcasters may not use "ignorance" of the new rule as a defense, just as with any other law. Therefore radio stations and personnel subscribe to a variety of industry magazines both in print and online to keep up with FCC actions.

For anyone who is opposed to the R&O, there is a thirty-day window from posting in which to file a petition for reconsideration. This simply requests that the FCC take another look at the policy. The FCC will then issue a memorandum opinion and order (MO&O) or an order on reconsideration that either makes changes to the rule or announces that the rule will remain as issued.[64]

Questions for Further Thought

1   Is the "marketplace of ideas" still a valid model?

2   Should the safe harbor hours be expanded, eliminated, or remain the same?

3   Why has the FCC and the courts seemingly reversed themselves on occasion?

4   Are the current limits on radio station ownership good or bad for the industry, owners, and consumers?

Shop Talk

Affiliates: Broadcast stations owned by individuals or companies other than the networks that air network programming.

Border blasters: Radio stations located on the Mexican side of the Rio Grande that were not limited in power by any treaty. Often heard as far away as Canada.

Brinkley, Dr. John (1885–1941): Innovator of border blaster radio stations. Many attribute his stations to spreading "hillbilly" music across the country.

Chilling effect: Theory that if one is afraid of punishment if a mistake happens, then he or she will avoid the situation entirely. Mainly related to libel cases such as *New York Times v. Sullivan.*

Fairness Doctrine: FCC statement that stations should cover controversial topics and that equal time had to be given to opposing viewpoints.

Federal Communications Commission (FCC): Body of the U.S. government charged with establishing rules and regulations governing broadcasting, cable television, telephone, satellite television, the Internet, and satellite and cell phones.

Federal Radio Commission (FRC): Predecessor of the FCC. Body organized to regulate the radio broadcasting industry (1927–1934).

General Order 40: Ruling that established clear channel radio stations across the country.

Media Bureau: Office within the FCC responsible for television and radio.

Owned and operated (O&O): Stations owned and operated by one of the networks.

Personal attack rule: FCC decision that if a person suffered a verbal attack he or she must be notified and offered time to respond.

Safe harbor: Time when content ruled to be indecent is permissible (10 P.M. to 6 A.M.).

Section 315: Part of Communications Act that places certain requirements on licensees with regard to political advertising.

Seven-seven-seven rule (7–7–7): Ruling that stated that no one person or company could own more than seven AM radio stations, seven FM radio stations, and seven TV stations. In addition, the stations could not reach more than 25 percent of the national audience. This was seen as a way to keep networks and others from controlling too much of the content.

Sustaining programs: Radio shows that are not funded by advertising. Usually community affairs programming.

Libel and Other Laws

Many laws that affect the radio industry are also relevant to all communications media. This chapter will delve into some of those issues with an eye to how they can affect the radio broadcaster.

It should be noted that most cases occur when the First Amendment rights of the media are weighed against the rights of individuals. Sometimes the media wins and sometimes the media loses. There are no set rules. A court may rule one way and the next week rule another way. In many instances, this results in a chilling effect.

Copyright

The governments of the United States and other countries have long recognized that intellectual property is as valuable as any other type of property. The ideas, and more importantly the expression of those ideas, take many forms. As an inventor may patent his or her invention, the artist can copyright his or her art. One may trace the copyright in various forms to shortly after the invention of moveable type. Copyright laws began in the United States around 1790. At that time, the law protected the author of any book, map, or chart for fourteen years, after which the copyright holder had the option of renewing it. The law's protection was slowly extended to include more media. By the 1870s,the law also included musical compositions, prints, paintings, and photographs.

In 1909 Congress revised the copyright law. The copyright law has continuously been adapted as new technology develops. The twentieth century saw the invention of radio, television, motion pictures, the phonograph, and the computer, to name just a few innovations. Congress began work on a new copyright law in the 1950s but didn't pass the current version until the Copyright Revision Act of 1976.

According to the law, things that are copyrightable are "original works of authorship fixed in any tangible medium of expression, now known or later developed, from which they can be perceived, reproduced, or otherwise communicated, either directly or with the aid of a machine or device."[1]

This means, first, that the work must be original. One cannot take a song or story that is the work of someone else and copyright it. While there are certain instances where one may use a portion of another's work, the protection of the creative process is the underlying theme of this law.

Second, the work has to be in a tangible medium; this includes photos, movies, newspapers, records, and tapes—anything that another person can see or hear. At first glance it may appear that a radio broadcast cannot be copyrighted because it is intangible. But if the DJ or station makes tapes of the show, those tapes can be copyrighted.

A person cannot copyright ideas or lists. If one could copyright a list or an idea, it would be easy to copyright all musical notes and all the words and letters in the alphabet. Then anyone using them would have to pay royalties. No one can copyright the note C# or a G-minor chord, but the Beatles song "Birthday" is copyrighted. The unique arrangement of the notes and words make it so. Most people do not realize it, but the song "Happy Birthday" is a copyrighted work. Anyone may write a song about birthdays, but they cannot use more than four bars of anyone else's music or use the exact wording of another's song or copyrighted work. The courts have ruled that this expression is where the creativity lies.

The law gives copyright owners certain rights, as the word implies. The copyright holder has the following rights:

1 To *reproduce* the work in copies or phonorecords;
2 To prepare *derivative works* based upon the work;
3 To *distribute copies or phonorecords* of the work to the public by sale or other transfer of ownership, or by rental, lease, or lending;
4 To *perform the work publicly*, in the case of literary, musical, dramatic, and choreographic works, pantomimes and motion pictures and other audiovisual work;
5 To *display the work publicly*, in the case of literary, musical, dramatic, and choreographic works, pantomimes and pictorial, graphic or

sculptural works, including the individual images of a motion picture and other audiovisual work; and

6   In the case of sound recordings, to *perform the work publicly* by means of a *digital audio transmission*.[2]

The copyright holder may also authorize another party to do any of the above.

For works created after January 1, 1978, the copyright lasts the length of the owner's life plus seventy years. If more than one person holds the copyright, as in a collaborative work, the copyright runs until seventy years after the last collaborator's death. The copyright for works made for hire is for ninety-five years from publication, or 120 years from creation, whichever is shorter.[3] However, the copyright owner or his or her heirs must continue to enforce the copyright.

Public Domain

After a copyright has expired, it is in the public domain. At this point anyone may use the work without paying royalties or obtaining permission. Works such as "Silent Night" are in the public domain. However, if an artist records and releases the song, they can claim that their arrangement is unique and therefore copyright their version of the song. They do not own "Silent Night," but do own their interpretation of it.

The movie *It's a Wonderful Life* is a good example of the public domain rule. When the movie was first made, copyright lasted for twenty-eight years and was then up for renewal. The movie had not been a hit, and the studio Republic Films decided to not renew the copyright.

Once the movie was in the public domain, television stations began airing it. It cost them nothing, and the movie became so popular that some stations aired it twenty-four hours a day leading up to Christmas. In 1993 a revised version of the copyright law allowed Republic to regain the rights, claiming that it owned the copyright to the original screenplay, and the movie was a derivative work.[4] Adaptations or derivative works are creations based on an original copyrighted piece. Only the copyright holder is allowed to make *Friday the 13th Part XX*, or a movie based on a novel or short story.

The right to perform the work is where ASCAP, BMI, and SESAC come into play. A performance may be live, on CD, broadcast, or recorded in any number of ways. The point is that the composer or author has the right to authorize the performance and receive payment for this use. The stations do not own the copyright, and in many instances they do not even own the CD. It is common for CDs that are distributed by record labels to have a sticker or printed message that the disc is "For promotional use only" or "Not for sale," or that "Sale or other transfer is prohibited," or that the disc "Must be returned on demand of record company." However, if a station buys a sound effects library or a commercial music library, it can purchase a buy-out. This means that the owner of the copyright, the company, is giving license to the station for unlimited use of the music for commercials, jingles, or other productions.

The author, owning the distribution rights, decides whether to publish, sell, lend, or rent the work.

Digital technology now allows for the copying of music or other digital formats without loss of quality. A file shared online should sound close to the original, which makes copyright infringement much easier.

The case brought against Napster in 2000 was one in which file sharing and downloading of music files were at issue. In the 1984 case of *Sony Corporation of America v. Universal Cities Studios*, the court ruled that having video cassette recorders (VCRs) was not an infringement of copyright laws, but instead, "It is intended to motivate the creative activity of authors and inventors by the provision of a special reward, and to allow the public access to the products of their genius after the limited period of exclusive control has expired."[5] The court saw the VCR as a way for the home viewer to record television programs for watching at a later time or rewatching later. This was before the widespread movie rental business and pirating of movies was even an issue.

Yet the Napster case was quite confusing to everyone. In the original case, the court ruled that Napster was guilty of copyright infringement, even though the owner was not directly violating the copyrights, and it had to cease operations.[6] Upon appeal, the Ninth Circuit Court of Appeals said that Napster could go back online as soon as it could stop the sharing of copyrighted music.[7]

A similar case is *MGM Studios, Inc., v. Grokster, Ltd., and StreamCast Networks, Inc.* Twenty-eight of the largest entertainment companies joined together in suing Grokster and StreamCast, saying that they were encouraging copyright infringement with their peer-to-peer (P2P) file-sharing programs. The same lower court that had ruled against Napster said it could not rule against the new companies because it needed proof that they had knowledge of specific instances of copyright infringement and did nothing to block them.[8] On June 27, 2005, the Supreme Court handed down its decision: those who develop and promote technology for copyright infringement can be sued.

> We hold that one who distributes a device with the object of promoting its use to infringe copyright, as shown by the clear expression or other affirmative steps taken to foster infringement, is liable for the resulting acts of infringement by third parties.[9]

With this decision the case was reversed and remanded back to the lower court for re-examination. As of this writing the case has not been reheard.

The Copyright Act of 1976 (amended in 1989) says that the copyright is applied the moment the creative product is "fixed in a copy or phonograph record for the first time." As soon as an artist types a script, writes a song on paper, or otherwise creates a piece, the artist owns the copyright.[10]

There are really several different types of copyright. An unpublished work is afforded copyright protection from its inception. One may use the copyright notice in the form of a copyright symbol, ©, the word *Copyright*, or in the case of broadcasting a statement such as "this broadcast is copyrighted," all followed by the year and name of the owner. For sound reproductions such as CDs, tapes, and the like, the © symbol is replaced by (p), indicating a registered work that includes these markings but has also been registered with the U.S. Copyright Office.

The first three assume that the creator of the work is the copyright holder. In this case it is in the best interest of the holder to register the work. If the work is properly registered and someone infringes upon the work for profit, the copyright holder is entitled to any money made off that work.

If a person writes something or produces a graphic design, or produces some other creative product as part of his or her job, it is considered work for hire. In these cases the person or company paying for the work owns the copyright. An applicant files two copies of the work, along with a simple form (downloadable at www.copyright.Gov/forms/), and a fee of thirty dollars with the U.S. Copyright Office in Washington, D.C., to register the work. Even if a work is not registered, two copies of all published works must go to the Library of Congress, although there are certain exemptions.

From time to time, broadcasters face charges of copyright infringement. In order for a lawsuit to be successful it is up to the plaintiff who files the suit to prove two main points:

1   That the person or company being sued had *access* to the copyrighted work. If the work was unpublished and no one ever had access to it, it is humanly impossible to steal from it. For this reason, most movie, television, and other media outlets will not accept unsolicited works.

2   Even if a person had access to a previous work, the plaintiff must prove that there was *substantial similarity* between the two works. There are hundreds of morning DJs doing a similar format, but it is not legal to have someone copy a radio program and mail it to another DJ in another town so that he may repeat the same comedy bits.

Fair Use

Broadcasters and academics have a special clause written into the copyright law, the concept of fair use. Congress notes that there are benefits to society in allowing parts of copyrighted works to be used at times. The fair use defense takes four things into account:

1   the purpose and character of the use;

2   the nature of the work;

3   the amount and substantiality of the work that was used; and

4   the effect on the potential market for that work.

Many things fall under the "purpose and character" of the use. A broadcaster covering an event as part of a newscast that includes any incidental copyrighted material in the broadcast is protected. It is also legal to read a short passage of copyrighted texts or to play a clip from a song if the purpose is to further discuss the work.

Another area that falls under the guise of fair use is parody. The courts have been unpredictable upon this matter. In some cases they have ruled that parodies of popular songs are a valid expression while at other times they have ruled that they are a copyright infringement designed to make money while the original work suffers. In a landmark ruling, the Supreme Court unanimously said that a 2 Live Crew song was a parody of the Roy Orbison song *Pretty Woman*. Applying the above fair use criteria, it said that the song was not the same as a bootleg copy because the new song would not hurt the sale of the older record.[11] But in a later case, it ruled that the book *The Juice Is NOT in the Hat* was a satire and not a parody of *The Cat in the Hat*.[12] The fine line between satire and parody is often hard to define. Generally in a parody one imitates the style of another's work for humorous effects, whereas in satire one uses a creative work to hold someone, or a group, up for scorn and to point out their faults. Academics and freelance writers may use copyrighted materials for teaching and research following the proper guidelines.

Copying a work for personal use does not fall under fair use, although software manufacturers often grant the right to make a backup copy or allow users to put one copy of a program on a desktop computer and another on a laptop. However, making a copy of a CD (music or software) to give a friend does keep the copyright owner(s) from making money.

The nature of the work is also a key deciding factor in judging copyright infringement suits. As mentioned earlier, lists are generally not copyrightable, as there is little creativity involved; however, a piece of art or literature is a creative work.

The amount of the work and the substantiality of the portion that is used can play a huge role in copyright suits. Reading one page from a 200-page book on the air is probably proper, but reading 150 pages over the course of several weeks is not. By the same token, reading one page of a two-page poem would probably be a violation.

In a famous television case, a television news crew videotaped and replayed a human cannonball who was appearing at a local carnival. The court ruled that even though the clip was only a few seconds, it showed the best part of his routine, so copyright had been violated. So one also has to be sure that the piece used is not vital.[13] This is akin to reading the last page of a mystery novel on the air and giving away who the murderer is. This will hurt sales of the book in that no one will want to read a mystery if the mystery has been ruined.

Libel

Defamation means words that damage a person's or business's reputation or standing in a community, that attack a person's or business's character and/or professional abilities. There are two types of defamation, but the most common one in media is libel. Written defamation is libel, while spoken defamation is slander. On the surface it may seem that radio defamation would be considered slander, but courts view broadcasting as a printed medium because portions are either prerecorded or scripted. Additionally, a person suing for slander must prove financial loss, whereas those suing for libel generally do not and usually can expect higher judgments.

Today's average libel suit costs a defendant thousands of dollars even if he or she wins the case. Just as doctors have malpractice insurance, most broadcasters have libel insurance, but with the costs skyrocketing, many can no longer afford it.

There are six things that a plaintiff must prove to win a libel suit:

1 that there was defamatory language, that the defendant was defamed;
2 that the defendant was identified in the statement;
3 that the statement was published (or broadcast);
4 that there is fault on behalf of the person or organization being sued;
5 that the statement(s) made were false; and
6 that there was personal harm inflicted upon the defendant.

Defamatory language is sometimes tricky to pin down. What may be defamatory in a newscast may not always seem so at first. One cannot say someone has been convicted of a crime unless they actually have been convicted. Many suits filed against broadcast stations come out of newscasts when an anchors or reporter says, "John Smith, who murdered the woman, was arrested today." For safety, the media assumes a person's innocence until a court proves otherwise. Thus, *accused murderer* and *police arrested a man they believe to be a murderer* are familiar phrases in the media.

There are many, many other ways to defame a person or business. Saying that a cigarette manufacturer was marketing its product to children resulted in a Chicago television station losing over $3 million in a lawsuit.[14]

Questioning a person's ability to do a job or his or her integrity, such as calling a lawyer a shyster or a doctor a quack can be defamatory. Usually saying someone is "all thumbs" isn't bad. If he or she is a neurosurgeon, however, this may be defamation.

Just a simple mix-up can be defamation in some cases. In one case, a reporter rushing to get a story on the air announced that a person living in a certain town had admitted to plotting to break into two businesses. What the reporter didn't realize was that there were two people with the same name, one living in a nearby town. He had chosen the wrong person.[15]

Saying Mary Smith was seen leaving *1224* Maple Lane for work this morning at 7 A.M., might be defamatory if Mary actually lives at *1226* and her neighbor's wife is out of town. It is implying that Mary did not spend the night in her own house.

Identification does not always have to be by name. One may defame a group of people if that group is not unduly large. For example, *Time* magazine printed a story saying that a town's depressed economy had led many business owners to burn down their buildings to collect insurance money. A group of men who owned two buildings that had burned tried to sue the magazine. But the court would not allow it because there had been over fifty fires that were attributed to arson in the past decade. The story did not name them and it could have actually applied to at least two hundred people.[16]

Neiman-Marcus v. Lait

The case of *Neiman-Marcus v. Lait* (1952) once again brought up this issue. Jack Lait and Lee Mortimer had written a book titled *U.S.A. Confidential.* In it they stated that some of the models and some of the Neiman-Marcus saleswomen were call girls and that most of the salesmen were gay. The court looked at the number of people from each group in making its decision.

There were 9 models, 25 salesmen, and 382 saleswomen in Neiman-Marcus's only store at the time. According to the court, the book had libeled all of the models. This was because they constituted a very small group. The same held true for the salesmen because of the word *most*. Lait did not libel the saleswomen, however. Their large number meant that no one could be identified according to the court. In announcing its decision, the court cited precedent where large groups had lost libel suits in the past.[17]

This case also set a precedent in saying that businesses may also be damaged by libel: "it cannot be said as a matter of law that a corporation cannot be damaged in a business way by a publication that it employs seriously undesirable personnel."[18]

A publication is anything that is printed, distributed, or broadcast. As soon as it hits the airwaves so that a third party or parties can hear it, it has met the broadcast standard. If one makes a comment to someone in private, it is neither slander nor libel. A third person must hear the comment.

Fault is more difficult to prove. The courts have given different media more leeway than others. If one can prove that a media outlet did not check sources, or in some other manner showed a disregard for the truth, fault may rest upon them. The court takes into account, however, the nature of the story and the medium used. If a story is breaking and a radio station rushes to get it on the air, the courts are usually a little more forgiving than if a story is a feature or documentary that took a month to produce. By the same token, a daily newspaper will have more freedom than a monthly magazine. If one has a month versus a day to prepare a story, the court expects more research. This does not, however, relieve daily media from responsibility.

In many cases the content of the actual news story may determine how much research should go into investigating it. For example, stories that seem outlandish will be given less leeway by the courts than stories that seem more viable. The plausibility that a person who has a long arrest record of past drug convictions has been arrested once again is quite high. The plausibility of a story based on an anonymous tip that the president of the local garden society, someone who has no arrest record, has been arrested for drug possession, should raise a red flag.

As you have undoubtedly learned elsewhere, the best defense is to have at least two corroborating accounts. This is the reason fact checking is stressed in newsrooms. This does bring up an interesting point. Some people are "libel proof." A person convicted of murder will not win a case against a station reporting that he or she owes back taxes, or parking fines. The courts consider a convicted murderer as having no reputation to protect.

The final item, harm to a person or business, is an intangible thing that is hard to prove or disprove.

Damages

The court does allow for general damages, the amount of money proven to have been lost because of the actions of the defendant (intangible items such as loss of business, embarrassment, and so on), as well as punitive damages, also known as exemplary damages. If a story is aired that a local restaurant was cited by the health department for vermin and other health violations, but in actuality it had not, the owner of the establishment may easily show a drop in the number of customers and revenue following the report and project future losses. The owner may also claim mental anguish, loss of standing with the industry, and so on. This would be an example of general damages.

Punitive damages are fines in excess of general damages. These fines are punishment to the defendant and may exceed millions of dollars.

Defenses for Libel Cases

The easiest and best defense against a libel case in the United States has been and will always be the truth. Usually if a case has reached the courts, there is a good chance that publication has occurred. Proving that the facts are true gives the defendant a perfect defense. A person reported to be a bigamist who indeed has two wives living in two different cities has no grounds for a libel suit.

A reporter who has more than two credible witnesses or sources can show that there was an effort made to verify the facts. The courts expect more accuracy from reporters who have had more time to work on a story or broadcast. A reporter may sometimes promise source anonymity. In this case giving that name will damage the reporter's ability to get information from sources in the future. Therefore one must weigh the pros and cons of such promises.

A reporter can use the identification defense. One argues in this instance that not enough information was given to identify any specific person or persons of a larger group. This can be a risky defense and is usually not one that is preferred.

In some cases both sides will settle on damages before the trial is finished. It is very hard to prove how much suffering a libeled person has gone through. If a lawyer knows that the case is lost, he or she may just try to argue that the amount requested is too high and settle out of court.

One may invoke other special defenses during a libel case. These defenses fall under the category of qualified privilege. Members of the press may report discussions during legislative and court proceedings, even if the information may be false or damaging. Members of the legislature and those in court are immune from libel and slander laws in those settings. The courts have ruled that such actions would hinder free and open dialogue. Therefore, reporters also have no burden when accurately reporting what was said.

Another defense is fair comment. Members of the media may, just like an individual, express opinions. An opinion cannot be true or false, because it is one's own views. A movie reviewer may say, "In my opinion that was the worst movie ever made." Because this not a news story but a criticism it is covered under fair comment. However, one cannot hide a personal attack behind fair comment. A DJ may say, for example, "In my opinion my neighbors are terrible parents and their kids should be taken from them." This is probably not fair comment, but libel. Even under fair comment there must be a component of truth. If there is no evidence of neglect or other wrongdoing this will probably be considered actual malice.

There is another important defense against libel. It will be useful to examine the case that gave birth to the defense. What is perhaps the most important case in media law occurred in 1968, a year that many consider to be a watershed year. Even though it was a newspaper case, it has relevance to all media.

The New York Times Co. v. Sullivan

This case involved a full-page ad taken out by a group of civil rights activists and celebrities entitled "Heed Their Rising Voice" that ran in the New York paper on March 29, 1960. The ad outlined civil rights abuses against African Americans in several cities. Among the cities mentioned was Montgomery, Alabama. The ad stated that "In Montgomery, Alabama, after students sang 'My Country, 'Tis of Thee' on the State Capitol steps, their leaders were expelled from school, and truckloads of police armed with shotguns and tear-gas ringed the Alabama State College Campus. When the entire student body protested to state authorities by refusing to re-register, their dining hall was padlocked in an attempt to starve them into submission."[19] Referring to Dr. Martin Luther King, it continued, "They have bombed his home almost killing his wife and child. They assaulted his person. They have arrested him seven times—for 'speeding,' 'loitering' and similar 'offenses.' And now they have charged him with 'perjury.'"[20]

One of the commissioners for the city of Montgomery, L. B. Sullivan, who oversaw the operation of the police department, requested a retraction to the ad. The *Times* refused, and Sullivan brought suit against the newspaper, citing what he claimed were inaccuracies in the ad. He claimed that the students actually sang the national anthem, not "My Country, 'Tis of Thee." He also said that the nine expelled students we expelled by the school board of education for demanding service at a lunch counter and not for the capitol protest, that the dining hall was not padlocked, that *most*—not *all*—of the students protested and that while the police were standing by, they did not "ring" the campus. Further, he claimed that Dr. King had been arrested only four times, that his assaults had come years earlier, that there was nothing linking the police to the bombings of his home, and that King had been cleared of his perjury charges.

In a landmark decision the court ruled that Sullivan was a public figure. As such he cannot expect the same degree of protection from libel as the average citizen. The court noted that if the media had to fear a lawsuit each time they reported about an elected official or public figure, they would be less likely to cover important issues and would therefore suffer a chilling effect.[21]

Subsequent cases went on to include celebrities such as actors and singers, as well as local public figures. Someone may be a public figure in one small town or on a campus but not in other areas. A person may be a public figure where one controversial issue is concerned but not in other parts of his or her life.

The only way for a public figure to win a defamation case is to show actual malice. Under actual malice a plaintiff must prove that the defendant knew that the information was false or showed a reckless disregard for the truth. Evidence that the defendant had doubts about a story's authenticity may also meet this criterion.

Censorship

Censorship is often synonymous with prior restraint. An attempt by the FCC or any other governing body to keep something from airing is prior restraint. Literally, it is trying to restrain the broadcaster from airing content. The Supreme Court says this is a direct violation of the First Amendment, as it is censorship. However, broadcasters may be subject to punishment for airing certain materials, such as obscenity, after the fact. One might compare this to the movie *Minority Report*, where the police are able to see into the future, predict murders, and apprehend the criminals in advance. We cannot see into the future so no one knows what will or will not be said or broadcast until it has gone over the air.

Interestingly, up to a third of censorship cases that do go to trial arise from local school boards and government bodies censoring library books or class content. These attempts at censorship are usually overturned when appealed to a court, but in the meantime the book, CD, video, or other material is off of shelf. Often materials may be off the shelf while the case works itself through the system, long enough for it to no longer be an issue. Some of the materials that have faced censorship include:

The Harry Potter Series	(J. K. Rowlins)
Of Mice and Men	(John Steinbeck)
I Know Why the Caged Bird Sings	(Maya Angelou)
The Adventures of Huckleberry Finn	(Mark Twain)
The Catcher in the Rye	(J. D. Salinger)
Goosebumps series	(R. L. Stine)
A Wrinkle in Time	(Madeleine L'Engle)[22]

Hazelwood School District et al. v. Kuhlmeier et al.

Students in Hazelwood, Missouri, were taking a high school journalism class that wrote and edited the school newspaper, *Spectrum*. The principal of the school routinely read the proofs of the newspaper before it went to the printer. In this case he deleted two articles he did not want appearing, one concerning pregnant students and the other about coping with the divorce of parents.

The students declared that this violated their First Amendment rights. The case made it all the way to the Supreme Court, where the justices ruled that the fact that the newspaper was part of a class assignment meant that there were no First Amendment issues and that students are not guaranteed the same rights afforded to adults in other settings.

The court said that it would look at three criteria when deciding this case. First, whether the newspaper (or one could infer radio station or other medium) is supervised by a faculty member; second, if the paper was designed to impart particular knowledge or skills to students and its audience; and, third, whether the school's name and resources are used.[23]

Generally speaking, however, obscenity is the only type of speech that is afforded no First Amendment protection.

Obscenity

In recent years a great deal of attention has centered on obscenity, indecency, and profanity on radio programs. These cases especially include shock jock programs like those of Howard Stern and Bubba the Love Sponge.

The number of complaints brought by the audience against broadcasters has risen substantially over the last several years.

Year	Shows	Complaints
2000	111 (85 radio)	111
2001	152 (113 radio)	346
2002	389 (185 radio)	13,922
2003	375 (122 radio)	202,032
2004	314 (145 radio)	1,405,419[24]

Until recently, the FCC could fine radio stations airing indecent programs up to $27,500 per day. The commissioners raised that number to $32,500 per day in 2004, with a cap of $325,000.[25] For small stations and local DJs, this fine can be quite a detriment. For some nationally syndicated programs, however, one can make an argument that the fines are worth the publicity. Each fine adds to the program's status, is much cheaper than buying advertising with any of the national media, and the amount of the fine can easily be made up by the charge one advertiser pays for a spot on the show. However, the FCC has recently added bite to back up the fines, as outlined later.

But before examining today's media, one must first look at how the present obscenity laws were developed. The main problem is how does one decide what is obscene and what isn't? Many people have used Supreme Court Justice Potter Stewart's statement "I know it when I see it." But that really isn't a good guideline to have when facing fines and a potential loss of a broadcasting license.

Two major cases decided by the Supreme Court give us our definition of what is obscene, and, in typical fashion, the definitions leave a wide margin for interpretation. Both of these cases resulted from the use of the mail, and not the media. More importantly, note that both cases involve the censoring of obscenity. This is because the First Amendment protects most types of speech.

Roth v. the United States

Roth mailed the books *American Aphrodite* and several circulars through the U.S. mail. He received a sentence of five years in jail and a fine of $5,000. The Supreme Court established several things in this case:

- Obscenity is not protected under the First Amendment.
- Obscenity is material "utterly without redeeming social importance."
- Sex and obscenity are not synonymous. Obscene material is material that appeals to the "prurient interest," according to the Roth test ("Whether to the average person, applying contemporary community standards, the dominant theme of the material taken as a whole appeals to the prurient interest").[26]

When identifying the average person the court noted that the trial judge had instructed the jury that "The test is not whether it would arouse sexual desires or sexual impure thoughts in those comprising a particular segment of the community, the young, the immature, or the highly prudish or would leave another segment, the scientific or highly educated or the so-called worldly wise and sophisticated indifferent and unmoved."[27] But that they should use their understanding of how the community as a whole would view the work: "you are to consider the community as a whole, young and old, educated and uneducated, the religious and the irreligious—men, women and children."[28] This was expanded upon in the case of *Miller v. California*.

Miller v. California

Miller was arrested and convicted, under a California state law, for conducting a mass mailing to advertise four books and a film. The ads were explicit, and the court found them to be obscene. The court in its ruling said that states can censor materials if they find them obscene under a three-part test:

1   The Roth test: it is necessary to establish that the average person, applying contemporary community standards, would find that the work as a whole appeals to the prurient interest.
2   Materials must depict or describe in a "patently offensive" way sexual conduct specifically defined by applicable state law.
3   The work, taken as a whole, must lack "serious literary, artistic, political or scientific value." This last section is commonly referred to as the SLAPS test.[29]

The court also said that all three criteria must be met before anything can be considered obscene. In delivering the opinion for the court, Chief Justice Burger wrote, "This case involves the application of a State's criminal obscenity statute to a situation in which sexually explicit materials have been thrust by aggressive sales action upon unwilling recipients who had in no way indicated any desire to receive such materials."[30]

So what does this mean and where does it leave broadcasters? First it draws a line between that which is pornographic and that which is obscene. According the court, these are not the same. Something that is simply sexually provocative, but not patently offensive, or if it has serious artistic qualities, or literary value, cannot be obscene. Often, excessive sexual detail or the repetitive nature of the description can make something obscene.

The first case to link obscenity to a sound recording occurred in Florida in 1987. A record-store owner was arrested for selling 2 Live Crew's album *2 Live Is What We Are* to a fourteen-year-old girl. Although charged with a felony, the court acquitted him. When the group's *As Nasty as They Wanna Be* became a hit in 1990, the American Family Association convinced the governor of Florida, Bob Martinez, to see if the album was indeed obscene. A decision by Judge Mel Grossman said that it was probably obscene, and the Dade County sheriff alerted record stores that selling the album could lead to arrest. Later that year, Judge Jose Gonzalez ruled it obscene. In the federal court ruling, the judge noted that the nudity itself isn't obscene, nor are four-letter words, but the audio message of the CD repeated over and over was analogous to a camera with a zoom lens. Police arrested another store owner for selling the album to an undercover officer. At an adults-only show in Hollywood, Florida, the police also arrested several band members. The courts once again acquitted everyone. Two years later, a court of appeals overturned the ruling that the record was obscene. The Supreme Court upheld the court of appeals' ruling stating that it was not obscene.[31]

Federal Communications Commission v. Pacifica Foundation

Another landmark broadcast case deals with indecency on a radio station owned by the Pacifica Foundation. On a Tuesday at 2 P.M. a DJ played a cut from a comedy album by George Carlin. The routine airing was entitled "Filthy Words." It is more commonly known as "The Seven Words That Can't Be Said on the Air." The routine aired for twelve minutes and went to great lengths to use the seven words in various funny configurations. A listener who was driving with his young son heard the broadcast and complained to the FCC. Pacifica's defense was that it had aired a warning before the broadcast. The court, in its ruling, indicated that it was possible the father did not hear it. Further, the FCC, after its investigation, said it had the authority to sanction the station under 18 U.S.C. 1464 (1976 ed.), which forbids "any obscene, indecent, or profane language by means of radio communications."[32] The FCC gave four reasons for broadcast content having different content regulations than other media:

1   the likelihood that children could tune in to a broadcast;
2   since radio receivers are in the home, the audience should be given extra protection from having something unwanted thrust upon them;
3   unconsenting adults may also tune in without a warning that offensive language is being used; and
4   because of the scarcity of the spectrum the government has to govern licensees in the public interest.

The Supreme Court agreed with the FCC. In part it said that it is unrealistic to think that a warning at the beginning of a program is sufficient, since listeners may be tuning in at any time. On this point the court also stated, "To say that one may avoid further offense by turning off the radio when he hears indecent language is like saying that the remedy for an assault is to run away after the first blow. One may hang up on an indecent phone call, but that option does not give the caller a constitutional immunity or avoid a harm that has already taken place."[33]

The court also noted that children have access to radio, and "Pacifica's broadcast could have been enlarged a child's vocabulary in an instant."[34]

In 1987 the FCC took action against three radio stations, issuing only warnings at the time. In the first case, a noncommercial station owned by Pacifica in Los Angeles aired excerpts from a play, *Jerker*, in which two homosexuals dying of AIDS discuss their sexual fantasies over the telephone. The FCC rejected the station's defense that the piece needed to be taken within the context of the program and surrounding discussion. The FCC found the material to be patently offensive.[35]

In the second case, the FCC found that a campus radio station had aired a song, 'Makin Bacon,' that had patently offensive descriptions of "sexual organs and activities as measured by contemporary community standards for the broadcast medium."[36]

The third case, an issue that is still ongoing, began when the commission cited the *Howard Stern Show* and Infinity Broadcasting airing its content. In this instance, the FCC said that it would "apply the *generic* definition of broadcast indecency."[37]

On reconsideration, the FCC decided to establish safe harbor hours for broadcasters. In the Pacifica case, the commission turned the case over to the justice department, but the department declined to prosecute.

Under Title 18 of the U.S. Code, "Whoever utters any obscene, indecent, or profane language by means of radio communication shall be fined under this title or imprisoned not more than two years, or both."[38] While the FCC is charged with overseeing such matters, it usually limits the penalties to cash forfeitures.

In the Infinity case, the commission decided that the content was not indecent. However, in the University of California case it ruled that the song was.

All three cases went to court on appeal, the plaintiffs stating that the FCC had in effect changed the rules without telling anyone. The court decided that the safe harbor hours were arbitrary in nature and overturned them. They agreed with the Infinity decision and questioned whether the audience of the college station was actually large enough for the broadcast to pose a risk.

In 2001 the FCC issued a policy statement concerning their interpretation of obscenity. First, it reiterated that obscenity is not protected speech and therefore is never allowed on the radio (or television). Then to define obscenity it went back to the Miller test. To be considered obscene, a work (1) must describe or depict sexual or excretory organs or activities; and (2) must be patently offensive as measured by contemporary community standards for the broadcast medium. The "contemporary community standards" criterion is a national standard that considers the sensibilities of the average broadcast member.

They also noted that "The determination as to whether certain programming is patently offensive is not a local one and does not encompass any particular geographic area. Rather, the standard is that of an average broadcast viewer or listener and not the sensibilities of any individual complainant."[39]

They also cited three things that they would consider in its decisions: (1) the explicitness or graphic nature of the description or depiction of sexual or excretory organs or activities; (2) whether the material dwells on or repeats at length descriptions of sexual or excretory organs or activities; and (3) whether the material appears to pander or is used to titillate, or whether the material appears to have been presented for its shock value.[40]

Over the course of radio's history there have been many instances of self-censorship by station owners and record labels. Station owners have historically censored songs that they were offended by, thought would offend the community and their listeners, or felt could bring action by the FCC. Some censored songs were denied airplay by stations only because someone thought they might have an alternate meaning. For example, "Puff the Magic Dragon," a song that many felt was a reference to smoking marijuana, was pulled from some stations. Yet the Beatles' "Lucy in the Sky with Diamonds" and "Lake Shore Drive" by Aliotta, Haynes, and Jeremiah—both songs about LSD—were not. Some songs were not played simply because the lyrics were unintelligible and therefore might be objectionable. The Kingsmen's "Louie Louie" is a prime example.

On television the *Ed Sullivan Show* was infamous for its censoring of musical acts. When Elvis Presley first appeared on the show the camera shot him only from the waist up because his hip gyrations were deemed inappropriate. When the Rolling Stones made an appearance they were told to change the lyric "let's spend the night together" to the less-provocative "let's spend some time together." Of course, being a live program, this strategy did not always work. When the Doors were told to replace the lyric "girl we couldn't get much higher" in the song "Light My Fire," they agreed, but then sang it as originally recorded. The same occurred when Elvis Costello performed on *Saturday Night Live*. Costello was told not to perform "Radio," his anti–radio industry song, but midway into the beginning of another song, he stopped the band and had them break into the forbidden song.

Some stations or groups may censor a song or list of songs due to what they feel is an inappropriate message. During the Vietnam war, some stations banned certain songs from airplay due to antiwar or antigovernment messages. "Ohio," a song by Crosby, Stills, and Nash, about the tragic killing of antiwar protesters by the National Guard on the Kent State Campus, and "I-Feel-like-I'm-Fixin'-to-Die Rag" by Country Joe McDonald are two such examples. Following the September 11, 2001, attacks on the World Trade Center, Clear Channel Communications issued a list of songs that stations were not to play. Included on the list were:

> Dave Matthews Band, "Crash into Me"
> Everclear, "Santa Monica (Watch the World Die)"
> Foo Fighters, "Learn to Fly"
> Savage Garden, "Crash and Burn"

Bangles, "Walk like an Egyptian"
Pretenders, "My City Was Gone"
Alanis Morissette, "Ironic"
Barenaked Ladies, "Falling for the First Time"
Fuel, "Bad Day"
Korn, "Falling away from Me"
Red Hot Chili Peppers, "Aeroplane"
Lenny Kravitz, "Fly Away"
Tom Petty, "Free Fallin'"
Bruce Springsteen, "I'm on Fire"[41]

Record labels realizing that stations would not give airtime to songs with profanity sometimes would supply stations a radio cut of a song with the objectionable word or words obscured or dubbed over. The Steve Miller Band's "Jet Airliner" was an interesting case, in that the original version usually was played on FM stations but a version with one word replaced with the word "stuff" was played on AM. The practice of offering alternate cuts still remains in practice today, some of it driven by the need to get airplay and some by pressure from retail giants like Wal-Mart that will only sell the "clean" version of songs.

Actions by the FCC over the past decade have left many broadcasters confused as to what does and does not constitute indecent content. In 2001 the FCC ruled that the version of Eminem's song "The Real Slim Shady" with the profanity edited out was indecent. Then, less than a year later, the commission reversed the decision.[42] While the FCC fined CBS stations for Janet Jackson's famous "wardrobe malfunction," the Enforcement Bureau said that it would not hold stations responsible for a profanity uttered by U2 singer Bono during an awards ceremony because it was "fleeting."[43] However, the commissioners revisited the case and overturned the earlier decision. In issuing the decision, Chairman Powell noted, "This sends a signal to the industry that the gratuitous use of such vulgar language on broadcast television will not be tolerated."[44] The commission also ruled that the airing of profanity during live coverage from a campaign headquarters was not to be penalized, and the profanity in *Saving Private Ryan*, aired on television, was acceptable because the film was considered art.

With increased scrutiny, more willingness to fine stations, and higher fines, more broadcast groups have begun to rein in some of their biggest on-air personalities.

Clear Channel Communications was fined $755,000 by the FCC for a broadcast on four Florida radio stations resulting from shows by shock jock Bubba the Love Sponge. Clear Channel entered into a $1.75 million consent decree to settle all complaints against the company for these and also fines incurred from airing the *Howard Stern Show* on some of its stations. Clear Channel also fired Bubba the Love Sponge and suspended the airing of the Infinity-syndicated *Howard Stern Show*.[45]

Infinity Broadcasting's parent company, Viacom, reached a $3.5 million settlement with the FCC, in part due to Stern's on-air comments. Part of the agreement included sensitivity training for all employees, plus the stipulation that Infinity fire Stern if the FCC brought further action. Shortly thereafter, Stern announced that he would be taking his show to Sirius Satellite Radio when his contract with Infinity expired or as soon as he was fired.

In another highly publicized case, Infinity fired syndicated shock jocks Opie and Anthony. The duo broadcast a show that involved a couple reportedly having sex in New York's St. Patrick's Cathedral. The broadcast group and stations received fines totaling $375,000. They are now on the XM Satellite radio service. However, in April 2006 it was announced that the duo had signed a deal to air on some CBS stations. CBS is owned by Viacom, also the owner of Infinity.[46]

This brings up two interesting points. In January 2005, the outgoing head of the FCC, Michael Powell, announced that the FCC had no interest in regulating the content of satellite radio.[47] However, in February the *Washington Times* reported that several members of the Senate would like to see satellite and cable content more strictly regulated.[48] To further complicate the matter, President Bush, in responding to a question asked at a gathering of newspaper editors in April, gave a confusing answer that appeared that he supported such regulation but at the same time preferred to let the issue be decided by the free market.[49]

The final decision may depend on whether the FCC views satellite radio as a broadcast medium or as a pay service. The FCC and the courts have given more leeway to media invited into the home, for pay, versus media available for free. The rationale is that subscriber-based media (magazines, newspapers, and cable and satellite television) are invited into the home and subscribers may decline service at any time. If satellite radio is not subject to the same regulations as broadcast radio, many fear it will give the new medium an unfair advantage.

While large companies immediately began to buy radio stations when the ownership rules were relaxed, did they also give the FCC an opening it never had before? The FCC has no direct power over networks, but can levy fines against individual stations. Clear Channel Communications has over twelve hundred stations. The FCC could easily levy fines on hundreds of its stations at once.

Other Types of Speech

The courts have ruled that various types of speech have different levels of protection. For instance, advertising is quasi free speech. While there is no reason to censor it, false or misleading advertising is subject to regulation of the Federal Trade Commission. Cases of false advertising fall under the FTC's jurisdiction.

Hoaxes

The FCC has taken a critical approach to hoaxes on the radio ever since the airing of the *Mercury Theater of the Air's* version of *War of the Worlds*, directed by Orson Wells. On Halloween night, 1938, Wells presented a radio adaptation of H. G. Wells's novel by the same name. The broadcast aired as if a series of breaking news reports were happening during a music program. While the broadcast was introduced as a radio drama at the beginning, many tuned in late and did not hear the disclaimer. Many people believed that alien spacecrafts were attacking earth and had landed in Grover's Mill, New Jersey.

The play took listeners from early announcements that scientists had witnessed a string of what appeared to be explosions on Mars to live on-the-spot coverage of the police and National Guard trying in futility to stop the aliens.

Police switchboards were jammed with calls, the *New York Times* reported 875 telephone calls to its offices, and highways were jammed with carloads of people fleeing New York. The Associated Press newswire issued an advisory that the invasion was just a radio play. While this broadcast made Wells a household name overnight, the FCC instituted a ruling that broadcasters could not use the words *news flash* or *bulletin* during the course of an entertainment program.

The issue really didn't start to resurface until the 1950s, when rock DJs started play upon the antiestablishment mentality of the music and the teenage audience. Contests were devised that created problems by stopping traffic, having people rushing to public spots looking for prizes, and generally disrupting society. In many ways the contests of the 1950s and '60s were similar to today's "flash mobs."

The FCC issued a policy against such contests and also about broadcasts that manufactured news stories. During the 1970s and '80s, the fake newscasts began to resurface, with stations faking the kidnapping or death of on-air personalities, fake crimes, and even a series of news reports stating that the United States was under nuclear attack from the USSR. One station faked a caller's confession to murder. The police spent over 150 hours investigating the false crime, and the incident received national attention. Several stations received the maximum fine at the time of $25,000.[50]

In a ruling against a station that broadcast a report that a city park was going to explode because it had been built over a landfill, the FCC stated:

> No licensee or permittee of any broadcast station shall broadcast false information concerning a crime or catastrophe if (a) the licensee knows this information is false, (b) it is foreseeable that broadcasting the information will cause substantial public harm. Any programming accompanied by a disclaimer will be presumed not to pose foreseeable harm if the disclaimer clearly characterizes the program as fiction and is presented in a way that is reasonable under the circumstances.[51]

As one can clearly see, areas in which radio-station owners, on-air personalities, and others may come into conflict with the rules and regulations of the FCC or Congress are many. For these and other reasons, most radio stations keep an attorney on retainer. Some attorneys specialize in media law and some specialize in dealing with the FCC. Only certain attorneys have permission to argue cases in front of the Supreme Court. This is one area where corporate owners truly have an advantage over the individual station owner.

Questions for Further Thought

1   Do obscenity cases hurt or harm shock jocks?

2   Do you agree with the ruling in the Hazelwood case or should *all* journalists be afforded the same protection under the First Amendment?

3   With satellite and the Internet, has the SLAPS test become outdated? Is there a better method of determining what is obscene?

4   Should members of the press have different defenses against libel cases? Why?

Shop Talk

Actual malice: Although public figures are "libel proof," actual malice is when a defendant is shown to have made remarks with a knowing disregard for the truth in an attempt to hurt or damage a defendant's reputation.

Defamation: Words that damage a person's (or business's) character, standing in the community, ability to conduct business, and the like. Forms of defamation are libel and slander.

Federal Trade Commission (FTC): An agency of the U.S. government charged with protecting consumers and business against unfair trade practices.

Intellectual property: Creative works as defined by the U.S. Copyright Office (scripts, songs, books, art, and so on).

Libel: Defamation that is written or broadcast.

Miller v. California: Expanding upon the Roth test, Miller introduced another part to the definition. The work, taken as a whole, must lack "serious literary, artistic, political or scientific value." Also known as the SLAPS test.

Plaintiff: One bringing a lawsuit against a defendant.

Public domain: A state in which a work no longer has a copyright, enabling its use without payment.

10

Media Ethics

Morals, Laws, and Ethics

Many ethical issues arise in the communications industry. Most of them are universal across the media, but some are unique to radio. In this chapter we will examine some of the larger issues.

Three concepts confuse many people: morals, laws, and ethics. *Morals* comes from the Latin *moralis*, or "customs and manners." Morals belong to a society. They are what society and custom dictate. Laws are society's way of dictating morals. In our culture stealing is morally wrong. But because this is such a large issue, we have developed laws and penalties to enforce them. Lying is generally morally wrong, but only under certain circumstances is it illegal (in court, or in a contract, for example). In day-to-day life, telling a lie will not get one arrested.

So what are ethics? One definition of ethics is that it is the study of morals. We then may talk about smaller cultures within our society. When we speak of communications ethics, we are referring to the study of the morals of the communications industry. Perhaps a better question to ask is, What do we mean when we say that something is "ethical"?

The word *ethics* comes from the Greek word *ethos*. Ethoses are the guiding principles or traditions that govern a culture. Because ethics are cultural, they may vary greatly among different cultural groups. The First Amendment grants freedom of speech and of the press, but we as a society assume that the media will act ethically.

While some ethical issues are industry questions, some are personal issues. One definition of ethics is "moral principles for living and making decisions."[1]

According to Frank Navran of the Ethics Resource Center, morals are values about what is right and what is wrong, while ethics refers to whether someone acts in a way that they and society deem as being moral.[2]

As a reporter, one must ask how he or she feels about interviewing the families of people recently killed in an accident or murder. If one finds this to be a problem, then there is a moral and ethical conflict that may mean that he or she should find a job outside of news.

The question of what is ethical and what is not has perplexed philosophers from ancient times until today, and will continue to be an area of study for generations to come.

Many great men and women have come up with their own ideas of how to define ethics and how to apply them. Brief descriptions of some of the more well known ethics frameworks follow.

The Golden Mean

Aristotle's feeling was that when one is faced with two possible decisions one should strive for a meeting halfway between the extremes. For example, a reporter with the assignment to cover a story about a recent murder may not be comfortable talking with the victim's family. At the same time, he or she knows that having an interview on tape will make the story much more interesting. Trying to find the middle ground, the reporter may interview neighbors, police, or other interested parties, without intruding upon the family.

Categorical Imperative

Simply stated, "Act as if the principle from which you act were to become through your will a universal law of nature."[3] In its basic form, Immanuel Kant was challenging one to think what would happen if everyone acted in the manner that he or she chose.

Utilitarianism

John Stuart Mills states that no one is better than anyone else. Therefore it is in everyone's best interest to seek the greatest good for the greatest number of people.

Christian/Judeo Belief

Known more commonly as the Golden Rule, the Christian belief comes from the New Testament ("And as ye would that men should do to you, do ye also to them likewise,"[4]) and the Jewish belief from the Talmud ("What is hateful to you, do not do to your neighbor"[5]). This is not to say that only these two religions hold this belief. In fact most religions have a tenet similar to these. Islam holds that you should "Do unto all people as you would they should do unto you, and reject for others what you would reject for yourself."[6] Buddhists adhere to "Hurt not others in ways that you yourself would find hurtful,"[7] and Hinduism states the same belief as "Treat others, as thou wouldst thyself be treated. Do nothing to thy neighbor, which hereafter Thou wouldst not have thy neighbor do to thee."[8]

Composite Characters and Fabrications

The public expects the media to be accurate and truthful. As the FCC ruling regarding hoaxes shows, there is an implied agreement between the media and the audience that the media should be honest. But what happens if there is a slip in this agreement?

Instances of lapses in truth develop from time to time. In 1980 *Washington Post* reporter Janet Cooke wrote a story called "Jimmy's World." The story discussed an eight-year-old boy who was a third-generation heroin addict: "Jimmy's is a world of hard drugs, fast money and the good life he believes both can bring. Every day, junkies casually buy heroin from Ron, his mother's live in lover, in the dining room of Jimmy's home. They 'cook' it in the kitchen and 'fire up' in the bedrooms. And every day, Ron or someone else fires up Jimmy, plunging a needle into his bony arm, sending the fourth grader into a hypnotic nod."[9]

However, people and organizations such as social services demanded to know who Jimmy was and where he lived. They wanted to help this poor child. Cooke insisted that she could not divulge the names of any of her sources, falling back on her First Amendment rights. Soon people began to suspect that Jimmy wasn't real, although Cooke and the *Post* insisted the story was true. The story won journalism's highest honor, the Pulitzer Prize, in 1981. Realizing that this story was not going to quickly fade from memory, the management of the *Post* asked Cooke about the story. They had recently learned that she had lied on her résumé saying that she was a graduate of Vassar and held a master's degree from the University of Toledo. In fact she had attended Vassar for only one year and had a bachelor's degree from the University of Toledo.[10] Cooke admitted that there was no Jimmy but that she had assembled a composite character from many different people. The prize was returned, Cooke was fired, and in a letter to its readers the *Post* admitted that it had run a false story, possibly alienating its readers. A "Where are they now?" article later profiled Cooke. She was working as a sales clerk in a store in Kalamazoo, Michigan, unable to get another job in journalism.

In 2003 two similar stories broke when it came to light that Jayson Blair, a reporter for the *New York Times*, had plagiarized a story about the family of missing soldier Jessica Lynch. Following his dismissal, the *Times* ran a series of stories outlining how a reporter, one that the editors admitted they had had suspicions about, was able to fake a story at such a prestigious newspaper. This resulted in the resignations of the executive editor and the managing editor.[11]

Stephen Glass was another rising young journalist, making it to the associate editor of *The New Republic* magazine. He ran into trouble when it was uncovered that part or all of twenty-seven of his stories were fabricated. The CBS newsmagazine *60 Minutes* noted in a prologue to an interview with Glass, "As *60 Minutes* first reported in May, he made up people, places and events. He made up organizations and quotations. Sometimes, he made up entire articles. . . . And to back it all up, he created fake notes, fake voicemails, fake faxes, even a fake Web site—whatever it took to deceive his editors, not to mention hundreds of thousands of readers."[12]

In all three of these instances, the journalists not only brought shame upon themselves, but also damaged the reputation of the institution they were working for. It is widely accepted that earning trust is harder than losing it. Once a particular newspaper, magazine, or radio station has lost the trust of its audience, it is hard to regain it.

Disinformation

In 1986 the Reagan Administration wanted to scare Libyan ruler Omar Qadhafi, so it began a disinformation campaign. Sources leaked information to the press saying that the United States intended to begin bombing Libya. In this case, the media did not know that it was airing untruths; the government was using it for its own means. Here one needs to ask if the media should be held responsible for airing information that has come from an otherwise credible source? As seen in libel cases, when the source seems credible, and there is a time element involved, the media may be excused.

Authorities have asked members of the press at times to broadcast or publish disinformation, to assist in an ongoing investigation or to keep a witness from harm. If a witness in an upcoming trial survives an assassination attempt, it may be in the interest of the courts, the witness, and the police to report that the person is dead. But how does this fit into a reporter's own sense of what is ethical?

Sometimes the police ask the media to hold back information to assist their investigations. They may wish a reporter to withhold pieces of information that only the true criminal knows. This is to keep copycat criminals or those who falsely claim to be the criminal from stalling the investigation.

In this case, the reporter must ask which option serves the greater good, and whether he or she can live with the decision.

The media are supposed to be fair. There is an implied impartiality in the press, even though it is difficult for a person to leave his or her biases at home. Even corporations and specific newspapers, magazines, radio stations, and television stations have biases. Some are liberal, some conservative, some middle of the road, but the biases do exist.

In a famous broadcasting case, well-known columnist and commentator George Will appeared on the ABC program *Nightline* following the 1980 presidential debate. Will raved about Reagan's skills, praising his "thoroughbred performance." What he did not disclose was that he had been Reagan's coach for the debate. This was seen by many as a breach of ethics.[13]

The *Wall Street Journal* fired a reporter for leaking information to his friends in advance of publication of a story concerning various businesses and stocks. These friends used the information to buy and sell stock. This type of action is insider trading. In addition to losing his job, the reporter was found guilty of fifty-nine counts of fraud and conspiracy, sentenced to eighteen months in jail with an additional five years' probation, fined $5,000, and sentenced to four hundred hours of community service.[14]

Payola

Another area of ethical concern is whether broadcasters and journalists should accept gifts. The original question arose in the 1950s when most DJs programmed their own shows. They played the music that they thought their audience would like, or that was on the charts. With hundreds of records arriving at radio stations every week, it was becoming harder to get a song on the radio. Record promoters quickly learned that the more airtime a record got, the more likely it was that the teen audience would buy it. They began a practice of bribing DJs to give a new record more airtime. Technically this was not a crime or even a violation of FCC policy. An investigation found the practice to be widespread across the country. By the time the investigation and House of Representatives hearings were through and the resulting FCC regulation against payola was put into place, many DJs, including some of the more famous ones, had either been fired or quit their jobs. Recently the specter of payola raised from the grave. In July 2005, Sony's BMG record label paid $10 million and admitted employees gave money, trips and other gifts in exchange for air play.[15]

Drugola

In the 1970s the practice returned in another form. Record companies hired promoters to push their records. In a slightly more complicated method, they identified the stations polled for the industry-wide charts listing which records were getting airtime. A station in Wisconsin might read the list, see what the stations across the country were playing, and add the hits to its playlist. In this way, the polled stations would report that a song was getting heavy airplay, even if it wasn't, and other stations would follow suit by airing it too. Instead of money, it was more likely that the bribe would be marijuana, LSD, or cocaine. This became the drugola scandal.

Plugola

There are many industry insiders who claim that payola is still very much alive. Instead of paying DJs, though, the money is going to the stations. In addition to money, stations may also demand free concerts, giveaways, or other perks.[16] Another version of promoting a product on the air without buying a commercial was plugola. This concept goes back to the early days of radio, television, and the motion pictures. Sheet music publishers would pay bandleaders or singers to perform their songs on the radio. Television programs would use products, often those sold by the sponsors, during the show. Today advertisers pay to have product placements in movies.

A concern in radio is that an on-air personality can easily drop in a good word or two about a product or business. If a popular talk show host says, "I just had a great lunch at my usual spot, Harry's Hash House—they have a really great chili, perfect for a cold day like today—so I'm ready to start the show," most listeners would never think that perhaps the host was being paid to say this, or possibly was a part owner of the restaurant. Therefore the FCC ruling in 1960 covering payola said that stations must announce any "promotional consideration" that was accepted.

Many morning shows will have local restaurants that bring in breakfast for the station. In exchange, the on-air personalities, while talking about the food, will say something along the lines of "We want to thank the folks at Harry's Hash House for providing our breakfast this morning." Most stations also have a limit set on the cash amount for gifts received by employees.

But what if a situation arises in which the opposite may occur? What if a reporter uncovers a story that a local car dealer has been turning back the odometers on used cars? Should the reporter run that story? What if the can dealer is one of the station's biggest advertising clients? Should that have an effect on the reporter's decision? Again, this is one of those ethical questions that has to be made by the individual based on his or her own sense of ethics. Many people may say that they would report it, regardless of the consequences. Would that decision be different if the station needed the advertiser's money to remain in business? What if the reporter is at risk of losing his or her job for airing the piece? Would the decision be different if the person was a new reporter, fresh out of school and without a family, versus an older person with children and all of the associated responsibilities and expenses (mortgage, insurance, and so on)?

Situational Ethics

This series of questions bring up the topic of situational ethics. Most ethical decisions cannot be made in a vacuum. One must take other external forces into consideration before making these decisions. In radio there are daily ethical decisions. Perhaps a salesperson may inflate the numbers of listeners just a bit. A friend may ask a DJ to put a plug in for his new store. A reporter may be assigned to cover a story that he or she has a personal interest in. Early on in everyone's career they are told to save money for the "Take this job and shove it" fund. The general consensus is that this should be at least three months' salary. If a person is placed in a position in which he or she is asked to go against his or her personal ethics, the financial safety net is there to fall back upon.

Another factor that may play into ethical decision making is the amount of the reward that is associated with the deed. One may not accept $100 to give a CD airtime, but what about $1,000 or the use of a new car for a year? A reporter may have a hard-set rule against interviewing families of victims, but if he or she thinks there might be a state broadcasting award, a promotion, or even a Pulitzer Prize in the offing the ethical decision may become more difficult. If you have ever watched a dog surrounded by an invisible electric fence, they sometimes will go through the fence if the incentive is there, knowing that they will get shocked. Often the dog then faces the dilemma of how to get back into the yard. The same situation may apply to people. They cross over the invisible ethical fence, only to wonder how they are ever going to get back to the other side.

Checkbook Journalism

Another ethical issue that arises from time to time concerns a practice known as checkbook journalism. If a journalist receives a phone call saying that a caller has "dirt on the mayor" but wants to be paid for the information, should the station pay the person? Some journalists think that paying for a good story is worth the money. The station's credibility rises when it can crack such stories, and after all, it is in the public interest to air them. And, since the station is a business, why shouldn't it pay for a source, just like any other business might pay for inventory or a consultant?

Critics of such practices, however, fear that a source that is paid for a story may start to sensationalize or even start to make up false stories in order to continue receiving money from the station. They also argue that if stations pay for stories, only the biggest stations with the deepest pockets will get the scoops. An additional argument is that sources who are paid do not hold the same weight in court as those who are not.

Privacy

The question of privacy also falls under ethical decision making. If a station knows the name of a rape victim, or an otherwise personal fact about a public figure, should it put it on the air?

In 1992 tennis player Arthur Ashe was diagnosed with AIDS after receiving a blood transplant during surgery. At this time AIDS wasn't as widely discussed as it is today. *USA Today* contacted Ashe and told him that they had documentation and were going to run a story. The reporter who had found out about Ashe's condition had three choices. He could (1) decide not report it; (2) report it; or (3) give Ashe the opportunity to make an announcement first. The reporter, by contacting Ashe, gave him the third option, but it still meant forcing Ashe to go public with a very personal aspect of his life. Some might see this as the Golden Mean in action, taking the middle ground. But to many others the question is, Should some parts of a person's life, even a celebrity's, be private? Ashe, who had retired from tennis, told reporters at a press conference, "Just as I am sure everyone in this room has some personal matter he or she would like to keep private, so did we."[17]

A long-standing practice among journalists is to not release the names of rape victims. However, in recent years some stations and newspapers have ignored this unwritten code. Critics of the practice say that news is news. They feel that since someone accused of the crime will have his name aired, so should the accuser's. Those against airing the names say it will have a chilling effect, in that victims will be hesitant to come forward or prosecute, fearing that their names will be made public.

The media have an obligation to act responsibly. As trustees of the airwaves, radio and television broadcasters are supposed to choose what to air while keeping the public interest in mind. In 1986 the state treasurer of Pennsylvania, R. Budd Dwyer, had been under investigation for bribery and had been convicted, although he maintained his innocence and many feel that he may have been framed.[18] The day before his sentencing, he called a press conference. Most members of the press expected him to announce his resignation. Instead he handed out envelopes that contained a suicide note, then removed a .357 Magnum from another manila envelope and told the reporters, "Please leave the room . . . if this will offend you." Reporters began pleading with him to stop as he started to place the gun in his mouth. "Stay away, this thing will hurt someone," he continued, he then put the gun in his mouth, pointed it toward his brain, and killed himself.

Radio and television outlets were covering the conference live. In this instance there wasn't time to make a snap decision about whether to air the incident or not. But during evening newscasts, only one local newscast aired the entire clip, while other outlets stopped the tape before the climactic ending.[19] ABC News sent the complete footage via satellite to its affiliate stations with the instructions to cut the video wherever they felt was suitable.

While this is a television case, radio sometimes faces similar situations. The question arises, How does one know if airing something is responsible journalism or not? If a talk show's topic is that it is too easy to obtain materials to make a homemade bomb, and the show has a guest who gives instructions in detail for how to build a pipe bomb, is that responsible programming?

Codes of Ethics

Most organizations have a code of ethics. Some of the professional organizations in the media with codes include the Society of Professional Journalists (SPJ), the Public Relations Society of America (PRSA), and the Radio-Television News Directors Association (RTNDA). Members are expected to use these codes as guidelines in their professions.

The National Association of Broadcasters (NAB) has a long history of a voluntary code or, at times, codes of ethics. Because codes of ethics are generally voluntary, there is little chance of penalization for violation of them. The original code called for station notification stating that it had violated the code. Later other stations were also notified of violations in the hopes that the announcement would shame violators. With television came a separate code. As is the case with most sets of rules and regulations, the codes must undergo periodic review and revisions to keep up to date. This was not the case with the television code, however, and eventually it became little more than a list of often-ignored suggestions.

However, in 1982, investigating a claim that television was operating in violation of antitrust laws, the justice department struck down the code because it said stations should limit the number of commercials. In 1990 the NAB finally issued what it calls a *Statement of Principles of Radio and Television Broadcasting*. The new document offers some broad guidelines about content and the responsibilities of broadcasters to their audiences in regards to programming. No mention is made of advertising limits. Additionally, the statement concludes with the following:

> This statement of principles is of necessity general and advisory rather than specific and restrictive. There will be no interpretation or enforcement of these principles by NAB or others. They are not intended to establish new criteria for programming decisions, but rather to reflect generally accepted practices of America's radio and television programmers. They similarly are not in any way intended to inhibit creativity in or programming of controversial, diverse or sensitive subjects.
>
> Specific standards and their applications and interpretations remain within the sole discretion of the individual television or radio licensee. Both

NAB and the stations it represents respect and defend the individual broad-caster's First Amendment rights to select and present programming according to its individual assessment of the desires and expectations of its audiences and of the public interests.[20]

As with most codes of ethics, there are no real penalties as a result of violating the rules. It is still up to the individual (licensee, on-air personality, producer, corporation, and so on) to make decisions that are in the public interest. Once again, the broadcaster has the role of deciding if what he or she is airing is good or bad.

Often, the case of what is right and what is wrong is not black and white, but rather a question whose answer falls into the gray area. Broadcasters are custodians of the airwaves, and, as such, they should ensure that all major sides of an issue receive airtime. Yet a broadcaster is sometimes faced with the reality of having to decide where his or her feelings end and those of the public interest begin.

 ## Questions for Further Thought

1 In your opinion, is there anything wrong with checkbook journalism if it means breaking a major story?

2 Where is the line between privacy and news?

3 Why would a journalist be tempted to use a composite character? What can be done to prevent it?

4 Can you think of a time when you have used situational ethics?

Shop Talk

Checkbook journalism: An ethical decision much debated: whether it is right to pay a source for a story or lead.

Code of ethics: Set of governing rules developed by professional organizations and businesses to help members and employees make the right choice when faced with options.

Composite character: An invented character that is based on several separate real people. This is an ethical problem if a reporter uses a composite character in a story and does not identify the character as such.

Disinformation: False information deliberately leaked to the press by the government or others.

National Association of Broadcasters (NAB): Professional organization of broadcasters founded in 1923.

Payola: Scandal in the radio industry during the late 1950s when it was found that

DJs and program directors were taking bribes to play records.

Radio-Television News Directors Association (RTNDA): Professional organization for journalists in the electronic media.

Product placement: Practice of placing a product in a motion picture in exchange for payment.

Privacy: Ethical question of where one's public life ends and private life begins.

Public Relations Society of America (PRSA): Professional organization for those working in the field of public relations or corporate communications.

Situational ethics: An acknowledgment that multiple variables affect ethical decisions and that one may change decisions based on a new set of variables.

Society of Professional Journalists (SPJ): Professional organization for newspeople working in print and electronic media.

11

Can Anyone Really Be Unbiased?

Everyone is in favor of free speech. Hardly a day passes without its being extolled, but some people's idea of it is that they are free to say what they like, but if anyone says anything back, that is an outrage.

—Winston Churchill

Left-Wing Liberals versus Right-Wing Conservatives

Perhaps the most controversial topic concerning the media is that of bias. Everyone has opinions about everything. This is a part of human nature. You like a song, a movie, or a certain person. You may align yourself with a political party, or register as an independent, which is still a choice. Perhaps your friends like the same set of things, or perhaps they don't. As the saying goes, there's no accounting for taste. You probably never get into arguments over such petty things. But, for many people, claims that the media are biased have become an obsession, a crusade, and for a few lucky people a career.

There are those who say the media are owned and run by liberals and therefore have a liberal bias, while others say just the opposite. Radio talk show host Michael Jackson had this to say in an interview: "Talk shows are dominated by conservatives, probably because they reflect the political leanings of station managers, who, in the main, come up through the ranks of sales rather than through news, entertainment and programming. Also, they are in the main, although not entirely, hoping to emulate the success of [Rush] Limbaugh."[1]

On the other side of the coin, former CBS News correspondent Bernard Goldberg told Rush Limbaugh that CBS News president Andrew Heyward told him, "Look, Bernie, of course there's a liberal bias in the news. All the networks tilt left. . . . If you repeat any of this, I'll deny it."[2]

Basic Model of Communication

It is important to look at the basic model of communication when discussing media bias. The model tells us, in its most simplistic form, that there is:

- a sender (a person with an idea),
- who translates that idea it into a recognizable code (language, symbols, and the like), and
- transmits it through a medium (voice, painting, radio, newspaper, and so on) to a
- receiver (a person who translates the coded message back into the idea).

Since so many other variables that come into play, communication, just like ethical decisions, does not occur in a vacuum. There is the environment that surrounds the communication. A noisy environment, a hot room, poor reception of a radio signal—all can make the message difficult to hear. We call this static, and it results in the receiver interpreting the message incorrectly. There are many types of possible distractions.

The above model is only a starting point. There can be other factors involved in the process.

Newcomb's A-B-X Model

Researcher Theodore Newcomb posited the Coorientation Model or A-B-X model. In the model there are two people (A and B) and a third variable (X). This variable can be another person, an issue, or a thing. The way A feels about B and the way B feels about A can be affected by how each feels about the variable X. If they both like X—say, football—then there is a common bond; the same holds true if they both don't like X.

If one person likes X and the other doesn't, however, it can put stress on the relationship. The bigger the issue (X), the more stress. If X is a highly controversial subject like abortion, euthanasia, or politics, it can have enough of an effect to override the initial feelings *A* and *B* shared for each other. The interesting part is that sometimes one may think he or she knows how the other feels, but in fact be in error. *A* and *B* may be in total agreement, but if they think that the other does not agree with their own assessment of *X*, the relationship is still stressed.[3]

This shows how the way people feel about issues can divide them. A division in ideology can divide the people of a town, a state, or the country. It certainly has pitted nation against nation during times of war.

When it comes to the media, two camps at opposite ends of the spectrum have emerged, the liberal left and the conservative right. Each of these camps feels that its views are right, and accuse the other group of controlling the media. As we will see in chapter 12, the agenda-setting model says that the media may tell people what to think about in the first place. Studies have also shown that the national media (magazines, television, newspapers, radio, the Internet, and so on) set the agenda for what the local media cover.

For instance, if the cover story in *Time* magazine is about the drop in the price of computers, the local news may do a story about the cost of computers at local stores. If the national media cover a story that has a political angle to it, perhaps the closing of military bases by the federal government in a cost-savings move, the local media may do a story about what the closing of a nearby base will mean to the economy, or interview a member of Congress representing the audience.

Magic Bullet Theory

As the agenda-setting theory states, the media don't tell people what to think, only what to think about. Yet there are many people who believe in the magic bullet or hypodermic needle effect of the media. They believe that the mass audience is comprised of individuals who believe everything that they hear or read, that the audience consists of the uninformed or innocent, or unintelligent. Their belief is that users of the media, lacking critical-thinking skills, need protection from erroneous messages. They have appointed themselves defenders of the people, there to protect the audience from anything that goes against their own belief systems. They believe that the media must constantly be monitored and any biases be brought to light.

Of course, the media are supposed to be unbiased. *The Society of Professional Journalists' Code of Ethics* states that journalists should be fair and honest, and the *Radio and Television News Directors Code of Ethics* clearly states that professional personal bias."[4]

There are many such watchdog groups. Examples of all of these groups include the Citizen's Coalition for Responsible Media, HearUsNow.org, Media Matters for America, the Media Research Center, the Poynter Institute for Media Studies, and the Project for Excellence in Journalism. This book attempts to remain neutral in its presentation so I will not identify groups by their ideology, although readers may access websites to read these for themselves.[5]

The following is an example of bias in our everyday lives. The majority of people in the United States are Christian. Therefore Christian holidays receive more attention than those of other faiths. Christmas has almost become the fifth season. One hardly ever sees a Hanukah sale or Eid specials at the local mall. We have biases toward what we are comfortable with and by what we are surrounded by.

People moving to foreign countries often acclimate to that culture out of necessity. Do members of the media also adapt their biases? Magazines, of all the media, are the most open about their biases. Magazines are published for specific groups of people based on politics, hobbies, cultural interests, and so on. Even those magazines that do not openly state a bias usually have one.

If a new radio-station reporter writes and produces three stories that are rejected for airing by the news editor, he or she may begin to see what stories get put on the air and begin to conform to that style or leave the station. One may say that the editor, then, is setting the bias of the station, but again, one must remember that the media are like any other business, and as such are profit-driven. Stations produce products that they believe will garner them the largest share of a target market. So in this case one must wonder are the media biased, or are they serving a biased public?

Ever since the 1950s, radio has become an increasingly narrowcast medium. The number of different specialized formats has been increasing over the years in hopes of finding an underserved niche audience. This is especially true today with certain syndicated programs. Rush Limbaugh is a conservative who makes his living by claiming that there is a liberal agenda and that the media are biased. Al Franken's show is positioned as an answer to Limbaugh's. Both of these broadcasters are intelligent, articulate, and persuasive. However, because of the nature of their programs, they are preaching to the choir. Most liberals do not tune in to Rush Limbaugh, nor do many conservatives listen to Al Franken. Again, are they examples of media bias, or are the audience members leading the way? Surely, without an audience, these personalities would be without shows.

Typical Reporter

Members of the news media are supposed to report news in an unbiased way. But the question arises of whether this can ever truly be done. In 1986 a study of newspaper journalists was conducted. It found that the average reporter was a thirty-two-year-old white, Protestant male who was married with children, had a bachelor's degree, and was politically middle-of-the-road. In 1991 the Freedom Forum funded a study to examine the typical radio newsperson. The findings of that study showed that the typical radio newsperson was a thirty-one-year-old married white man. A study conducted in 1994 found little difference.

Data from 1991 Study

Race	Median Age
White, 89%	Men, 34
Black, 6%	Women, 28
Hispanic, 3%	Total, 31
Asian, 1%	
Native American, 1%	

Gender	Married
Male, 69%	Men, 61%
Female, 31%	Women, 40%
	Total, 51

College Education
Degree earned, 70%
Only some college, 25%
No college, 5%[6]

A 2004 report issued by the RTNDA found some improvement in diversity but not much. The new study found that radio newsrooms were about 88 percent white, as were 92 percent of radio news directors. Further, over half of the newsrooms were male only.[7]

The question is, Can this "typical" reporter cover a story about women or minorities or people of other faiths without his or own biases coming into play? Can a reporter ignore his thirty-two years of history, and his political, religious, and ethical beliefs while reporting? Conversely, can a reporter who is a minority, female, or of a less prevalent faith shut out his or her own biases in the same situation? We all like to believe that we are unbiased and just. However, a debate remains as to where our biases even come from.

Behaviorists hold that all biases come from our environment—that is, our past experiences, society's reactions, perhaps our teachers, parents, and other role models when we were children. Others claim that our individual biases are just that: individual and unique to us because we are born with them. All babies are born with a fear of falling. They will not crawl on a piece of glass extending over the edge of a table. This is a "visual cliff" fear. Babies are also born with a dislike for loud noises and a desire for nourishment. Some like certain foods while others reject them. This all occurs before they are old enough to be influenced by another's feelings. A third school argues that our biases are a combination of our innate and learned behaviors.

Back, then, to the question, Can any media ever be unbiased? If one assumes that each medium consists of individual stations, each station comprised of individual people with different histories and biases, the answer is no.

But what if the effects of all of the individual biases cancels each other out? If a child takes every crayon out of a box and colors a piece of paper, the result will always be black, for black is the combined presence of all colors. Each individual color blends together with the other colors, resulting in none being dominant. Another way of looking at this theory is imagining a seesaw or a druggist's scale. If there is an equal amount of bias put on each side, the result will be an even, middle-of-the-road approach without a tilt to either side. For those familiar with statistics, this follows the normal distribution. In a normal distribution chart, the majority of people fall in the middle, with an equal number of people falling to one side of the line as the other, resembling an arch with a slow outward curve at the bottom. If this were true, then the majority of people would not have views that are extremely conservative or liberal but would be closer to middle-of-the-road. Each of the extremes cancels the other out, so that for every liberal there is a conservative and vice versa.

If one assumes that the media are controlled by large corporations and that these corporations set policies, then the answer may still be no. Karl Marx stated that the ruling class wishes to retain the economic status quo. If one sees the large media conglomerates as being the media ruling class, then what rewards could they gain from pursuing changes to the system?

Types of Bias

Regardless of whether the aforementioned watchdog groups are liberal, conservative, or neutral, they all have rules or certain criteria. The groups use these rules when searching for media biases.

FairPress.org is a group dedicated to finding biases. While the Fair Press website specifically states that these criteria are to be used in identifying biases of a particular ideology, one may easily adapt them as criteria for finding any media bias. Using these criteria and the basic definitions of the Free Press group, the following may be said (it should be noted that these definitions are the author's interpretation and attempt to offer neutral guidelines; the organization's exact definitions may be accessed at: www.FreePress.org/identify.htm). The group lists the following categories of bias:

Bias by commission: When only one side of a story is given without a dissenting viewpoint.

Bias by omission: When parts of a story are left out, especially those that would disagree or discredit the point of the story as told by the reporter.

Bias by story selection: Harkens back to the gatekeeper theory. This criterion states that bias can be seen in which stories are told and which are not.

Bias by placement: Where a story is given space. If a story runs at the beginning of a newscast, the audience will believe it to be more important and tend to remember it longer. The same is true for the print media. Front-page stories are presumed to be the ones that are most important.

Bias by sources: A reporter is biased if he or she has more sources for one side of a story than the other, giving it more credibility.

Bias by spin: Much like the agenda-setting model, bias by spin is when a reporter gives attention only to an aspect of a story that supports one side while ignoring those that support the other.

Bias by labeling: According to Fair Press, bias by labeling involves giving the label of "conservative" to a person but not labeling. This can easily be adapted to say that the labeling of liberals and not conservatives, or labeling anyone by his or her political beliefs when not relevant to a story, is bias.

Bias by policy recommendation or condemnation: Goes against the basic tenet of journalism. Journalists are not to take sides in matters unless they are writing a column or editorial. In a news story they should neither support nor condemn a policy. [8]

A Rhetorica.net website article states the media have both a liberal and a conservative bias. The article states that perhaps what is more important is to examine the frames "that structure what journalists can see and how they can present what they see."[9]

Commercial bias: As noted earlier, the media are businesses and as such present news and other content that they feel will bring in more viewers, listener, or readers, resulting in higher advertising sales and therefore increased revenue.

Temporal bias: Radio has an advantage over other traditional media in that news can be updated and reported constantly throughout the day. But this also drives the need to constantly update the news so that it is the latest version possible, dropping stories that lack immediacy.

Visual bias:
This has no relevance to radio, but is important to consider in television and print media. Television is unlikely to cover a story that doesn't have a visual aspect, even if it means having a reporter standing by the side of the road to say it is raining or snowing. However, radio does have an aural bias. News reports that offer good actualities and natural or "nat" sound are more likely to be aired. This is especially true for feature stories.

Bad news bias: Good news is boring; news that makes the world seem scary is more luring to the audience. If a DJ says, "We'll have a news report coming up at the top of the hour that says everything is fine," fewer listeners will stay tuned in than if the DJ had said, "We have some terrible news coming up, about a multiple homicide," more will stay tuned. This brings to mind the journalism mantra "If it bleeds, it leads."

Narrative bias: Narrative deals with the story's structure. A good news story has all the elements of any good literature. Drama is a vital part of a story, so many journalists may create drama by finding a certain angle, or find experts or groups who disagree with each other. Once a journalist finds a style, it is hard to resist using it. Many talk shows will purposefully pit opposing sides against each other because it is "good radio" or "good television." In essence, it creates drama.

Status quo bias: This bias asserts that the American press believes in the American system. Journalists do not often question whether the system is broken or if other countries can show us a better way of doing things.

Fairness bias: This is the basis of journalism. Members of the press, as seen in the codes of ethics, are supposed to be fair. In cases where a member of one side of an issue makes an announcement or accomplishes something, one's sense of fairness says that a member of the other side should be contacted and given response time. This may give the appearance that the press is being fair, but it may also appear that the two sides are attacking each other.

Expediency bias: As with the temporal bias, the media strives to get news on the air first. In this endeavor there is often a drive to rely on those who are easily accessible for comment, or readily available press releases. Certain "experts" may be repeatedly interviewed for multiple stories, limiting the number of voices on any given issue.

Glory bias: In an effort to seem involved in the story, reporters often file stories from exotic locations. On radio this is more often a tactic of NPR, which has reporters located around the globe.[10] An anchor could read a story about a car bombing from NPR's newsroom in Washington, D.C. Somehow, it seems more exciting, however, if the reporter is in the same country or, better yet, the same city as the bombing.

What about non-news material? Someone has to pick the topic or guest for a talk show. If asked to choose between interviewing his or her favorite movie star and a Nobel Prize–winning scientist, the sad fact is that most people would pick the movie star—and that includes DJs and music directors. If you work for a country station but prefer rock, you may tend to choose music that is more crossover than if you preferred traditional country. Is this a case of musical bias?

With all of these possibilities for bias, can broadcasters avoid them? Is it possible to be value neutral or will the media forever be doomed to be biased?

Many radio talk show hosts are biased. Some make their living as being the unofficial spokesperson for the conservatives and others for the liberals. The difference in these cases is that the hosts are not claiming to be unbiased. As long as one admits biases, then most people, even if they don't agree with them, will not criticize one for hiding their agenda.

One thing is certain: whether the media are biased or not, they have become scapegoats for both liberal and conservative groups. Whether this bias truly exists or is just a perception on the part of the groups is hard to say. However, with an increasing amount of group ownership in radio and competition from multiple alternative sources, broadcasters must work harder than ever to overcome the perception of bias, whether true or not. As Benjamin Franklin wrote, "If all printers were determined not to print anything till they were sure it would offend nobody, there would be very little printed."[11]

Questions for Further Thought

1   Will the ever growing multitude of media sources help reduce or increase media bias?

2   Do radio listeners give more importance to a story based on where it is placed in the broadcast?

3   Do members of the media unconsciously add bias by using the same sources for multiple stories?

4   How can members of the media ensure that they are not being biased?

Shop Talk

Bias: A personal view or opinion that impedes one from being impartial.

Coorientation or A-B-X model: Posited by Theodore Newcomb, it holds that the way two people feel about each other may be influenced by how they feel about a third person, object, or issue and also how they believe the other person feels about the same.

Magic bullet theory: Idea that the audience is all believing and holds no resistance to media messages. Also known as the hypodermic needle theory.

The Big Dogs

Who Are the Big Players (Owners) in Radio?

Ten companies own 18 percent of the all of the radio stations in the United States today and 23 percent of all commercial stations. As mentioned throughout this text, the trend over the last decade has been a move toward media concentration. This hasn't always been the case. For most of radio's history the FCC preferred more people owning stations, equating this to a greater diversity of voices.

With the Telecommunications Act of 1996, however, the subsequent lifting of the cap on the number of stations one person or company may own, and the elimination of the requirement that a station must be owned for a certain amount of time, radio stations in the past few years have been bought and sold like baseball cards. The buying frenzy seems to have leveled off, however. According to one industry source, "The year 2004 was one of unusual stability for media owners. After a decade of consolidation, the level of acquisition of activity was the lowest in years."[1]

Trends

Several trends characterize media concentration.

1 A concentration of ownership within one industry. A company putting all of its eggs in one basket. Infinity Broadcasting, for example, has concentrated its resources on electronic media.

2 Cross-media ownership has also opened up under deregulation. Now it is common for one company to own radio stations, television stations, newspapers, magazines, cable providers, and even billboards. Instead of concentrating on one medium, they have branched out into others.

3 Conglomerate ownership has also been increasing. Conglomerates are companies that have diversified into many different industries. One example is Vulcan Northwest, Inc. In addition to radio stations, the company also owns the Seattle Seahawks, Portland Trailblazers, the *Sporting News*, several real estate holdings, and the Science Fiction Museum and Hall of Fame.[2] Two of the biggest conglomerates are Viacom and Disney.

4 Some companies may attempt to achieve vertical integration within the industry. This is more common in the print media than in radio or television but has happened with radio owners as well. Clear Channel Communications not only owns radio stations, but outdoor concert venues, a research company, *Inside Radio Magazine*, a marketing group, and a company that sells promotional items.[3]

All of these trends have had an effect on the media landscape. As the following summary of the top players indicates, each of the conglomerates has taken a different approach to the stations that they acquire and whether they diversify or concentrate on one particular medium.

Clear Channel Communications

The company that owns the most radio stations is Clear Channel Communications. With over 1,190 stations, this company owns almost 9 percent of the nation's 13,660 radio outlets. Clear Channel also operates a concert booking company, outdoor concert venues, a format consulting company, several syndicated programs and services, and a research arm.[4] Clear Channel is the largest operator of Hispanic radio stations in the United States and owns more than one hundred stations in Mexico.[5]

Citadel Broadcasting Corporation

Citadel Broadcasting Corporation is the fifth-largest group, owning 213 stations in forty-six midsized markets. Much like Cumulus, the Citadel belief is that midsized markets have many local advertisers without the competition presented to major market stations.[6] It too ranks number one or number two in the majority of the markets it serves.

Cox Radio, Inc.

Cox Radio is involved in the operation of 79 stations in one form or another. They not only own stations, but also operate and/or provide sales and marketing for other station owners. Cox claims to be the third largest radio chain based on sales.[7]

Cumulus Broadcasting, Inc.

The second-largest radio company, though far behind Clear Channel, is Cumulus Media, Inc., which subscribes to the idea that midsized markets allow for the greatest opportunity. The company website states that the company believes that midsize markets are better because of:

- a greater use of radio advertising as evidenced by the greater percentage of total media revenues captured by radio than the national average;
- rising advertising revenues, as the larger national and regional retailers expand into these markets;
- small independent operators, many of whom lack the capital to produce high-quality locally originated programming or to employ more sophisticated research, marketing, management and sales techniques; and
- lower overall susceptibility to economic downturns.[8]

Cumulus owns 310 radio stations in sixty-one midsized markets and five in the Caribbean. The company's strategy is to cluster stations in and around these areas. The group claims to hold the number one or two share of audience and revenue in each of its markets in this way.

Entercom Communication Corporation

Entercom owns more than 103 radio stations. Among the big players in radio group organizations, Entercom is unusual in that it is 95 percent family owned and operated.[9]

Infinity Broadcasting

Infinity Broadcasting is another of the major players in radio broadcasting. Owning 179 radio stations in top markets, Infinity differs a great deal from the Clear Channel business model. Viacom owns Infinity, along with CBS, Paramount Pictures, Paramount Home Entertainment, Paramount Amusement Parks, Simon and Schuster Publishing, BET, MTV, VH1, Showtime, CMT, TV Land, Nickelodeon, and Comedy Central, among other things. Infinity is just one small piece of the larger company.[10]

Pros and Cons of Media Concentration

Good arguments exist for and against the concentration of media. There are distinct advantages of a large company owning a radio station, just as there are advantages of a single station owner.

Pro

Perhaps the advantages are easier to find than the disadvantages. Large companies usually mean more money and resources are available for a station. While a small station might not be able to send someone to the National Association of Broadcasters (NAB) meeting in Las Vegas every spring, it is probable that the larger companies will have multiple representatives. If they do not send someone from each station, there will be at least someone to report back on new technology, trends, and so on. By the same token, large companies may afford better benefits, such as insurance, retirement funds, and higher salaries, than a small station. Working for a large company can also give one a better chance of moving up the ladder to a larger market.

Larger companies tend to have better research data available and better training programs for sales and management staff, and they offer a chance for employees in different markets to share anecdotal stories of what has worked and what has not in their markets. Group owners may even allow stations more time to make adjustments during lean times; if a station that is owned by a large corporation is changing formats, for instance, the larger group may willing to sustain the loses in the short run, for long-term profits. A single station owner cannot afford to lose money for very long.

Con

While the group-owned station might be able to sustain short-term losses, there is more pressure for stations to perform. Instead of an individual owner, a group-owned station has corporate headquarters to report to, which in turn reports to the board of directors. Generally, group-owned stations are under more pressure to turn a higher profit margin than others.

A recent study in *The Communicator* found that while, on average, news directors who oversaw three or more stations made more money than those who oversaw one station, the opposite was true for reporters and sports anchors. News anchors announcing on one station made salaries comparable to those of anchors working on three or more stations. When looking at group-owned stations versus single stations, the only people that benefited from a single station were reporters, who earned substantially more.[11]

In some small markets, the local radio station may be the only source of news. If the only news report is national news from the network feed, can the station truly be serving the public interest? Radio stations run by large companies may not have a local community's best interests at heart. Whereas the old FCC regulations gave preference to a local person applying for a license, that is no longer the case. Today, while the day-to-day management personnel at most local stations may live in the same community as the station's audience, the owners and higher-level management do not.

While it may seem that chains would require newspapers or radio stations to follow the "company line" and endorse the same presidential candidate, research has shown this to be untrue. Most media owners feel that the local management has a better feel for what is best for the community. In the world of newspapers, the lone exception had been the Scripts Howard chain, which recently ended the practice. Today only one small chain remains that enforces a chain-wide endorsement, Copley Press.[12] Yet the question of plurality still needs to be raised. In some markets, as noted in chapter 6, large companies that own more than one station may combine offices and jobs. If a company owns four stations in a market, the same music or, more important, the same news will be going over all four stations. Until the concept of gatekeeping is introduced this may not seem like a problem.

Gatekeeping

Gatekeeping is an idea that was first proposed by Kurt Lewin in 1947 and later adapted to the study of communication by David Manning White. As discussed in chapter 6, there are literally millions of items that could be covered by the press or discussed on air every day. Of those millions, say that there are one hundred stories that are "real" news stories. Further whittle down that number to twenty-five that are seen as important local stories. Now say that you are the news director of a radio station. You have four minutes in which to present the news at the top of the hour. You must decide which stories make it on the air, how much time each is given, and in which order you air them. Listeners have been trained over the years to know that stories that lead are more important and stories that are given more time are more important than those that are given less. This means that you are in charge of the gate, deciding which stories get in like the bouncer at a trendy club. Gatekeeping doesn't just happen in news. The program director decides which songs get airtime, a talk show host decides which guests to invite, his or her producer decides which callers to put on the air, and so forth. Really, one could make a case by saying that if salespeople call only on large businesses in hopes of making a big sale, they are acting as gatekeepers by not calling on smaller companies and stores.

Agenda Setting

At the same time, as someone in charge of the gate, you are also telling the audience what is important. A story has made it on the air, so therefore it must be important. The idea came from research performed by Maxwell McCombs and Donald Shaw in 1972. They interviewed undecided voters in Chapel Hill, North Carolina, during the 1968 elections. The researchers also did a content analysis of local television and newspapers. They found that what the voters identified as being the most important issues during the election were also the ones that the media were covering. This did not mean that the media were changing anyone's attitudes, but, as one researcher put it, "While the press isn't always successful at telling people what to think, it is stunningly successful at telling its readers what to think about." This theory of agenda setting has withstood further testing; one study found that what the media chose as important became important to the consumer within four to six weeks.[13]

Critics of chain ownership of radio stations fear that one news director may have too much control over what goes on the air and therefore what the listeners will believe are important issues. Perhaps this is true. Yet, little discussion occurs about towns with one newspaper, which has become the norm in today's market.

The Big Names in Radio

In today's world of giant radio conglomerates and syndicated programming, only a handful of names jump out as being "stars" of radio. The early radio personalities that were household names became that way because they were on network radio programs—Jack Benny, George Burns and Gracie Allen, Orson Wells, and Edgar Bergen had weekly programs. Today we seem to have gone full circle. Big names in radio are nationally syndicated, often controversial, and use television to either simulcast their program or to give them additional audiences. Whether you agree with them or not, most are great communicators. Controversy may arise from the fact that they are shock jocks, or that they have extremely conservative or liberal views. Maybe they don't have to become controversial to achieve fame, but it seems to help. Below are just a few of the more well-known radio personalities.

Howard Stern

The self-proclaimed "King of All Media" is the most famous and probably the most shocking of the shock jocks. Stern began his radio career at his college radio station. After jobs at various stations along the East Coast, Stern landed a job at WNBC. However, he soon found himself released from the position in 1985 when he refused to obey the station's on-air rules. WXRX, a New York station owned by Infinity Broadcasting, hired him next. Stern's show continued to be a hit with males eighteen to forty-nine.[14]

Soon the show was being simulcast to Philadelphia, then Washington,

D.C., soon reaching a total of sixty-two stations.[15] But Stern's brand of radio brought down the wrath of the FCC on more than one occasion. In 1986 the FCC issued a notice of apparent liability. The notice to Infinity said it must either control Stern or be fined. The FCC fined Infinity stations $6,000 in 1988. Over the next several years, the total amount of fines levied against Infinity was $1.7 million.

In 1998, Stern brought his radio show to cable television. The program, an edited videotape of the radio program, often involves nudity, frank sexual discussions, and other controversial content. Stern wrote an autobiography entitled *Private Parts* (the fastest-selling book in Simon and Schuster history at that time, judged by units sold in the first week), and his New Year's Eve pay-per-view special was the most watched pay-per-view program in history. *Private Parts* was also made into a successful movie. In 1998 Stern began a television program on CBS in an attempt to counterprogram NBC's *Saturday Night Live*. The program was one of Stern's rare failures.[16]

In 2004 the FCC warned Clear Channel Communications they might face penalties for airing the *Howard Stern Radio Show*. Clear Channel reacted by suspending the program from its stations. Clear Channel still received a record $1.75 million fine from the FCC relating to the Stern show and others that aired over its stations.[17] Infinity, as part of an agreement with the FCC, began sexual sensitivity training for its employees. Stern read the rules on the air and vowed to not abide by them.[18]

After not appearing on the show for a week, Stern returned with an announcement that he was in negotiations with Sirius to bring his program to the satellite provider as soon as his contract with Infinity expired at the end of 2005. Citadel Broadcasting, meanwhile, pulled Stern off of four stations because of his touting of his move to satellite radio on his current program.[19] He said that he would not quit the show on Infinity, but faced with restrictions he might resort to just playing music.[20] The move to satellite would remove all content limitations from Stern, as the FCC has said that it would not regulate content delivered over satellite. Such an acquisition would be a coup for the new provider, as Stern has extremely loyal listeners, many of whom will subscribe to the service just to hear his program.

Don Imus

Often considered radio's original shock jock, Imus quickly shot up to the top market. Imus worked in Palmdale, Stockton, and Sacramento, California; then Cleveland and then New York within three years. He quickly gained notice with his outrageous stunts, crude humor, and interesting guests. Soon after moving to New York, Imus developed a substance abuse problem that resulted in his being fired. The man who was once was at the top of his business found himself without a job, and no one was willing to take a risk on him. He got the opportunity to return to Cleveland and take an on-air position. He was soon offered his old job with the same New York station that had fired him, WNBC (now WFAN).[21] In 1993 the program began syndication and in 1996 it started being simulcast on MSNBC. The tone of the program has matured. Imus now discusses serious topics of the day and appeals to an older audience. One of the original VJs on VH-1, Imus operates a ranch for seriously ill children. The ranch has often been a point of heated discussion on the *Howard Stern Show*, with Stern strongly expressing his opinions against Imus and the ranch.[22]

Opie (Gregg Hughes) and Anthony (Cumia)

As mentioned in chapter 9, the once popular shock-jock duo were fired by Infinity Broadcasting when they reportedly aired, via cell phone, a couple having sex in St. Patrick's Cathedral, New York, during a worship service. The FCC levied a $357,000 fine.[23] The pair, syndicated to seventeen stations, could not seek jobs at other stations because of their contract's noncompete clause. They were still paid but could not broadcast for the two remaining years of their deal. Presently the may be heard on XM Satellite Radio.[24] The team has recently signed a deal to air on some CBS stations, rejoining Viacom, the parent company of Infinity Broadcasting.[25]

Al Franken

If anyone had a question about how the one-time writer for *Saturday Night Live* felt about Rush Limbaugh, it was answered by Franken's best-selling book *Rush Limbaugh Is a Big Fat Idiot*. Because of all the conservative talk-show hosts, Franken decided to start a liberal radio network, Air America Radio, presently heard on fifty-three stations as well as XM and Sirius satellite services. In addition to Franken's program, the network has programs such as *Morning Sedition* (a play on the name of the NPR show *Morning Edition*), The Majority Report, The Laura Flanders Show, and *The Kyle Jason Show*.[26]

Sean Hannity

Hannity's three-hour daily radio program is carried on 420 stations with an audience of 12 million listeners. He also cohosts the television program *Hannity and Colmes* on the Fox News Network. The conservative Hannity began his career at his college radio station. Upon graduation, he found a job in Alabama, then moved to a station in Atlanta and finally to New York City. He has received numerous awards, including Radio and Records' Talk Show Host of the Year (2003, 2004) and the NAB's Marconi Award for Talk Show Host of the Year in 2003. Hannity is also an author of two *New York Times* best-selling books.[27]

Rush Limbaugh

Limbaugh is heard on approximately six hundred stations through syndication on the Premiere Radio Networks (a subsidiary of Clear Channel Communications). His show is produced by his Excellence in Broadcasting (EIB) Network. While Howard Stern refers to himself as "King of All Media," Limbaugh settles for the self-given title of "A Man, a Legend, a Way of Life."

Limbaugh may not have invented the one-sided style of programming, since Father Charles Coughlin had an estimated audience of 40 million on the CBS network during the 1930s. Limbaugh's father was a partner in a radio station in Rush's hometown of Cape Girardeau, Missouri, where he first got started as a DJ. After dropping out of college, Limbaugh worked for a number of stations and as the stadium announcer for the Kansas City Royals.

Eventually settling in California, his ratings became so high that WABC, New York, offered him a position. His became known for one-sided attacks against the "liberal media" and the "liberal agenda" of Democrats, feminists (or "feminazis," as he calls them), environmentalists, and others. Following back surgery in 2003, Limbaugh became addicted to prescription painkillers. He underwent treatment for addiction to the pills purchased through illegal sources. Noting that Limbaugh had often criticized celebrities and others who have gotten away with breaking the law, many media outlets referred to a 1995 Limbaugh quote: "Too many whites are getting away with drug use. The answer is to . . . find the ones who are getting away with it, convict them, and send them up the river."[28]

Although Limbaugh has a strong and loyal following, his television program *The Rush Limbaugh Show*, which was also syndicated, failed to reach and maintain the numbers of his radio program. Limbaugh is a member of the Radio Hall of Fame, winner of the NAB's Marconi Award for Syndicated Radio Personality of the Year, and has also written two best-selling books.[29]

Bill O'Reilly

O'Reilly's show airs on four hundred radio stations. He has taken an unusual path to radio fame, however. While many begin in radio and eventually add television to their repertoire, O'Reilly began in television in 1975. He then made several moves to larger markets, eventually landing in New York. He worked for CBS News as a reporter, moved to ABC, and eventually became the host for *Inside Edition*. O'Reilly, who has a bachelor's degree in history and a master's in broadcast journalism, then decided to leave the media and study at Harvard's Kennedy School of Government, where he earned a master's degree in public administration. After graduation, he got his own program on the Fox News Network. In addition to his television and radio presence, O'Reilly writes a syndicated column and has had three books reach number one on the *New York Times* bestsellers list.[30]

Michael Reagan

The oldest son of President Ronald Reagan, Michael Reagan first came to radio as a guest host on the Michael Jackson program in Los Angeles. He was soon the host of his own radio show in San Diego. In 1992 the show went into national syndication. The Radio America Group distributes Reagan's show to over 5 million listeners on over two hundred stations. The author of several books and a weekly syndicated column, he presently has two programs on the air, *The Michael Reagan Show*, which airs Monday through Friday, and *Michael Reagan Weekend Edition* on Saturday mornings.[31]

Melissa Block

Block is a host of NPR's afternoon drive-time program *All Things Considered*. Since joining NPR, Block has worked in almost every position, including director, editor, producer, and reporter. A graduate of Harvard with a degree in French history and literature, she became a host of the popular show in 2003.[32]

Terry Gross

When William Siemering wrote the NPR mission statement, he included the phrase "Acquire and produce cultural programs which can be scheduled individually by stations." Perhaps no show does this better than *Fresh Air*, hosted by Terry Gross. The program, heard weekdays, covers a range of topics from art exhibits to interviews with rap artists. Gross, who has a bachelor's degree in English and a M.Ed. in communications is a winner of the prestigious George Foster Peabody Award for excellence in radio broadcasting.[33]

Garrison Keilor

Keilor is one of the most popular public radio personalities. Creator and host of PRI's *Prairie Home Companion*, he is heard weekly on over 550 stations. The program distributed by PRI is part music and variety show, part barn dance, and part old-time radio. Performed live each Saturday evening, Keilor spins tales of his mythical hometown of Lake Wobegon. The segment begins each week with "It was a quiet week in Lake Wobegon" and ends with "And that's the news from Lake Wobegon, where all the women are strong, all the men are good looking, and all the children are above average." In addition to the weekly program, Keilor has written several books and hosts a daily five-minute segment called *The Writers Almanac* that mixes a little bit of the "today in history" format with literature and a reading from a poet or author. His latest offering is *Literary Friendships*, a program that invites authors to talk about their friendships with each other and each other's works.[34]

Michael Feldman

Feldman's audience participation show *WhadYa' Know?* is a combination quiz show (where callers team up with audience members), music show (he has a three-piece house band), and interview show.

On his own website, Feldman, who at one time was a schoolteacher, describes his start in radio: "Soon I had my very own Friday night call in for the undateable, bedridden and geriatric called 'Thanks for Calling,' wherein people called in seeking comfort and instead found me. One thing led to another, and within a year I was doing a 6 to 9 AM show from a greasy spoon, Dolly's Fine Foods, which I called 'The Breakfast Special.'"[35]

He left radio to drive a cab, but soon returned to radio, this time working for Wisconsin Public Radio. From there he received and accepted an offer to host a show on Chicago's WGN, only to be let go from that position. Wisconsin Public Radio offered him a spot once again, and in 1985 his program went on the air. Today it is usually broadcast live from Madison, Wisconsin, on Saturdays.

Diane Rehm

In a story that reads like a movie script, Rehm volunteered for American University's WAMU radio station, and on her first day a program host called in sick. The station manager asked her to assist him with the show. Having no background in radio, Rehm agreed. Several months later she was the assistant for that program. Six years after first walking into the station, she began hosting a program, and when one of her guests didn't show, she did an "open phones" show. The question that she asked, and still asks guests, is, "Tell me what you do." Her show became immensely popular. She began to syndicate her program through NPR after she raised her own funds to purchase satellite time. She was a hit on NPR, and things were going well, until she was stricken with spasmodic dysphonia, a neurological disorder that makes speaking difficult. After intensive, painful therapy, she returned to the air, but instead of trying to hide her affliction she brought it to the forefront. Her program remains a popular NPR show, and she has written two books.[36]

Carson Daly

Executive producer and original host of MTV's *Total Request Live (TRL)*, Daly also hosts the NBC program *Last Call with Carson Daly*. Recently Daly launched a syndicated radio program, *Carson Daly Most Requested*, via Clear Channel Communications' Premiere Radio Networks, on over one hundred stations.[37]

Matt Drudge

A man who seemingly came from nowhere, Drudge began his media career as a hobby. His career began by posting rumors that he heard while managing the CBS studio gift shop online. Soon people across the country read his website as he started to get into "hard news" and began breaking major stories. His Drudge Report website, although at first ignored by the mainstream media, became recognized as a viable news medium.

In a talk before the National Press Club in 1998, Drudge summed up the power of the Internet: "The difference between the Internet, television and radio, magazines, newspapers is the two-way communication. The Net gives as much voice to a 13-year-old computer geek like me as to a CEO or speaker of the House. We all become equal."[38]

Besides his extremely barebones website, Drudge also has a daily e-mail and newsletter, and hosts a Sunday-evening radio program. While his name is usually linked to his website, the recognition brings listeners to his show.

Dr. Dean Edell

An M.D. by profession, Dr. Edell was one of the first doctors to host a radio program. Beginning his broadcast career in 1978, he has combined television and radio to become one of the most popular radio personalities. He is on over four hundred radio stations, both as the host of his own show and also on *Medical Minutes*, a series of brief medical reports. In addition, Edell is syndicated to television stations in seventy-five markets with his ninety-second *Medical Report*.[39]

Bob Edwards

This Radio Hall of Fame member was the host of NPR's *Morning Edition* from the show's inception in 1974 until 2004. His casual yet authoritative style helped make the program one of the most listened-to, with more than 13 million listeners per week. Edwards began his radio career at a small station where, like many others at small stations across the country, he did a little bit of everything. He was a DJ/sales/newsperson. As a member of the army stationed in Seoul, he produced and anchored the news for television and radio on American Forces Korea Network (AFKN). Returning to the United States, he was hired to anchor the news on WTOP TV in Washington, D.C. While working at the station, he earned a master's degree in broadcast journalism from American University. The winner of numerous awards, including the George Foster Peabody award, Edwards was replaced on NPR in 2004. He now can be heard on XM Radio.[40]

Michael Jackson

Jackson is one of the most awarded talk show hosts in radio today, and is listed as number eleven on one list of "The 25 Greatest Radio Talk Show Hosts of All Time." He also has seven Emmy Awards for his television program and four Golden Mikes. In addition, he has the French Legion of Merit and a star on the Hollywood Walk of Fame, and Queen Elizabeth honored him with the Most Excellent Order of the British Empire (MBE). Jackson began broadcasting in his native South Africa before moving to England and then to the United States. Eventually he moved to Los Angeles, where he broadcast for thirty-two years at KABC-AM.[41] When the station abruptly pulled the plug on his program, more than a few people were confused. The liberal program host soon was on the air at KNS-AM. Guests on his program include everyone from rock stars to politicians to scientists and economists. He also may be heard through his website, www.michael-jacksontalkradio.com.

Tom Joyner

A member of the Radio Hall of Fame, Joyner hosts the *Tom Joyner Morning Show*, one of the few nationally syndicated urban programs. It is carried in over one hundred markets, and its 5 million listeners make the program the highest rated urban show in the country. Working his way up from Alabama, to Memphis, and eventually to Chicago by way of St. Louis, Joyner became one of the top DJs in the city. After working for almost every urban station in Chicago at the time, Joyner took a position in Dallas. When his contract with the Dallas station was up, he began negotiations with the station and also his former station in Chicago. While most radio stations require on-air personalities sign a contract with an exclusivity clause, neither station included one. Joyner decided to take both contracts, working Dallas in the morning and Chicago in the afternoon, taking advantage of the time difference and the ease of flying between the two major airports. Known as the Fly Jock, Joyner continued this relentless schedule from 1985 to 1993. In 1994 his show became the first live syndicated program produced by an African-American DJ.[42] Joyner recently announced that he will produce a weekly television variety-comedy television show to be nationally syndicated.[43]

Larry King

The first person to simulcast a television call-in talk show on television, King set the standard for talk shows. A member of the Radio Hall of Fame, King took the advice of a veteran announcer and moved to Florida, where the industry was beginning to flourish. He got his start at a radio station in Miami. While working for the station, he started hosting a television program. He also added a newspaper column, making him a "triple threat." After it came to light that he was involved in some questionable financial dealings, King lost all three jobs. After a few years working in California writing magazine articles and at a radio station, he was able to work his way back onto the air in Miami.[44] Soon the Mutual Network was nationally syndicating his program. This led to the new Cable News Network (CNN) offering him a one-hour spot each weeknight. His intense yet casual interview style gives one the impression that he is passionate about knowledge and his guests. His show is an oddity in that it is a television talk show that takes phone calls from listeners around the world. King has interviewed royalty and rock stars, politicians and authors. His *Larry King Live* is the highest rated program on CNN. He has won the Peabody award for both his radio and television programs.[45]

Kim Komando

One of the most popular syndicated programs is the *Kim Komando Show*. Each week, Komando, known as the "Digital Goddess," gives advice about computers, technology, and software. Her program may be heard in all fifty states on more than four hundred stations. Her three newsletters have over 1 million subscribers, and her syndicated column appears in more than one hundred newspapers.[46] Komando became interested in computers after her father asked her to do some research on what different careers paid. She quickly abandoned architecture for computers. After several years of selling computer and telephone systems for AT&T, IBM, and Unisys, she began her own business in 1992. Using her savings to produce an infomercial, she became an overnight sensation. She then moved on to AOL and Fox News. Wanting to do a radio program, she approached the major networks but could not find a taker. Finally, she formed WestStar TalkRadio Network with Barry Young, a talk show host in Phoenix.[47]

Eric "Mancow" Muller

Mancow's talk show has ratings consistently better than Howard Stern's in his home market of Chicago. He insists that his program is not shock, but instead is issue-oriented. After starting as a child model and actor, he received a degree in theater but took a job in radio following graduation.[48] Mancow chose his nickname from a character that he once played that was half man, half cow. Muller has appeared on Broadway in several long-running shows. As a DJ in San Francisco, he once blocked traffic on the Bay Bridge while he got a haircut, in a publicity stunt/protest to a $200 haircut that President Bill Clinton had received aboard Air Force One while it sat on a runway at Los Angeles International Airport. A lawsuit resulted in the radio station paying a $1 million settlement.[49] In perhaps the first case of its kind, Muller sued a person who made numerous complaints to the FCC which resulted in

Muller and his station being fined $42,000. Muller filed a $3 million law-suit arguing that the man had filed more than sixty FCC complaints with the intent to harass him only later to drop the complaint after a judge reviewed it.[50] Presently in limited syndication, his Chicago-based program will be syndicated on the new Talk Radio Network.[51]

Dr. Laura Schlessinger

Schlessinger is the first woman to win the Marconi Award for Network/Syndicated Personality of the Year. *The Dr. Laura Schlessinger Program* is on more than three hundred stations and claims over 12 million listeners. Often criticized for her conservative views and abruptness with callers, Dr. Laura has also written seven books that have appeared on the *New York Times* best-sellers list, as well as four children's books. Numerous organizations have bestowed honors upon her. Schlessinger holds a Ph.D. in psychology and is a licensed marriage, family, and child counselor.[52]

In Summary

Radio broadcasters face many issues today. Consolidation of stations by major media chains, challenges from new media technologies like satellite radio and podcasting, declining profits, a loss of listeners, tightening of regulations by the FCC, and other concerns. But radio has faced many challenges in the past and will more than likely get through these as well. However, radio of tomorrow may be as different to us as the radio of the past is.

 Questions to for Further Thought

1   Looking at the bios of the big names in radio, do they share any traits?

2   Ultimately, is radio concentration good or bad? What is the best and worst thing about it?

3   Do the media tell people what to think about?

4   Should the FCC reregulate the industry or should the market determine which stations and owners prosper and which do not?

Shop Talk

Agenda setting: Communication theory that states that while the media do not tell the audience what to think, by covering an issue they are telling the audience what the important issues are, therefore influencing what they think is important.

Clear Channel Communications: The largest owner of radio stations in the United States.

Concentrated ownership: A company strategy to hold businesses in only one field.

Conglomerate ownership: A strategy in which one company holds several diverse business interests.

Counterprogramming: To place a different type of program in direct competition with another station's, hoping to draw audience members away.

Cross-media ownership: Possession of more than one type of media, especially in the same market.

Exclusivity clause: Common in broadcasting, part of a contract that bans on-air talent from appearing on other stations.

Gatekeeping model: Idea that there are many stories, songs, guests, and so on vying for airtime, and someone must decide which are worthy.

Notice of apparent liability: FCC warning to a licensee.

Peabody awards: Named for George Foster Peabody, the annual awards given by the University of Georgia's College of Journalism and Mass Communication honor excellence in broadcasting and journalism.

Plurality: More than one opinion or voice.

Radio Hall of Fame: Housed in Chicago's Museum of Broadcast Communications, inductees are nominated in one of four areas: Pioneer Network or Syndicated; Active Network or Syndicated; Pioneer Local or Regional; and Active Local or Regional.

Vertical integration: An attempt by a company to own all aspects of the supply, production, and distribution aspects of its endeavor.

VJ: Host for music video program. Name coined by MTV and VH-1.

Notes

1

1. Radio Advertising Bureau (2005), *2006 Radio Marketing Guide and Fact Book*, p. 4.

2. www.fcc.gov/mb/audio/totals

3. News Generation, Inc., "Radio Resources" @ http://www.newsgeneration.com/radio_resources/resources.htm.

4. Washington State University (2002), "Extension Reaches Out on the Hispanic Airwaves" @ http://caheinfo.wsu.edu/focus/2002spring/hispanic.html.

5. National Association of Broadcasters (2004), *2003–2004 Marketing Guide and Fact Book for Advertisers*, p. 8.

6. Sterling, C. and Kittross, J. (1990), *Stay Tuned: A Concise History Of American Broadcasting*, Wadsworth, p. 19.

7. www.wikipedia.com.

8. Marconi Calling @ http://www.marconicalling.com/html/index.html.

9. Marconi Corporation, GEC Collection @ http://www.marconi.com/Home/about_us/Our%20History/GEC%20Heritage/GEC%20Collection.

10. "Electrical Experimenter," August 1919, p. 372, quoted @ http://earlyradiohistory.us/1919bwtp.htm.

11. Howeth, L. (1963), "The Navy and the Radio Corporation of America," *History of Communications- Electronics in the United States Navy*, Bureau of Ships and Office of Naval History.

12. PBS (2004), "Tesla, Master of Lightening" @ www.pbs.org/tesla/11 /11 _america.html.

13. Ibid

14. Ibid.

15. Ibid.

16. Fry, M., "History in the Making" (Reprinted from: *The Cat's Whisker, Vol. 3*, No. 1, March 1973) @ http://www.hammondmuseumofradio.org/fessenden-bio.html.

17. F.C.C. History Project, "The Ideas that Made Broadcasting Possible" @ www.fcc.gov/omd/history/radio/ideas.html.

18. Lewis, T. (1991), *Empire of the Air: The Men Who Made Radio*, HarperCollins.

19. ibid.

20. *Scientific American Supplement*, No. 1665, November 30, 1907, pp. 348–350 @ http://earlyradiohistory.us/audi1907.htm.

21. Hilliard, R. and Keith, M. (2005), *The Broadcast Century and Beyond: A Biography of American Broadcasting*, 4th ed. pp. 8–9.

22. Maclauren, W. R. (1949), *Invention and Innovation in the Radio Industry*, Macmillan.

23. Venti , N. and Scudder, M. (2003), "About WHRW" @ http://www.whrwfm.org/about.php

24. Tsividis, Y. (2002), "Edwin Armstrong: Pioneer of the Airwaves" @ www.Columbia.edu/cu/alumni/magazine/spring2002/Armstrong.html.

25. Edwin Armstrong: The Creator of FM radio @ www.wsone.com/fecha/armstrong.htm.

26. "Nathan Stubblefield: 1858–1928," *Adventures in Cybersound* (1998) @ www.acmi.net.au/AIC/STUBBLEFIELD_BIO.html.

27. Hoffer, T. (1971), "Nathan B. Stubblefield: The Real Father of Radio," *Journal of Broadcasting*, Summer.

28. Jacks, M., "The History of Long Distance: A Communications Revolution" @ http://www.thehistoryof.net/history-of-long-distance.html.

29. Sterling, C. and Kittross, J. (1990), *Stay Tuned: A Concise History Of American Broadcasting*, Wadsworth, p. 61.

30. "David Sarnoff: 1891–1971," *Adventures in Cybersound* (1998) @ http://www.acmi.net.au/AIC/SARNOFF_BIO.html.

31. Benjamin, L. (1993), "In search of the Sarnoff 'Radio Music Box Memo,'" *Journal of Broadcasting and Electronic Media, Vol. 37* (Summer) Issue 3.

32. David Sarnoff Library, "1941–1945: The Making of the General"@ www.davidsarnoff.org/ds05.htm.

33. Lewis, T. (1991), *Empire of the Air: The Men Who Made Radio*, HarperCollins.

34. Sterling , C. and Kittross, J. (1990), *Stay Tuned: A Concise History of American Broadcasting*, Wadsworth, p. 68.

35. NASA, Consumer Price Index (CPI) Inflation Calculator @ http://www1.jsc.nasa.gov/bu2/inflateCPI.html.

36. "Golden Age Spotlight on Networks," *The Digital Deli On-line* @ http://www.digitaldeliftp.com/LookAround/la_networkspot_nbc.htm.

37. Sterling , C. and Kittross, J. (1990), *Stay Tuned: A Concise History of American Broadcasting*, Wadsworth, p. 110.

38. Popik, B., "Tiffany Network (C.B.S.)" @ http://www.barrypopik.com/article/335-/tiffany-network-cbs.

39. FCC, Order #37, 1938.

40. Museum of Broadcast Communications, "Flashback, The 50th Anniversary of ABC" @ http://www.museum.tv/exhibitionssection.php?page=88.

41. Richter, W. (2003), "Television Broadcasting Networks," *Encyclopedia of International Media and Communications*, Routledge, p. 397.

42. ABC Press Release, March 29, 1945.

43. "Mutual Broadcasting System," Wikipedia @ http://en.wikipedia.org/wiki/Mutual_Radio_Network.

2

1. Gould, J. (1958), *All About Radio And Television*, Random House, pp. 58–71.

2. "Bob Hoke's Radio Memorabilia" @ http://www.radioattic.com/attics/hoke_memorabilia.htm.

3. Kallis, S. (2003), "Captain Midnight," *Encyclopedia of Radio*, Fitzroy Dearborn, p. 299.

4. Scharrer, E. (2003), "Children's Programs," *Encyclopedia of Radio*, Fitzroy Dearborn, p. 320.

5. Allen, R, C. (2004), "Soap Opera," *Encyclopedia of Television, 2nd ed.*, Routledge, p. 2116.

6. Museum of Broadcast Communications, "Soap Opera" @ http://www.museum.tv/archives/etv/S/htmlS/soapopera/soapopera.htm.

7. Crook, T. (2003), "Drama on U.S. Radio," *Encyclopedia of Radio*, Fitzroy Dearborn, p. 493.

8. Library of Congress, "The American Women" @ http://memory.loc.gov/ammem/awhhtml/awrs9/daytime.html.

9. BBC, "What's On: Soaps on the BBC" @ http://www.bbc.co.uk/cgi-perl/whatson/search/genre.cgi?start=20&genre=ent_soaps&tstart=now.

10. Ellis, S. (2004), "Radio Soap Operas Raise HIV/AIDS Awareness in Africa," *Talking Drum Studio Sounds Message of Hope, Community* @ http://usinfo.state.gov/gi/Archive/2004/Mar/31–263172.html.

11. For an audio clip: www.radiohof.org/adventuredrama/fredfoy.html.

12. Stryker, F., "The Lone Ranger's Creed" @ http://www.write101.com/lrcreed.htm.

13. Radio Hall of Fame, "Fran Stryker" @ http://www.radiohof.org/adventuredrama/franstriker.html.

14. French, J. (1997), "Sound Effects" @ www.old-time.com/sfx.html.

15. Bell, A. (2003), "Comedy," *Encyclopedia of Radio*, Fitzroy Dearborn, p. 360.

16. Sterling, C. and Kittross, J. (1990), *Stay Tuned: A Concise History of American Broadcasting*, Wadsworth, p. 116.

17. Brason, M, Ed. (1988), *Flywheel, Shyster, and Flywheel: The Marx Brother's Lost Radio Show*, Pantheon Books, p. 11.

18. Marx, H. and Barber, R. (1961), *Harpo Speaks*, Bernard Geis.

19. Sterling, C. and Kittross, J. (1990), *Stay Tuned: A Concise History of American Broadcasting*, Wadsworth, p. 119.

20. "Beulah," Wikipedia @ http://en.wikipedia.org/wiki/Beulah_%28show%29.

21. Gans, H.J. (2005, reprint), *Deciding What's News:* A Study of CBS Evening News, NBC Nightly News, Newsweek, and Time, Northwestern University Press.

22. Morrison's report can be heard at "Hindenburg Disaster" @ http://www.otr.com/hindenburg.shtml. The famous passage is about three minutes and forty nine seconds into the clip.

23. Moore, B. (2003), "Schechter, A. A. (1907–1989)," *Encyclopedia of Radio*, Fitzroy Dearborn, p. 1240.

24. Moore, B. (2003), "White, Paul (1902–1956)," *Encyclopedia of Radio*, Fitzroy Dearborn, p. 1515.

25. A clip of Winchell is available @ http://www.radiohof.org/news/walterwinchell.html.

26. "Father of Talk Radio," *Talkers Magazine On-Line* @ http://www.talkers.com/greatest/8rgray.htm

27. Baseball Almanac @ http://www.baseball-almanac.com/prz_qrr.shtml.

3

1. Sterling, C. (2003), "American Federation of Musicians," *Encyclopedia of Radio*, Fitzroy Dearborn, p. 64.

2. § 506, *Communications Act of 1934*, amended 1946 @ www.fcc.gov/Bureaus/OSEC/library/legislative_histories/213.pdf.

3. Radio Hall of Fame, "Wolfman Jack, Radio" @ http://www.radiohof.org/discjockey/wolfmanjack.html.

4. "Wolfman Jack," Wikipedia @ http://en.wikipedia.org/wiki/Wolfman_Jack.

5. Ibid.

6. Fong-Torres, B., "Like a Rolling Stone, Richard Fatherly Knows Best" @ www.reelradio.com/storz.

7. Ibid.

8. Friedwald, W. (2005), "Elvis Today," *American Heritage*, Feb-Mar 56/1, p. 25.

9. Rock and Roll Hall of Fame, "Barry Gordy Jr." @ http://www.rockhall.com/hof/inductee.asp?id=111.

10. "Barry Gordy and Motown" @ http://history.sandiego.edu/gen/recording/motown.html.

11. Universal Motown Records Group @ www.universalmotown.com/.

12. Bower (2002), *2002–2003 Broadcasting and Cable Yearbook*.

13. Radio Advertising Bureau (2006), *2006 Radio Marketing Guide and Fact Book*, p. 38.

14. Arbitron Corporation (2005), *Radio Today*, p. 15.

15. Ibid., p. 16.

16. Ibid., p. 23.

17. Ibid., p. 27.

18. Country Music Hall of Fame, "Origins of Country" @ www.countrymusichalloffame.com/explore/history.

19. Gomery, D. (2003), "Grand Ole Opry," *Encyclopedia of Radio*, Fitzroy Dearborn.

20. "Country Music Not Singing The Blues," *CMA World*, December 6, 1996 @ http://www.cmaworld.com/news_publications/pr_archive/pr_96_dec6.asp.

21. "Country Music Formats," TVRadioWorld @ http://www.tvradioworld.com/directory/Radio_Formats/radio_formats_country.asp.

22. Arbitron Corporation (2005), *Radio Today*, p. 35.

23. Ibid., p. 43.

24. Ibid., p. 51.

25. Armstrong, L. @ http://www.worldofquotes.com/topic/Advice-_-Experience-_-Wisdom/11/.

26. Watkins, T., "GMA's 'New' Definition of Gospel Music" @ http://www.av1611.0rg/crock/gmalyrics2.html.

27. Powell, M. (2002), *Encyclopedia of Contemporary Christian Music*, Hendrickson Publishers.

28. Arbitron Corporation (2005), *Radio Today*, p. 51.

29. Ibid., p. 55.

30. Ibid., p. 59.

31. Patterson, D., "Breaking the Line" @ http://rockradioscrapbook.ca/black.html.

32. Arbitron Corporation (2005), *Radio Today*, p. 63.

33. Interep, "ABC Radio Sales" @ http://www.interep.com/services/profile.php?compID=1.

34. Bachman, K. (2003), "Teen continues falloff as Internet beckons," *MediaWeek*, *Vol. 13* (Dec. 8) i45, p. 10.

35. Arbitron Corporation (2005), *Radio Today*, p. 14.

4

1. Bernard Berelson (1949), "What 'Missing the Newspaper' Means," in Paul F. Lazarsfeld and Frank N. Stanton, Eds., *Communications Research, 1948–1949*, Harper & Brothers, pp. 111–112.

2. Arbitron Corporation (2005), *Radio Today*, p. 6.

3. www.fcc.gov/mb/audio/totals

4. Buzzard, K. (2003), "Hooperatings: Radio Rating Service," *Encyclopedia of Radio*, Fitzroy Dearborn, pp. 721–723.

5. Museum of Broadcast Communications, "A.C. Nielsen" @ http://www.museum.tv /archives/etv/A/htmlA/acnielsen/acnielsen.htm.

6. "Prime Time," *Time Magazine* (March 22, 1963) @ www.time.com/time/archive/pre-view/0,10987,896676,00.html.

7. Ibid.

8. A. C. Nielsen (2005), "A.C. Nielsen, Our History" @ http://www2.acnielsen.com/com-pany/history.shtml.

9. Buzzard, K. (2003), "Arbitron: International Media Research Firm," *Encyclopedia of Radio*, Fitzroy Dearborn, pp. 90–92.

10. Arbitron, "National Radio Services" @ www.arbitron.com/national_radio/home.htm.

11. Ibid.

12. "Navigauge Launching New Standard of Broadcast Measurement" @ http://www.navigauge.com/pressrelease.aspx?releaseID=news_pr_081704.

13. Arbitron (2002), "Arbitron Radio Market Report Reference Guide" @ www.arbitron.com/downloads/purplebook.pdf.

14. "Metro Survey Area (Metro or MSA)" @ http://www.krgspec.com/Library/MSA.cfm.

15. Arbitron (2001), "Rating Distortion & Rating Bias," p. 5.

16. Arbitron (2001), "Rating Distortion & Rating Bias."

17. SRI Consulting Business Intelligence (2005), "The Vals Segments" @ www.sric-bi.com/VALS/types.shtml.

18. Hinman, D and Brabazon, J. (1994), *You Really Got Me: An Illustrated World Discography of the Kinks 1964–1993*, Douglas E. Hinman.

19. "The History of Sound Recording Technology: Cassette Culture" @ http://www.recording%2Dhistory.org/.

20. "Sony History, Please Listen to This" @ http://www.sony.net/Fun/SH/1–18/h3.html.

21. "Compact Disc," Wikipedia @ http://en.wikipedia.org/wiki/Compact_disc.

22. Crawford, K. (2005), "A sneak peek at Super Bowl ads Advertisers are shelling out a record $2.4M per spot; 4 controversial ads have been pulled," CNN Money (February 4) @ http://money.cnn.com/2005/02/02/news/fortune500/superbowl_ads/.

23. "2003 AFTRA Radio Recorded Commercials Contract Schedule of Minimum Fees" @ http://www.aftra.org/contract/crates2.htm.

24. Arbitron (1005) *Radio Today: How America Listens to Radio 2005 Edition*, p. 5.

25. Reuters (2004), "Clear Channel Radio cuts commercials to gain ad dollars," USA Today (July 18) @ http://www.usatoday.com/money/media/2004–07–19-clear-channel_x.htm?POE=MONISVA.

5

1. Mitchell, J. (2005), "Public Radio Since 1967," *Encyclopedia of Radio*, Fitzroy Dearborn, p. 1132.

2. Thompsen, P. (2001), "Noncommercial Radio Broadcasting," in *The Radio Broadcasting Industry*, Pitts and Albarran, Eds., Allyn and Bacon, p. 140.

3. "Remarks of President Lyndon B. Johnson Upon Signing the Public Broadcasting Act of 1967" @ http://www.cpb.org/aboutpb/act/remarks.html.

4. "Internet History—Defense Advanced Research Project Agency" @ http://living-internet.com/i/ii_darpa.htm.

5. *The Public Broadcasting Act of 1967* as Amended, Subpart D–Corporation for Public Broadcasting, Sec. 396 [47 U.S.C. 396] Corporation for Public Broadcasting @ http://www.cpb.org/aboutpb/act/.

6. Ibid.

7. Siemering, W. (1970), "National Public Radio Purposes," *Public Broadcasting PolicyBase* @ www.current.org/pbpb/documents/NPRpurposes.html.

8. Ibid.

9. Dvorkin, P. (2004), "Bob Edwards Reassigned: Ageism or Just Change?" *NPR.org* (April 28, 2004) @ http://www.npr.org/templates/story/story.php?storyId=1854657.

10. "Public Radio International," *Inside PRI* @ www.pri.org/PublicSite/Inside/index.html.

11. Mitchell, J. (2003), "Public Radio Since 1967," *Encyclopedia of Radio*, Fitzroy Dearborn, p. 1136.

12. Stavitsky, A.G. (1993), "Listening for Listeners: Educational Radio and Audience Research," *Journalism History, Vol. 19*, 1.

13. Stavitsky A.G. (1994), "The Changing Conception of Localism in U.S. Public Radio," *Journal of Electronic Media, Vol. 38*, 1.

14. *NPR Annual Report 2003*, Pg 22.

15. Lasar, M. (2003), "Hill, Lewis 1919–1957: U.S. Founder of KPFA-FM and Pacifica Foundation," *Encyclopedia of Radio*, Fitzroy Dearborn.

16. *United States* v. Dunifer, 997 F.Supp. 1235 (N.D.Cal. 1998).

17. *United States v. Stephen Paul Dunifer*, 219 F.3d 1004 (9th Cir. 2000).

18. F.C.C., "Low Power Broadcast Radio Stations" @ www.fcc.gov/mb/audio/low-pwr.html.

19. Ibid.

20. Ibid.

21. F.C.C., "FM Translators and Booster Stations" @ www.fcc.gov/mb/audio/

translator.html.

22. GEN Docket No. 87–839, In the Matter of Revision of Part 15 of the Rules regarding the operation of radio frequency devices without an individual license— LPB et al Joint Petition or Partial Reconsideration, Adopted November 16, 1990; Released December 28, 1990 @ www.radiosystems.com/PDF/radiate.PDF.

6

1. Wells, T. and Wilson, H. (1978), *WKRP in Cincinnati Theme*.

2. Hopkins, T. (1982), *How to Master the Art of Selling*, Champion Press.

3. Voice tracking is the practice of having one announcer record multiple segments that can be aired between songs at one or more stations, thus removing the live element and often the local aspect as well. This saves multiple-station owners money by eliminating the need for numerous DJs.

4. Hughs, C. Email correspondence, March 25, 2005.

5. McConnell, M., Email correspondence, March 29, 2005.

6. Lynch, S., Personal Interview, April, 25, 2005.

7. Data from U.S. Advertising Market Shows Strong Growth In 2004, Radio Inc. (April, 30, 2005) @ http://www.radioink.com/HeadlineEntry.asp?hid=127629.

8. "Advertising," *Encyclopedia of Radio*, 2003, Fitzroy Dearborn, p. 6.

9. U.S. Department of Labor, Bureau of Labor Statistics (2004), "Announcers" @ www.bls.gov/oco/ocos087.htm#earnings.

10. Warner, C. and Spencer, J., "Radio and Television Sales Staff Profiles, Compensation and Practices" @ www.charleswarner.us/rtvsls.html.

11. U.S. Department of Labor (2004), Bureau of Labor Statistics, Employer Costs for Employee Compensation: December 2004 @ http://economics.about.com/od/employ-mentcostindex/a/eci_04_Dec.htm.

12. BMI (2005), "The BMI Backgrounder" @ http://www.bmi.com/about/.

13. ASCAP (2005), "Customer Licensees" @ http://www.ascap.com/licensing/about.html.

14. SESAC, "About Us" @ www.sesac.com/aboutsesac/about.html.

15. ASCAP (2005), "Frequently Asked Questions about Licensing" @ www.ascap.com/licensing/radio/radiofaq.html.

16. BMI (2005), "Royalty Information Booklet" @ http://www.bmi.com/songwriter/resources/pubs/royaltyradio.asp.

17. ASCAP (2005), "About ASCAP" @ http://www.ascap.com/about/payment/royalties.html.

18. Exemptions Established Under "Fairness In Music Licensing Act" of 1998 17 U.S.C. § 110 @ http://cyber.law.harvard.edu/is02/readings/17usc110.html.

19. U.S. Department of Labor, Bureau of Labor Statistics @ http://bls.gov/oco/ocos087.htm.

20. Chuday, L. (2005) *NAB's Guide to Careers in Radio*, National Association of

Broadcasting, pp. 48–49.

21. "The State of the News Media 2004: Radio," *Journalism.org* @ http://www.stateofthenewsmedia.org/narrative_radio_newsinvestment.asp?cat=6&media=8.

22. Ibid.

7

1. D'Ambrose, C. (2003), "Frequency Range of Human Hearing" @ http://hypertextbook.com/facts/2003/ChrisDAmbrose.shtml.

2. Peck ,K. (2001), "H.E.A.R. Force Delivers Sonic Survival" @ http://www.audiologyonline.com/articles/arc_disp.asp?id=302.

3. The Who: Trivia and Random Facts @ http://classicrock.about.com/od/triviagames/p/whotrivia.htm.

4. Webb, J., "Twelve Microphones That Changed History" @ http://www.vintageking.com/12mics.htm.

5. Adams, C. (1976), "The Straight Dope" (March 12) @ http://www.straightdope.com/classics/a1_258b.html.

6. "Goldmark, Peter Carl," *The Columbia Encyclopedia*, Sixth Edition (2001) @ http://www.bartleby.com/65/go/GoldmrkP.html.

7. Brewster, M. (2004), "Peter Goldmark: CBS's In House Genius, Business Week On-Line" @ http://www.businessweek.com/bwdaily/dnflash/aug2004/nf20040825_9715_db078.htm.

8. Narrative by Edward "Ted" Wallerstein @ http://www.musicinthemail.com/audiohistoryLP.html

9. Rushin, D., "The Magic of Magnetic Tape" @ http://www.tvhandbook.com/History/History_tape.htm.

10. "The History of Recording Technology" @ http://www.tvhandbook.com/History/History_recording.htm.

11. Sony Corporation (2005), "Sony History" @ http://www.sony.net/Fun/SH/1–20/h5.html.

12. OneOff Media Inc., "History of CD Technology" @ www.oneoffcd.com/info/historycd.cfm.

13. The ENIAC Museum On-Line @ http://www.seas.upenn.edu/~museum/.

14. Famously Wrong Predictions @ http://www.wilk4.com/humor/humore10.htm.

15. McNulty, J. (2005), "Digital Divide Project Finds Evidence that Computers at Home Improve High School Graduation Rates," *U.C. Santa Cruz Currents On-Line* (April 11) @ http://currents.ucsc.edu/04–05/04–11/divide.asp.

16. Shankland, S. (2005), "Barrett: No end in sight for Moore's Law," *CNET News.com* (March 1) @ http://netscape.com.com/Barrett+No+end+in+sight+for+Moores+Law/2100–1006_3–5594779.html.

17. Find more information @ http://library.thinkquest.org/27887/gather/fundamentals/broadcasting.shtml.

18. F.C.C. (1993), "History of Wire and Broadcast Communication" (May) @ http://www.fcc.gov/cgb/evol.html.

19. Reuters (2005), "Clear Channel Overhauls its Net Strategy," *CNET News.com* (March 24) @ http://news.com.com/Clear+Channel+overhauls+its+Net+strategy/2100-1027_3-5635625.html.

20. Center for Media Research (2005), "Online Radio Midday Audience Tops a Million" (May 22).

21. "Podcasting," Wikipedia @ http://en.wikipedia.org/wiki/Podcasting.

22. Acohido, Byron (2005), "Radio to the MP3 Degree: Podcasting," *USA Today* (February 9).

23. Searls, D. (2004), "DIY Radio with PODcasting" (September 28) @ http://garage.docsearls.com/node/462.

24. BMI (2005), "Web Site Performance Agreement" @ http://www.bmi.com/licensing/forms/Internet0105A.pdf.

25. *Space and Tech* (2000), "Proton Successfully Launches Sirius Radio 3" @ http://www.spaceandtech.com/digest/flash-articles/flash2000-090.shtml.

26. www.sea-launch.com.

27. Ray, J. (2005), "Sea Launch Rocket Puts Radio Satellite Into Space" (February, 28) @ http://www.spaceflightnow.com/sealaunch/xm3/.

28. Sirius Satellite Radio, "FAQs" @ www.sirius.com/servlet/ContentServer?pagename=Sirius/CachedPage&c=Page&cid=1018209032792.

29. XM Satellite Radio, "Learn About XM" @ http://www.xmradio.com/learn/programming.jsp.

30. Bunkley, N. (2004), "More Tuning Into Satellite Radio," *Detroit News* (December 28).

31. "U.S. Households with Cable Television 1977–1999" @ www.tvhistory.tv/Cable_Households_77–99.JPG.

32. Media Info Center @ http://www.mediainfocenter.org/compare/penetration/printable.asp.

33. Satellite Broadcasting and Communications Association (2003), "US Satellite Television Subscribers Tops 20 Million Mark," Press Release (August 20) @ www.spaceref.com/news/viewpr.html?pid=12360.

34. IT Facts, "Advertising, U.S. Radio Advertising Budgets Grow 2% in 2004, Driven by Local Radio" @ http://www.itfacts.biz/index.php?id=P2613.

35. IT Facts, "Advertising, US advertising market up 9.8% in 2004, generated $141 bln" @ http://www.itfacts.biz/index.php?id=P2847.

8

1. Report and Order, MM Docket 94–130, 10 FCC Rcd 11479.

2. *Hoover v. Intercity Radio Co.*, 283 F.10003 (DC Cir. 1923).

3. Government Printing Office in Washington, D.C. for the Department of Commerce, *Proceedings of the Fourth National Radio Conference and Recommendations for Regulation of Radio*, November 9–11, 1925, [C1.2: R11/925].

4. Ibid.

5. *U.S. v. Zenith Radio Corp. et al.*, 12 F. 2nd 614[ND Ill. 1926].

6. Franklin, M. and Anderson, D. (1990), *Mass Media Law: Cases and Materials*, 4th ed., The Foundation Press, Inc., p. 756.

7. Siebert, F., Peterson, T., and Schramm, W. (1963), *Four Theories of the Press*, University of Illinois Press.

8. U.S. National Archives, "Bill of Rights" @ http://www.archives.gov/national_archives_experience/charters/bill_of_rights_transcript.html.

9. Franklin, M. and Anderson, D. (1990), *Mass Media Law: Cases and Materials*, 4th ed., Foundation Press, pp. 36–37.

10. Caristi, D. (2003), "Federal Radio Commission," *Encyclopedia of Radio*, Fitzroy Dearborn, p. 381.

11. F.C.C., "FCC Fiscal Year 2006 Budget Estimates Submitted to Congress February 2005" @ http://www.fcc.gov/Reports/fcc2006budget_main.pdf.

12. *Technical Radio Laboratory v. FRC*, 59 App. D.C. 125, 36 F.2d 111 (1929).

13. *United States v. Gregg et al.*, 5 F. Supp. 848 (S.D. Tex. 1934) at 857.

14. Schwarcz, J., "The Goat Gland Doctor: The Story of John R. Brinkley" @ http://www.quackwatch.org/11Ind/brinkley.html.

15. *KFKB Broadcasting Association v. Federal Radio Commission*, 47 F 2nd 670 [D.C. Cir. 1931].

16. Agreement Between the Government of the United States of America and the Government of the United Mexican States Relating to the AM Broadcasting Service in the Medium Frequency Band, 1986

17. Lee R. (2002), *The Bizarre Careers of John R. Brinkley*, University Press of Kentucky.

18. Zwonitzer, M. and Hirshberg, C. (2002), *You Will Miss Me When I'm Gone: The Carter Family and Their Legacy in American Music*, Simon and Schuster.

19. *Modification of FM Broadcast Station Rules to Increase the Availability of Commercial FM Broadcast Assignments*, 94 FCC 2d MM Docket 80–90 (1980).

20. FCC Commissioner Chong, R., "Trends in Communications and Other Musings on Our Future" @ http://law.indiana.edu/fclj/pubs/v47/no2/chong.html.

21. F.C.C. (1993), "History of Wire and Broadcast Communication" @ http://www.fcc.gov/cgb/evol.html.

22. F.C.C., "Commissioners" @ www.fcc.gov.

23. "Communications Act of 1934 §308," in Compilation of Selected Acts Within the Jurisdiction of the Committee On Energy and Commerce: Communications Law As Amended Through December 31, 2002, 108TH CONGRESS 1st Session, April 2003.

24. In the Matter of Rules Relating to Multiple Ownership, 22 F.C.C. 2d 306, 18 R.R. d 1735 (1970).

25. Multiple Ownership (12–12–12 Reconsideration), 100 F.C.C.2d 74, 57 R.R. 2d 967 (1985).

26. Kirby, K. (2003), "Freedom of Information: A Primer on the FCC's New Ownership Rules," (2003), RTNDA website @ http://www.rtnda.org/foi/fcc_primer_2003.html.

27. Foreign Ownership Guidelines for FCC Common Carrier and Aeronautical Radio Licenses: Section 310 of the Communications Act of 1934, as Amended. "Initial Authorizations and Transfers of Control and Assignments of Common Carrier and Aeronautical Radio Licenses": International Bureau, November 17, 2004, DA 04–3610.

28. In the Matter of Amendment of Section 1.80 of the Commission's Rules, FCC 97–002, January 1997.

29. Mishkind, B., "Canadian Radio History" @ http://www.oldradio.com/archives/stations_c/canada.html.

30. "Call Letter Origins" @ www.oldradio.com.

31. Stock, R. (1996), "Reaching Over The Border: Canadian & U.S. Firms Realize Growth Opportunities in Post- NAFTA Market," *Legal Management*, May/June.

32. "Canadian Content Rules" @ http://www.media-awareness.ca/english/issues/cultural_policies/canadian_content_rules.cfm.

33. Reighard, P. (2003), "Cuba," *The Encyclopedia of Radio*, Fitzroy Dearborn, p. 430.

34. Price, M., "Public Diplomacy and Transformation of International Broadcasting," *Comparative Media Law Journal*, Vol. 1, Issue 1, January-June.

35. Associated Press (2004), "U.S. Overcomes Cuban Jamming of Radio Broadcasts," Monday, August 23.

36. Sterling, C. and Kittross, J. (1990), *Stay Tuned: A Concise History of American Broadcasting*, Wadsworth, p. 304.

37. FCC, Order #37, 1938.

38. *National Broadcasting Company et al. v. United States*, 319 U.S. 190 (1943).

39. Report and Statement of Policy re: Commission En Banc Programming Inquiry, 25 Fed. Reg. 7291 (1960).

40. Mayflower Broadcasting Corp., 8 F.C.C. 333 (1940).

41. Report on Editorializing by Broadcast Licensees, 12 F.C.C. 1246 (1949).

42. *Communications Act of 1934*, § 315

43. *Communications Act of 1934*, § 315(a)

44. *Farmers Educational & Cooperative Union v. WDAY*, Inc., 360 U.S. 525 (1959).

45. Times-Mirror Broadcasting Co., 24 P & F Radio Reg. 404 (1962).

46. *Red Lion Broadcasting Co., Inc. v. FCC*, 395 U.S. 367 (1969).

47. Ibid.

48. Ibid.

49. *Miami Herald Publishing Co. v. Tornillo*, 418 U.S. 241 (1974).

50. In the Matter of the Handling of Public Issues Under the Fairness Doctrine and the Public Interest Standards of the Communications Act, 48 FCC 2d 1 (1974).

51. Ibid.

52. *Communications Act of 1934*, § 315 (a) 7.

53. Nicholas Zapple, 23 F.C.C. 2d 707 (1970).

54. *Branch v. Federal Communications Commission*, 824 F. 2d 37, 14 Med.L.Rptr. 1465 (D.C.Cir. 1987).

55. *Communications Act of 1934*, § 315 (b).

56. Fairness Report, 102 F.C.C.2d 142, 246 (1985).

57. Syracuse Peace Council, 2 F.C.C.R. (1987).

58. *Telecommunications Research and Action Center v. FCC*, 801 F. 2d 501 (D.C. Cir. 1986).

59. *Fairness in Broadcasting Act of 1987* in Bill Summary & Status for the 100th Congress.

60. "EBS," Broadcast History website @ http://www.oldradio.com/current/bc_conel.htm

61. "The EBS Authenticator Word List" @ http://www.akdart.com/ebs.html

62. Mishkin, B., "What was Conelrad? EBS? EAS?" @ http://www.oldradio.com/current/bc_conel.htm.

63. F.C.C., "The Emergency Alert System (EAS)" @ http://www.fcc.gov/cgb/consumerfacts/eas.html

64. F.C.C. (1998), *A Glossary of Telecommunication Terms*, Public Service Division, Office of Public Affairs.

9

1. *Copyright Law of the United States of America Title 17 of the United States Code*, § 102.

2. *Copyright Law of the United States of America Title 17 of the United States Code*, § 106.

3. *Copyright Law of the United States of America Title 17 of the United States Code*, §-302.

4. Alsdorf, M. (1999), "Why Wonderful Life Comes but Once a Year," Slate (December 21) @ http://slate.msn.com/id/1004242 /.

5. *Sony Corporation of America v. Universal Cities Studios*, 464 U.S. 417 (1984).

6. *A&M Records, Inc. v. Napster*, 114 F. Supp. 2d 896, 900 (N.D. Cal. 2000).

7 Summary of *A&M Records, Inc. v. Napster* opinion @ http://www.ce9.uscourts.gov/web/ocelibra.nsf/504ca249c786e20f85256284006da7ab/cc 61d7c45e059bd4882569f100620da0?OpenDocument.

8. Smolla, R. (2004), "You Say Napster, I Say Grokster," *Slate* (Dec 13) @ http://slate.msn.com/id/2110982/.

9. MGM Studios Inc., et al. v. Grokster Ltd., et al., No. 04–480, argued March 29, 2005.

10. 17 U.S.C. Section § 101.

11. Campbell v. Acuff-Rose Music, Inc., 972 F. Supp. 2d 1429, reversed and remanded (1994).

12. Sostek, B., Yoo, T. (2003), "But I Know It When I See It," Fort Worth Business Press (Jan. 10–16) @ http://www.tklaw.com/website.nsf/WEBnewx/ E9C2CAE7D8D7B97786256CC40060291E.

13. *Zachinni v. Scripps-Howard Broadcasting Co.*, 433 U.S. 562 (1977).

14. *Brown & Williamson Tobacco Corporation v. Walter Jacobson and CBS, Inc.*, No. 82-648 (N.D. Ill.) (1984).

15. *Liquori v. Republican Co.*, 396 N.E. 2d. 726, 5 Med.L.Rptr. 2180 (Mass. App. Ct.) (1979).

16. *Granger v. Time, Inc.*, 568 P. 2d. 535, 3 Med.L.Rptr. 1021 (1977).

17. *Neiman-Marcus v. Lait*, 13 F.R.D. 311 (S.D.N.Y. 1952).

18. Ibid.

19. *New York Times v. Sullivan*, 376 US 254 (1964).

20. Ibid.

21. Ibid.

22. "ALA 100 Most Frequently Challenged Books of 1990–2000" @ http://www.ala.org/ala/oif/bannedbooksweek/bbwlinks/100mostfrequently.htm.

23. Hazelwood School District v. Kuhlmeir, 108 S. Ct. (1988).

24. Table of Indecency Complaints and NALs: 1993–2004 @ http://www.fcc.gov/eb/broadcast/ichart.pdf.

25. *Debt Collection Improvement Act of 1996*, 28 U.S.C. § 2461 § 180(b).

26. *Roth v. United States*, 354 U.S. 476 (1957).

27. Ibid.

28. Ibid.

29. *Miller v. California*, 413 U.S. 15 (1973).

30. Ibid.

31. 2 Live Crew @ http://www.ftppro.com/library/2_Live_Crew.

32. *Federal Communications Commission v. Pacifica Foundation*, 438 U.S. 726, (1978).

33. Ibid.

34. Ibid.

35. Pacifica Foundation, Inc., 2 F.C.C. Rcd 2692, (1987).

36. Regents of the University of California (Santa Barbara), 2 F.C.C.Rcd. 2703, (1987).

37. Infinity Broadcasting Corp. of Pennsylvania, 2 F.C.C.Rcd. 2705, (1987).

38. U.S. Code Title 18, § 1464: Broadcasting Obscene Language.

39. In the Matter of Industry Guidance On the Commission's Case Law Interpreting 18 U.S.C. § 1464 and Enforcement Policies Regarding Broadcast Indecency ("Indecency Policy Statement"), 16 FCC Rcd 7999, 8002 (2001)..

40. Ibid.

41. "The Clear Channel Banned Songs List" @ http://radio.about.com/library/weekly/blCCbannedsongs.htm.

42. In the Matter of Citadel Broadcasting Company Licensee of Station KKMG (FM), Pueblo, Colorado, File No. Eb-00-IH-0228, NAL/Acct. No. 200132080057, (2002).

43. Golden Globes Awards Order, 19 FCC Rcd. at 4982.

44. In the Matter of Complaints Against Various Broadcast Licensees Regarding Their Airing of "The Golden Globe Awards" Program, FCC 04–43.

45. Deitz, C. (2204), "F.C.C. Rips Up All Complaints Against Clear Channel for $1.75 Million" (June, 9) @ http://radio.about.com/od/sternindecency/a/blaa060904a.htm.

46. Associated Press (2006) "Shockjocks May Replace Roth on Radio."

47. Hinckley, D. (2005), "Powell, More Technocrat Than Crusader," *New York Daily News* (January 24).

48. Baker, C. (2005), "On The Offensive at the FCC," *The Washington Times* (February 6).

49. Eggerton, J. (2005), "Bush Backs Indecency Standard, Broadcasting and Cable," *Broadcasting & Cable* (April, 14).

50. Levine, J. (2000), "A History and Analysis of the Federal Communication Commission's Response to Radio Broadcast Hoaxes," *Federal Communication Law Journal, Vol. 52*, p. 273–219, (January 31) @ http://classes.lls.edu/s2000/manheimk/com-law/coursematerials/hoax2.pdf.

51. Part 73 Regarding Broadcast Hoaxes, *Communications Act*, Report and Order, 7 FCC Rcd. 4106 (1992).

10

1. Leslie, L. (2004), *Mass Communication Ethics: Decision Making in Postmodern Culture*, 2nd Ed, Houghton Mifflin, p. 6.

2. Navran, F., "Ask the Expert" @ http://www.ethics.org/ask_e4.html.

3. Kant, I (1901). Translated by Watson, J., *The Metaphysics of Morality*, cited in *Ideas of the Great Philosophers*, Sahakian, W. and Sahakian, M. (1993), Barnes and Noble, p. 45.

4. *Holy Bible King James Version*, Luke 6:31.

5. *Talmud*, Bavli, Shabbat 30b-31ª.

6. *Mishkat-ul-Masabih.*

7. Udana-Varga, 5:18.

8. Mahabharata, Ganguli, Book 13 CXIII.

9. Cooke, J. (1980), "Jimmy's World," *Washington Post*, (September 28), p. A1.

10. Maraniss, D. (1981), "Post Reporter's Pulitzer Prize is Withdrawn; Pulitzer Board Withdraws Post Reporter's Prize," *Washington Post* (April 16).

11. "Top New York Times Editors Quit, Arce, R. and Troetel, S.," *CNN.com* (March, 1, 2001) @ http://www2.cnn.com/2003/US/Northeast/06/05/nytimes.resigns/.

12. Kroft, S. (2003), "Stephen Glass: I Lied for Esteem," *CBS News 60 Minutes Interview*, (August 17) @ http://www.cbsnews.com/stories/2003/05/07/60minutes/main552819.shtml.

13. Solomon, N. (2004), "George Will's Ethics: None of Our Business?" (January 3) @ http://www.antiwar.com/solomon/?articleid=1873.

14. "Winans Gets 18-Month Term in Trading Case," *Wall Street Journal* (August 7, 1985).

15. Starkman, D. "Sony BMG Settles Radio Payola Probe," (2005). *The Washington Post*, July 26.

16. Goldman, T. (1992), "Tennis Great Ashe Reveals He Has Aids," *Los Angeles Times* (April 9).

17. "Budd Dwyer," *Anwers.com* @ http://www.answers.com/topic/budd-dwyer.

18. Gottlieb, S. (1990), "Media Ethics: Some Specific Problems" (February) @ http://library.educationworld.net/a7/a7–94.html.

19. Ibid.

11

1. Hennessy, T. (2002), "Pulling the mike on L.A.'s dean of talk a big mistake," *Press Telegram* (November 30).

2. Kovacs, J. (2001), "'Bias' aired out on Rush Limbaugh," *WorldNetDaily* (December 5) @ http://www.worldnetdaily.com/news/article.asp?ARTICLE_ID=25556.

3. Newcomb, T. (1953), "An approach to the Study of Communicative Acts," *Psychological Review*, 60: 393–404.

4. RTNDA, "Code of Ethics and Professional Conduct Radio-Television News Directors Association" @ http://www.rtnda.org/ethics/coe.shtml.

5. Fairpress.org @ www.fairpress.org/mbn/blog.htm, Media Research Center @ www.mediaresearch.org, Media Matters for America @ http://mediamatters.org/, Journalism.org @ www.journalism.org, Poynter Institute @ www.poynter.org.

6. Stone, V. (2000), "Radio Newspeople" @ http://www.missouri.edu/~jourvs/radioers.html.

7. Papper, B. (2004), "Recovering Lost Ground," *RTNDA/F Research* @ http://www.rtnda.org/research/research.shtml.

8. Ibid.

9. "Media/Political Bias," *Rhetorica* @ http://rhetorica.net/bias.htm.

10. Ibid.

11. Franklin, B. @ http://quotes.forbiddenlibrary.com/

12

1. "The State of the News Media, 2005," Project for Excellence in Journalism @ http://www.stateofthenewsmedia.org/2005/narrative_overview_ownership.asp?cat=5& media=1.

2. "Who Owns What, Vulcan, Inc.," *Columbia Journalism Review* @ http://www.cjr.org/tools/owners/vulcan.asp.

3. Clear Channel Communications website @ http://www.clearchannel.com/Corporate/ PressRelease.aspx?PressReleaseID=1170&p=hidden

4. Ibid

5. http://www.clearchannel.com/IntRadio/mexico.aspx

6. www.citadelbroadcasting.com.

7. www.coxradio.com.

8. www.Cumulus.com.

9. Entercom Communications @ http://www.hoovers.com//free/co/factsheet.xhtml? COID=58022&cm_ven=PAID&cm_cat=OVR&cm_pla=C04&cm_ite=entercom.

10. Viacom Website @ http://www.viacom.com/thefacts.tin.

11. Papper, B. (2005), "Salary Survey," *Communicator* (June), RTNDA, p. 28.

12. Strupp, J. (2004), "A Few Choice Words," Editor & Publisher, Vol. 137, Issue 11 (November).

13. Winter, J. and Eyal, C. (1981), "Agenda Setting For The Civil Rights Issue," *Public Opinion Quarterly* (Fall) V.45, Issue 3, p. 381.

14. Deitz, C. (2004), "Howard Stern Announces Impending Jump To SIRIUS Satellite Radio" (October, 6) @ http://radio.about.com/mbiopage.htm.

15. Howard Stern @ http://www.answers.com/topic/howard-stern

16. Freeman, M. (1998), "Howard Gets a Tweaking," *Media Week* (Sept. 7), p. 9.

17. "Clear Channel to Pay Record Fine for Indecency Charges," *On-Line NewsHour* (June 9, 2004) @ http://www.pbs.org/newshour/updates/clearchannelfine_ 06–09–04.html.

18. "Stern, Still Talking, Still Feisty," *CNN/Money* (January 4, 2005) @ http://money.cnn.com/2005/01/04/news/newsmakers/stern/.

19. "Poor Howard Stern — 2 More Words He Can't Say On Show: 'Satellite Radio'" @ http://radio.about.com/od/sternindecency/a/aa010605a.htm.

20. "Howard Stern Makes Threat," *CNN/Money* (December 10) @ http://money.cnn.com/2004/12/10/news/newsmakers/stern/.

21. Don Imus @ http://www.answers.com/topic/don-imus.

22. Lawrence, W. D. (2003), "Imus, Don," *Encyclopedia of Radio*, Fitzroy Dearborn, pp. 743–744.

23. "F.C.C. Slams Infinity With Fine Over Opie & Anthony Stunt" @ http://radio.about.com/library/weekly/aa100503a.htm.

24. Opie and Anthony @ http://www.answers.com/topic/opie-and-anthony

25. Associated Press (2006) "Shockjocks May Replace Roth on Radio."

26. www.airamericaradio.com.

27. Sean Hannity @ http://www.wabcradio.com/showdj.asp?DJID=1725.

28. Thomas, E. (2003), "I Am Addicted To Prescription Pain Medication," *Newsweek* (October 20).

29. Rush Limbaugh @ http://radio.about.com/library/blprofiles/blpro-rush.htm.

30. Bill O'Reilly @ www.billoreilly.com.

31. The Michael Reagan Show @ www.radioamerica.org/Program2003/reagan.htm.

32. Melissa Block @ http://www.npr.org/templates/story/story.php?storyId=2100245.

33. Terry Gross @ http://www.npr.org/templates/story/story.php?storyId=2100593.

34. Prairie Home Companion @ http://prairiehome.publicradio.org/.

35. "The Fastest Mike in the Midwest" @ http://www.notmuch.com/Show/Bios/michael.html.

36. Diane Rehm @ www.wamu.org/programs/dr/diane_rehm.

37. "Carson Daly Most Requested" @ www.premrad.com/carsondaly.html.

38. Matt Drudge @ http://www.vikingphoenix.com/public/rongstad/bio-0002/MattDrudge.htm.

39. Dr. Dean Edell @ http://www.wlsam.com/showdj.asp?DJID=1650.

40. "Bob Edwards: 30 Years at NPR" @ http://www.npr.org/about/specials/bedwards/biography.html.

41. Michael Jackson @ http://radio.about.com/library/blprofiles/blpro-michaeljackson.htm.

42. Williams, G .A. (2003), "Joyner, Tom," *Encyclopedia of Radio*, Fitzroy Dearborn, p. 790–791.

43. Speight, K. (2005), "Litton tapped for 'Joyner' distrib'n," *The Hollywood Reporter.com* (April 15) @ www.hollywoodreporter.com/thr/search/article_display.jsp?schema=&-vnu_content_id=1000883809.

44. Larry King @ http://www.achievement.org/autodoc/page/kin0bio-1

45. Larry King @ http://www.cnn.com/CNN/anchors_reporters/king.larry.html.

46. Kim Kamando @ www.kamando.com/index.asp.

47. Kim Kamando @ http://www.sheridanmedia.com/site/staff.html.

48. Kim, J. (1997), "A night in Cow town: No anonymity for shock jock," *Chicago Sun-Times* (November 14).

49. Mancow @ http://www.nndb.com/people/462/000022396/.

50. Masterson, K. (2004), "'Mancow' Sues Man Who Complained to the FCC," *Chicago Tribune* (March 24).

51. "Mancow Ready to Make His Move," *Talkers Magazine*, 54, Dec 2004/Jan 2005.

52. Laura Schlessinger @www.drlaura.com.

Index

Media Industries

General Editor
David Sumner

The Media Industries series offers comprehensive, classroom friendly textbooks designed to meet the needs of instructors teaching introductory media courses. Each book provides a concise, practical guide to all aspects of a major industry. These volumes are an ideal reference source for anyone contemplating a career in the media.

To order other books in this series, please contact our Customer Service Department:

(800) 770-LANG (within the U.S.)
(212) 647-7706 (outside the U.S.)
(212) 647-7707 FAX

Or order online at www.peterlang.com